Everyday Life and Cultural Theory

'Ben Highmore's engaging and readable study of how modern and contemporary theories have defined and examined everyday life provides a lens for students and scholars alike through which to examine a central issue in cultural studies and social thought.'

Ivan Karp, *Emory University*

'Highmore has produced a valuable resource for teachers in all the disciplines that are concerned with the study of culture. He addresses the key thinkers who have defined the major variants of this crucial construct of cultural theory, and he has done so both accessibly and brilliantly.'

George Marcus, *Rice University*

Everyday Life and Cultural Theory provides a unique critical and historical introduction to theories of everyday life. Ben Highmore traces the development of conceptions of everyday life from the cultural sociology of Georg Simmel, through the Mass-Observation project of the 1930s to contemporary theorists such as Michel de Certeau.

Individual chapters examine:

- Modernity and everyday life
- Georg Simmel and fragments of everyday life
- Surrealism and the marvellous in the everyday
- Walter Benjamin's trash aesthetics
- Mass-Observation and the science of everyday life
- Henri Lefebvre's dialectics of everyday life
- Michel de Certeau's poetics of everyday life
- Everyday life and the future of cultural studies

Ben Highmore is a Senior Lecturer in Cultural and Media Studies at the University of the West of England. He is editor of the *Everyday Life Reader* (forthcoming, Routledge 2002).

For Wendy Bonner

Everyday Life and Cultural Theory

An Introduction

Ben Highmore

London and New York

First published 2002
by Routledge
11 New Fetter Lane, London EC4P 4EE

Simultaneously published in the USA and Canada
by Routledge
29 West 35th Street, New York, NY 10001

Routledge is an imprint of the Taylor & Francis Group

© 2002 Ben Highmore

Typeset in Perpetua and Bell Gothic by
Florence Production Ltd, Stoodleigh, Devon
Printed and bound in Great Britain by
Biddles Ltd, Guildford and King's Lynn

British Library Cataloguing in Publication Data
A catalogue record for this book is available from the British Library

Library of Congress Cataloging in Publication Data
Highmore, Ben, 1961–
    Everyday life and cultural theory : an introduction/Ben Highmore.
        p.cm.
    Includes bibliographical references and index.
    1. Life. 2. Civilisation, Modern—20th century. 3. Culture—Philosophy
    —History—20th century.
    BD431 .H475 2001
    306—dc21   2001034793

ISBN 0–415–22302–4 (hbk)
ISBN 0–415–22303–2 (pbk)

Contents

Illustrations

Preface and acknowledgements

This book is an introduction to 'everyday life and cultural theory'. It is an introduction, not so much because it is written in an introductory style (though I hope that it is written in a way that avoids some of the more unappetizing conventions of academic writing), but because work on the everyday is, as I argue, only just beginning. The 'everyday life theory' that I write about here is both an introduction and an invitation to start thinking about an arena of life that manages, for the most part, to avoid scrutiny. Or rather, the kinds of interventionist scrutiny that it has received have often been undertaken in the name of governing the everyday. Here, instead, a form of inventive and critical attention allows, potentially at least, another 'everyday' to begin to appear.

The order of the chapters in this book may seem a little odd. Chapter 2 (which tells you what the rest of the book is about, and tries to knit together some of the main arguments) might seem more like an introductory chapter than chapter 1. My decision to place a very general chapter about 'everyday modernity' in front of this is because I wanted to be able to ground the arguments with some historical description of a world 'out there', which cultural theory might be seen as responding to. After chapter 2 the book progresses in the usual chronological fashion.

The choice of which theorists and theories are included within this account probably also needs a word or two. This book is a route-map of one particular path through the many varied possibilities that are suggested by connecting the terms 'everyday life' and 'cultural theory'. It strikes me that 'theory' (a much overused term, of course) could be the name we reserve for the most insistent puzzling about aspects of life that are taken as problematic. Now while there is a whole variety of theorists who deal with problematics *and* the everyday (Erving Goffman, Harold Garfinkel, Martin Heidegger, Agnes Heller, Dorothy E. Smith – to mention just some of the most obvious ones), they don't necessarily deal with the *everyday as a problematic*. As such the everyday often becomes the occasion, the territory for a puzzling that is often directed elsewhere. The theorists and theories chosen here seem to me to be characterized by a much more directed attention to the everyday as a problematic. They all seem to bring the everyday into an awkward focus.

The writing of any book voraciously consumes vast swathes of everyday life. This book was no exception. So my first acknowledgement must be to Wendy Bonner who has had to endure God knows how many hours (days, years) of this book. For suffering bad moods, garbled monologues, missed meal times, and much besides, I dedicate this with all my love. Our children have probably not come out of this unscathed either. To the question 'Where's daddy?' the answer 'He's in his working room' became something of a haunting and guilt-inducing refrain. So thanks then to Molly for not taking any of this too seriously and for continually 'disturbing' me with new tricks and new ways of wearing clothes. Thanks also to Zebedee who came along just at the right time.

From the start Steven Connor helped shape this project and kept it on course as it weaved (sometimes precariously) about. His unflagging enthusiasm and pertinent advice made writing this book much less onerous than it could have been. A number of people have read part or all of earlier versions of the book (some were hoodwinked into it, others volunteered themselves; all of them helped). So I'd like to thank Ian Buchanan, Barry Curtis, Iain Hamilton Grant, Michelle Henning, Alan Read, Simon Sadler and Morag Shiach. Various anonymous readers read some of this with an eye to its publication – their support gave me the encouragement to finish it. Thanks as well to Rebecca Barden and Alistair Daniel at Routledge for getting the book to publication. I want to thank everyone in the School of Cultural and Media Studies at the University of the West of England and especially all those involved in the 'everyday life research group'. Finally I want to thank my parents, who have supported a career which for so many years must have seemed invisible.

Chapter 1

FIGURING THE EVERYDAY

Whatever its other aspects, the everyday has this essential trait: it allows no hold. It escapes.

(Blanchot [1959] 1987: 14)

Investigating the everyday

THERE IS NO ESCAPE: to launch an investigation into the theoretical practices of those who attend to everyday life requires attention to the everyday 'itself'. To trace the troubled career of 'the everyday' as it is mobilized by a disparate collection of intellectuals from the late nineteenth century to the late twentieth century necessitates an attempt to gauge the specific gravity of the term, its connotations and its references. Unspecific gravity might be a better phrase. As the notion of 'everyday life' circulates in Western cultures under its many guises (*Alltagsleben, la vie quotidienne*, run-of-the-mill and so on) one difficulty becomes immediately apparent: 'everyday life' signifies ambivalently. On the one hand it points (without judging) to those most repeated actions, those most travelled journeys, those most inhabited spaces that make up, literally, the day to day. This is the landscape closest to us, the world most immediately met. But with this quantifiable meaning creeps another, never far behind: the everyday as value and quality – everydayness. Here the most travelled journey can become the dead weight of boredom, the most inhabited space a prison, the most repeated action an oppressive routine. Here the everydayness of everyday life might be experienced as a sanctuary, or it may bewilder or give pleasure, it may delight or depress. Or its special quality might be its lack of qualities. It might be, precisely, the unnoticed, the inconspicuous, the unobtrusive.

This ambivalence vividly registers the effects of modernity. If the everyday is that which is most familiar and most recognizable, then what happens when that world is disturbed and disrupted by the *unfamiliar*? If the 'shock of the new' sends tremors to the core of the everyday, then what happens to the sense of the everyday as familiar and recognizable? In modernity the everyday becomes the setting for a dynamic process: for making the unfamiliar familiar; for getting accustomed to the disruption of custom; for struggling to incorporate the new; for adjusting to different ways of living. The everyday marks the success and failure of this process. It witnesses the absorption of the most revolutionary of inventions into the landscape of the mundane. Radical transformations in all walks of life become 'second nature'. The new becomes traditional and the residues of the past become outmoded and available for fashionable renewal. But signs of failure can be noticed everywhere: the language of the everyday is not an upbeat endorsement of the new; it echoes with frustrations, with the disappointment of broken promises.

The heterogeneous and ambivalent landscape of everyday modernity needs investigating. This investigation starts, like all investigations should, with a detective. For Sherlock Holmes 'everyday life' is decidedly undecided. While never in doubt about the correctness of his own investigative methods, Holmes' relationship to the everyday is marked by a passionate ambivalence that takes us to the heart of the problem of everyday life in modernity. Sherlock Holmes gets bored. He gets bored when the mysterious and enigmatic side of life is not taxing his rationalistic intelligence. Conan Doyle's detective is a man who is often bored. For him the world of the everyday is associated with the dull and the humdrum: 'I know, my dear Watson, that you share my love of all that is bizarre and outside the conventions and humdrum routine of everyday life' (Doyle [1892] 1993: 45). To what extent Dr Watson shares this love is an open question: one thing is for sure, his love of the bizarre does not have the passionate intensity of Holmes'. Nor does he suffer so much when faced with the everyday. Holmes is repulsed by the everyday and can only deal with its atrophying force by taking refuge in cocaine:

> 'My mind,' he said, 'rebels at stagnation. Give me problems, give me work, give me the most abstruse cryptogram, or the most intricate analysis, and I am in my own proper atmosphere. I can dispense then with artificial stimulants. But I abhor the dull routine of existence.'
>
> (Doyle [1890] 1995: 89–90)

Written over four decades (1887–1923), Sir Arthur Conan Doyle's stories frequently picture Sherlock Holmes collapsing under the weight of the everyday. His friend, Dr Watson, fears for his physical health and sanity, hoping that some new case will appear to break through the life-threatening torpor that besets him. But this image of the everyday as a deadening force is only one of the elements of everydayness in the cosmos of the Holmes stories.

The everyday is also the home of the bizarre and mysterious. The 'commonplaces of existence' are filled with strange occurrences:

> life is infinitely stranger than anything which the mind of man could invent. We could not dare to conceive the things which are really mere commonplaces of existence. If we could fly out that window hand in hand, hover over this great city, gently remove the roofs, and peep in at the queer things which are going on . . . the wonderful chain of events, working through generations and leading to the most *outré* results, it would make all fiction with its conventionalities and foreseen conclusions most stale and unprofitable.
>
> (Doyle, quoted in Langbauer 1993: 94)

The non-everyday (the exceptional) is there to be found in the heart of the everyday. Indeed many of the Sherlock Holmes stories start with what seem to be ordinary, petty occurrences that hardly warrant the attention of the great detective. But for Holmes the everyday is not what it seems. Or rather the everyday is precisely the route to be taken in solving the mystery he is investigating. And here we come to the very core of Holmes' relationship to the everyday: however much he loves the strange and bizarre, his entire being is dedicated to puncturing its mystery. Holmes works his disenchantment at various different levels. His power to solve cases works to bring the bizarre firmly down to earth: seemingly magical or ghostly events turn out to be ordinary acts of greed, spite, love, jealousy and other manifestations of 'human nature'. In this, Holmes could be seen as demystifying the bizarre and returning events to the everyday. But it is Holmes' method of detection that most captures the peculiar figuring of the everyday in Conan Doyle's fiction.

Holmes is a genius; he is not ordinary. He continually astounds Watson and his clients by his uncanny divination of the details of a person's life through the mere observation of an everyday object or the outward appearance of a person. In 'The Adventure of the Blue Carbuncle' (1892), Holmes has been given a hat to examine, and draws the following conclusions about the wearer of the hat:

> He had foresight, but has less now than formerly, pointing to a moral retrogression, which when taken with the decline of his fortunes, seems to indicate some evil influence, probably drink, at work upon him. This may account also for the obvious fact that his wife has ceased to love him.
>
> (Doyle 1993: 168)

Holmes takes the most everyday of objects and seems to have an extraordinary gift of being able to discover (*as if by magic*) the stories of those associated with them. But here again, what appears to be extraordinary is brought back within the realm of the ordinary and everyday. When Holmes explains his reasoning it appears banal, *elementary*; it seems to be merely a matter of being attentive to the most insignificant of details. As one client remarks: ' "I thought at first you had done something clever, but I see that there was nothing in it after all" ' (Doyle 1993: 48). Like the mysteries that Holmes solves, the mystery of Holmes' abilities turns out to be very ordinary indeed. Not that this stops us from being amazed. What appeared to be the gift of foresight is merely the systematic application of a method. But it is a method that transforms the insignificant into its opposite. Such a method should, according to Holmes, be dealt with by a proper scientific treatise, not via the frivolous and melodramatic form of detective fiction. To the mystery of the everyday, Holmes brings the disenchantment of rationalism. His 'gift' is nothing more or less than the extension of rationalistic and scientific principles to the seemingly unfathomable cases he investigates. If he loves the bizarre and mysterious side of the everyday, he loves its disenchantment through rationalism even more. Yet it is precisely this rationalism that transforms the insignificant and everyday into ciphers for the bizarre. Holmes' approach to the everyday generates mystery at the same time as it demystifies it.

But Sherlock Holmes' relationship with the everyday is clearly privileged: apart from occasionally being overcome by it, he spends most of his time analysing it, observing it and mastering it. While the particular mix of boredom, mystery and rationalism that he puts in play is central to figuring everyday life, we need to look elsewhere to see how this mix is related to everyday modernity. We need to disentangle this contrary mixture of forces to see how their entanglement figures the everyday as both known and unknown, comfortable and uncomfortable. This constellation needs to be related to ideas and practices that are central to modernity. Boredom, for instance, will connect us to the peculiar temporal experiences that seem to emerge from the patterns and arrangements of modern working life. From the 'emptying' of time in the modern factory to the extensive bureaucratization of governance, from the atomized working practices in the office to the industrialization of the home, the modern world seems characterized by routines, by systems and regulatory techniques. But Western modernity is also characterized by mystery. Whether it is the mystery of the unconscious and the gothic narratives it reveals, or the 'exotic' cultures of 'other people' (the 'poor' for the Western bourgeois, the 'native' for the West in general), mystery takes everyday forms. Freudian 'slips' are everyday occurrences. Popular anthropology renders the daily practices of other cultures as at once both strange and mastered.

Rationalism, the third term in our mix, binds these two aspects together, not in some kind of explanatory grid, but as an engine driving these forces. It too has two sides and we will need to see its multiform reflection in both 'boredom' and 'mystery'. Paradoxically, rationalism holds within it an irrational kernel: it seeks to disenchant the world through an unquestioned belief in its own value. Rationalism is not the antidote to myth and ritual, but the emergence of new myths and rituals under the banner of the 'true'.

Boredom: the emptying of time

If Western modernity can be seen as the emergence of new and different temporal experiences, then, for the most part, these experiences are connected to an institutionalized world of work and organized instruction. The prehistory of modern temporalities can partly be found in the gradual standardizing of time. Mechanical clocks, as they emerged in the fourteenth century, standardized the units of time and were dynamically related to changes in working patterns. As Richard Biernacki argues: 'The introduction of the modern method of calibrating hours in a metric independent of tangible occurrences, with units that are interchangeable and uniform across the seasons, coincided with the expansion of urban wage labor during the fourteenth century' (Biernacki 1994: 62). Clocks alone cannot account for the particularity of modern time. Dramatic changes in the representation and experience of time (the 'nature' of time) can also be related to the standardizing practices of the Church, the school and the hospital, which impacted fundamentally at the level of the everyday (see Adam 1995). So, for instance, at the beginning of the nineteenth century a school day could include an accounting of all the activities that had been scheduled for the day: the pupil 'every day puts down in his book the day of the month, at the termination of his day's tasks. And on a page at the end of his book, he daily registers the number of lessons said, pages written, sums wrought, etc.' (Andrew Bell [1813] quoted in Jones and Williamson 1979: 74). This daily monitoring and accounting was a routine that marked each and every day, but it also continually divided and catalogued the day into countable segments. Such practices emphasized the routinization and regimentation of daily life.

Standardized time developed unevenly. Prior to the late nineteenth century standardized time was regulated only at a local level: to travel was to enter non-synchronized time. Steven Kern writes that in the 1870s 'if a traveller from Washington to San Francisco set his [sic] watch in every town he passed through, he would set it over two hundred times' (Kern 1983: 12). Unsurprisingly, perhaps, it would be the railway and telegraph systems in the 1880s that would set the pace for establishing a global standardization of time (Kern 1983: 11–15). Networks designed to increase the speed of communication and commerce, and to overcome the physical distance of space, reconfigured the tempo of the everyday. The everydayness of everyday modernity is a synchronization based on minutes and seconds. The modern spectacle of thousands of commuters converging on the metropolis by train each morning is dependent on timetables synchronized to the minute, even if these trains are *regularly* late.

Perhaps the most common analogy for characterizing 'everyday life' within modernity (its uniformity, its dullness and so on) is the assembly line. In an essay that explores the relationship between everyday life and boredom, Laurie Langbauer writes: 'The boredom of everyday city life is the boredom of the assembly line, of one thing after another, of pieces locked in an infinite series that never really progresses: the more it changes, the more it remains the same' (Langbauer 1993: 81). Similarly Susan Stewart writes:

> The prevailing notion that everyday time is a matter of undifferentiated linearity may be linked to the prevailing forms of experience within the workplace. Such a notion presents us with an assembly line of temporality, an assembly line in which all experience is partial, piecemeal.
>
> (Stewart 1993: 13)

Siegfried Giedion, in his evocatively titled book, *Mechanization takes Command: A Contribution to Anonymous History*, dates the assembly line (*avant la lettre*), not to Henry Ford in the early twentieth century, but to the continuous production line implemented by Oliver Evans at the end of the eighteenth century (Giedion 1969: 77–127). Continuous production, in whatever form, follows the logic of industrial capitalism in its drive to maximize output; it does so by 'an uninterrupted production process' which is characterized by 'the inexorable regularity with which the worker must follow the rhythm of the mechanical system' (Giedion 1969: 77). In seeing this form of work as exemplifying something fundamental about everyday modernity, the particularities of different 'line' systems are less important than the way continuous production in general can be seen to affect workers' everyday lives. Karl Marx in the first volume of *Capital* (first published in 1867) sketches the transformation that such systems brought about:

> In handicrafts and manufacture, the worker makes use of a tool; in the factory, the machine makes use of him [*sic*]. There the movements of the instrument of labour proceed from him, here it is the movement of the machine that he must follow. In manufacture the workers are the parts of a living mechanism. In the factory we have a lifeless mechanism which is independent of the workers, who are incorporated into it as its living appendages. 'The wearisome routine of endless drudgery in which the same mechanical process is ever repeated, is like the

torture of Sisyphus; the burden of toil, like the rock, is ever falling back upon the worn-out drudge.'

(Marx 1976: 548)

For Marx the shift in relationships, whereby the worker becomes the mere appendage to the machine, is part of the intensification of alienation brought about by modern capitalism. But rather than giving an abstract account of this alienation, Marx insists on the sensory-mental condition it generates:

> Factory work exhausts the nervous system to the uttermost; at the same time, it does away with the many-sided play of the muscles, and confiscates every atom of freedom, both in bodily and in intellectual activity. Even the lightening of the labour becomes an instrument of torture, since the machine does not free the worker from the work, but rather deprives the work itself of all content.

(Marx 1976: 548)

Just as work is emptied of 'all [creative] content', so time is emptied of any significant markers that would differentiate one moment from the next (figure 1). In the varied literature on assembly line work the theme of regulated activity and the slowness of time are continually evident. In Ben Hamper's account of life on the rivet line at the General Motors plant at Flint in Michigan, the clock becomes the number one enemy:

Figure 1   The inexorable regularity of modern work – photograph by Gjon Milli

> But the clock was a whole different mammal altogether. It sucked on you as you waited the next job. It ridiculed you each time you'd take a peek. The more irritated you became, the slower it moved. The slower it moved, the more you thought. Thinking was a very slow death at times.
>
> (Hamper 1992: 95)

Earlier in the book Hamper explains the relationship between the assembly line and the stretching out of time: 'the one thing that was impossible to escape was the monotony of our new jobs. Every minute, every hour, every truck and every movement was a plodding replica of the one that had gone before' (Hamper 1992: 41).

The repetition-of-the-same characterizes an everyday temporality experienced as a debilitating boredom. What makes the assembly line such a telling exemplification of everyday modernity is not the specificity of the factory environment, but the generalized condition that it points to: 'plodding', 'monotony' – the emptiness of time. What makes continuous production register so vividly is the regulating of time within the widespread conditions of industrialization. From the point of view of the everyday, industrialization is not something limited to factory production, but something registered in nearly all aspects of life. Writing about the cultural effects of railway travel, Wolfgang Schivelbusch subtitled his book 'the industrialization of time and space' (Schivelbusch 1977). The extensiveness of industrialization needs to be noted, not simply as a technological condition, but as a sensory-mental experience. 'The salaried masses' (the salariat) of clerks, secretaries, executives and stenographers, wielding typewriters, telephones and now, of course, computers, operate within an industrial and rationalized environment (see Kracauer [1929] 1998). Giedion finds intensified mechanization in nearly every form of everyday culture: bread, chairs, death, washing and so on (Giedion 1969). The uneven extension of industrialization brought industrial technologies and management techniques into the home, and under the guise of efficiency and ease, worked to regulate and rationalize home life. The results of this have been well documented and synoptically signposted by the title of Ruth Schwartz Cowan's book *More Work for Mother* (Cowan 1989). Industrialization in general is locked into the uneven and unequal experiences of social difference in a dynamic that homogenizes and differentiates at the same time (see, for instance, Kramarae 1988). The experience of homogenized time is unevenly distributed across social differences: the boredom of factory work is differentiated from the boredom of the computer operator, which is differentiated from the boredom of the domestic worker, and so on.

The phrase 'marking time' brings with it some of the flavour of everyday modernity in its ambiguous play on the literal process of 'marking' (differentiating, discriminating) and its everyday meaning of dull waiting, of boredom. The standardizing of time and the routinization of daily life that accompanies it operate across this ambiguity:

> The pages falling off the calendar, the notches marked in a tree that no longer stands – these are the signs of the everyday, the effort to articulate difference through counting. Yet it is precisely this counting that reduces differences to similarities, that is designed to be 'lost track of.' Such 'counting', such signifying, is drowned out by the silence of the ordinary.
>
> (Stewart 1993: 14)

To account for this peculiar monotony (the deadening routinization of everyday modernity) a technological account is not enough. Written at the beginning of the twentieth century Max Weber's investigation of the 'spirit' of modern capitalism suggests that the 'modern Western form of capitalism has been, at first sight, strongly influenced by the development of technical possibilities' (Weber [1904–5] 1991: 24). Weber goes on to suggest that 'technical possibilities' are in themselves not enough to encourage the development of modern capitalism. Weber emphasizes the importance of social structures: 'among those of undoubted importance are the rational structures of law and administration. For modern rational capitalism has need, not only of the technical means of production, but of a calculable legal system and of administration in terms of formal rules' (1991: 25).

A world governed by the exhaustive protocols of bureaucracy and the administrative rigour of 'official life' figure, not only a different framework for understanding modern capitalism, but also an everyday life continually plagued by government. In the fictions of Franz Kafka, the everyday is invaded by a maze of bureaucratic officialdom that seems entirely designed to frustrate and destroy (Kafka [1925] 1994, [1926] 1997). The everyday is caught in a web of administration with terrifying effects. Administrative government in modernity permeates the everyday, from the collection of taxes to the 'policing of families' (Donzelot 1980). For Weber, the 'iron cage' of bureaucratic rationality is the opposite of spontaneous enjoyment and he nostalgically pictures it as a 'renunciation, a departure from an age of full and beautiful humanity' (1991: 181). Tracing the cultural conditions that have allowed this form of life to dominate, Weber recognizes the mark of a Puritanical asceticism. Modernity, for Weber, is asceticism secularized, generalized and enforced:

> The Puritan wanted to work in a calling; we are forced to do so. For when asceticism was carried out of monastic cells into everyday life, and began to dominate worldly morality, it did its part in building the tremendous cosmos of the modern economic order. The order is now bound to the technical and economic conditions of machine production

which to-day determine the lives of all the individuals who are born into this mechanism, not only those directly concerned with economic acquisition, with irresistible force. Perhaps it will so determine them until the last ton of fossilized coal is burnt. In Baxter's view the care for external goods should lie on the shoulders of the 'saint like a light cloak, which can be thrown aside at any moment'. But fate decreed that the cloak should become an iron cage.

(Weber 1991: 181)

Weber's 'iron cage' is everyday modernity as machine-like and bureaucratic. It is an everyday life governed by asceticism. If the result of Weberian and Marxian everyday modernity is boredom, this is a boredom that is cut through with a murderous insistence.

But 'boredom' is also a subtle tool for forms of cultural discrimination aimed at differentiating everydayness. Writing about boredom, Patricia Meyer Spacks states:

Although the spread of boredom has coincided with and reflected an increasing stress on subjectivity and individualism, the state of mind carries social as well as personal meanings. From the eighteenth century on, one can note a tendency to attribute boredom to members of groups other than the writer's own. Middle-class journalists in the eighteenth century believe the nouveaux riches to be bored. In the nineteenth century (encouraged by Lord Byron) the middle class assigns the condition to the aristocracy. The old think the young are bored.

(Spacks 1995: x–xi)

The designation of particular classes and their gendered variations as bored and boring nearly always centred on a notion of everyday life. Seen from the point of view of an emergent middle class, aristocratic everyday life was decadent (luxury and excess as daily routine) and lacking in the kind of differentiation that could enliven it. Such a condition produced boredom as a sign of the historical redundancy of the class. Boredom was a sign for denigrating the everyday life of other social groups. In *London Journal: A Survey of London Life in the 1830s*, Flora Tristan, a French writer visiting London, sees the signs of boredom everywhere: 'on the one hand there is the busy population of the city whose only motive is desire for profit, on the other there is the haughty, disdainful aristocracy who come to London each year to escape from boredom' (quoted in Spacks 1995: 15). And later in the same journal: 'English women's lives are unbelievably monotonous, sterile and drab. Time has no meaning for them – the days, months and years bring no change to this oppressive uniformity' (in Spacks 1995: 164). The use of boredom to differentiate between everyday lives is directed, here, through an idea of national differences. Social difference is writ large in the 'boredom' of the everyday. But just as it can be used to denigrate, it can also be used to diagnose: boredom can become a sign of social critique.

In the culture of modernity the boredom of women offers a vivid example of this. Often portrayed as the bored housewife, the middle-class woman of nineteenth-century representation was often portrayed as fickle and unable to occupy herself with serious projects. Her everyday life was cluttered with cultural debris that showed her as an easy target for the peddlers of an inferior and industrial culture. The classic example of such a portrayal is Emma Bovary's fondness for reading romantic novels in Flaubert's *Madame Bovary*. Andreas Huyssen describes the fictional Emma Bovary as 'a woman who tried to live the illusions of aristocratic sensual romance and was shipwrecked on the banality of bourgeois everyday life' (Huyssen 1986: 45). A banal and boring everyday life is mingled with a desire for a cultural form that is seen as, ultimately, boring. But boredom could also be used as an index of unfulfilled desires and unnamed anxieties. It could work as a synecdoche for more general, critical dissatisfactions within culture (seen as exploitative, patriarchal, capitalistic). The boredom of everyday life can be, and often has been, an area of social and political struggles. Coupled with the rational analysis of exploitation is the great mumbled scream of boredom. In the 1960s, heralding a second wave of feminism, Betty Friedan attempted to give voice to this muffled scream and 'the problem that has no name':

> Each suburban wife struggled with it alone. As she made the beds, shopped for groceries, matched slipcover material, ate peanut butter sandwiches with her children, chauffeured Cub Scouts and Brownies, lay beside her husband at night, she was afraid to ask even of herself the silent question: 'Is this all?'
>
> (Friedan 1965: 13)

The use of 'boredom' both to mark social distinctions and to diagnose cultural domination points to one inescapable factor: everyday life (like any other aspect of life) is marked by difference. Such differences in the experience of everyday life (differences most obviously noted by class, gender, 'race', sexuality, etc.) will also be marked in the different approaches to theorizing the everyday. As Naomi Schor suggests:

> Two widely shared but diametrically opposed views inform what theories we have on the everyday: one, which we might call the feminine or feminist, though it is not necessarily held by women or self-described feminists, links the everyday with the daily rituals of private life carried out within the domestic sphere traditionally presided over by women: the other, the masculine or masculinist, sites the everyday in the public

> spaces and spheres dominated especially, but not exclusively, in modern
> Western bourgeois societies by men.
>
> (Schor 1992: 188)

It will become evident, as this book progresses, that the masculinist perspective predominates: it is the street rather than the home that is seen as the privileged sphere of everyday life.

Strangeness at the heart of the everyday

To see everyday modernity as boring or relentlessly routinized is to capture only one side of its general articulation. Alongside this, and overlapping with it, is the everyday as mystery. If a certain form of 'spiritual' rationalism can be seen as the motor of deadening routines, rationalism can also be seen to generate more mysterious forms. Indeed some of the most productive guides to everyday modernity (as both boredom and mystery) operate, like Sherlock Holmes, within the terms of a disenchanting rationalism. But, also like Sherlock Holmes, the material that they dredge up is both mysterious and 'banal'. Writing about the ethnological orientation of Durkheim, Marx and Freud, Nancy Bentley comments:

> It is hard to overlook the fact that the writings of these three thinkers, for all their rational mastery, helped to make strange and almost unfathomable the territories of self and society that are usually the most familiar to us from everyday life. A certain irony obtains: ethnological analysis always makes partly alien what it masters.
>
> (Bentley 1995: 77)

It is the ability of 'making strange' within a culture of rationalism and of finding the strange within everyday life that is central to this study of everyday life and cultural theory. In his *Introductory Lectures on Psychoanalysis* (published 1917), Freud rhetorically defends his insistence that psychoanalysis is of central importance for understanding everyday life. In attending to the parapraxes of everyday life (slips of the pen, of the tongue, of the body and the memory), Freud imagines his audience as complaining that there are 'so many marvels in the field of mental disorders, which require and deserve to have light thrown upon them, that it does really seem gratuitous to waste labour and interest on such trivialities' (Freud 1973: 51). To investigate the everyday world and 'consider why a speaker at a banquet uses one word instead of another or why a housewife has mislaid her keys' would seem commonplace and paltry in relation to the 'marvels' of 'madness'. Freud, in what could be read as a homage to Sherlock Holmes, replies:

And if you were a detective engaged in tracing a murder, would you expect to find that the murderer had left his photograph behind at the place of the crime, with his address attached? or would you not necessarily have to be satisfied with comparatively slight and obscure traces of the person you were in search of?

(1973: 52)

The revolutionary theories of Freud conjure up a world of repressed desire; they articulate stories that, because of their claimed ubiquity, can be seen as everyday but are made up of materials that seem a world away from the humdrum routines of everyday life. Freud identifies an intimate link between psychoanalysis and the everyday:

It is true that psychoanalysis cannot boast that it has never concerned itself with trivialities. On the contrary, the material for its observations is usually provided by the inconsiderable events which have been put aside by the other sciences as being too unimportant – the dregs, one might say, of the world of phenomena.

(1973: 52)

Such a picture of psychoanalysis figures it as a very ordinary science, or rather a science of the ordinary, a ' "surface psychology" of everyday life' (Ferguson 1996: vii).

The everyday life that Freud describes is a world of everyday manners and conventions, continually disrupted by repressed thoughts. Here the propriety of custom can at times seem to be a mere patina on more 'basic instincts'. In the examples that Freud offers, the everyday is animated by a dynamic contest between the forces of propriety and the unmanageable material of repression, as, for example, in the professor who remarks: ' "In the case of the female genitals, in spite of many *Versuchungen* [temptations] – I beg your pardon, *Versuche* [experiments] . . ." ' (Freud 1973: 52).

While Freud will not be a specific focus of this book, his work is of singular importance for the everyday. On the one hand, the idea of the 'Freudian slip' has entered everyday language, insisting that everyday communication is continually betraying unintended desires. On the other, the idea of the unconscious as something that is both everywhere and nowhere offers a compelling analogy for the everyday. Although theorists of the everyday don't explicitly apply the full machinery of psychoanalysis, there is often an insistence that the realm of consciousness doesn't exhaust the everyday.

The everyday as non-conscious life is a vivid aspect of the tradition that I will describe. In another reference to detective fiction, Freud recognizes that 'science' flirts uneasily with sensationalism: 'I am aware that – in this city, at least – there are many physicians who (revolting though it may seem)

13

choose to read a case history of this kind ["Dora"] not as a contribution to the psychopathology of the neuroses, but as a *roman à clef* designed for their private delectation' (Freud [1905] 1977: 37). Setting himself up as a figure of propriety it may be that Freud protests too much and that sensationalism is more fundamental both to the project of psychoanalysis and to everyday modernity. Both Freud and Holmes have a distaste for sensationalist forms of representation, yet both struggle to pursue the fantastic in the most seemingly banal places.

Alongside the dull routines of existence, modernity invades the everyday as 'phantasmagoria'. For Marx the phantasmagoria of modernity is characterized by the commodity, which disguises human social relationships in 'the fantastic form of a relationship between things' (Marx 1976: 165). The daily life of modernity is, of course, saturated with commodities, and some of the most vivid aspects of the phantasmagoria were to be found in shop window displays and exhibitions (figure 2). Both of these instances push the 'magical' to the forefront of the everyday. In Emile Zola's 'phantasmagoric hymn to the marvels of modern commerce' (Kristin Ross in her introduction to Zola 1992: v) the department store is animated by fantastic relationships. Zola's *Au bonheur des dames* (*The Ladies' Paradise*) (1883) describes a big Paris department store as seen through the eyes of an enamoured provincial shop worker:

> Groups of women pushing and squeezing, devouring the finery with longing, covetous eyes. And the stuffs became animated in this passionate atmosphere: the laces fluttered, drooped, and concealed the depths of the shop with a troubling air of mystery; even the lengths of cloth, thick and heavy, exhaled a tempting odour, while the cloaks threw out their folds over the dummies, which assumed a soul, and the great velvet mantle particularly, expanded, supple and warm, as if on real fleshly shoulders, with a heaving of the bosom and a trembling of the hips.
>
> (Zola 1992: 16–17)

Here mere 'product' takes on magical properties and comes to life. Modern everyday life is 'sensational' (alive with desire) even if the ability to purchase the commodities on offer is highly regulated.

In the phantasmagoria things appear to be alive and people appear as objects of display. In modern exhibitions (ethnographic and 'folk' museums, World's Fairs, and so on) the everyday is put on display as phantasmagoria. Crucial to this phantasmagoric representation is an exoticism: not everyday 'everyday life', but the everyday life of 'others'. Historically, geographically and ideologically distant, the phantasmagoria of modernity offers an image, a simulation of 'other' everydays. The visitor to the Paris Exposition Universelle of 1889 would find 'human showcases' in 'the Senegalese, the

Figure 2 'The fantastic form of a relationship between things.' *Magasin, avenue des Gobelins* – photograph by Eugène Atget (1925). Albumen-silver print from a glass negative, 8 1/8 × 6 5/16" (20.6 × 16 cm). The Museum of Modern Art, New York. Abbott-Levy Collection. Partial gift of Shirley C. Burden. Copy Print © 2001 The Museum of Modern Art, New York

Congolese, New Caledonians, Gaboonese, Dahmeyans, a Cochin-China and a Kampong-Javanese settlement' (Greenhalgh 1988: 88). The *Pall Mall Gazette* describes these living exhibitions:

> Each village is built in its own grounds, enclosed by a fence, and inhabited by its own natives . . . All these natives have been specially imported for the exhibition. They have brought with them the materials for their huts, their tools, and everything for them to reproduce in the capital of the civilised world the everyday life of Africa, the Pacific, and the Further East.
>
> (quoted in Greenhalgh 1988: 88)

The intensive and relentless cataloguing and displaying of the everyday lives of 'others' is, of course, a central aspect of the culture of colonialism: colonial capitalism that imports 'exotic lives' as 'exotic goods'. The 1908 Franco-British Exhibition shows how extensive this was in its inclusion of both a Senegalese and an Irish village (Coombes 1994: 187–213). The spectacularization and exoticizing of everyday life should be seen as a far-reaching aspect of modernity, bringing together such distinct materials as the work of someone like Henry Mayhew with his *London Labour and the London Poor* (Mayhew [1861–2] 1967), with the 'life group' displays in ethnographic museums, folk museums and heritage museums (Jacknis 1985; Sandberg 1995). Using reportage, mannequins, 'pretend' or 'real' actors, everyday life is 'experienced' (as directly as possible) as something other.

The everyday offers itself up as a problem, a contradiction, a paradox: both ordinary and extraordinary, self-evident and opaque, known and unknown, obvious and enigmatic. In seeing the everyday as bizarre and mysterious, while at the same time distancing himself from such a world ('hover over this great city'), Sherlock Holmes can be seen as figuring the peculiarity of everyday modernity as phantasmagoria. In seeing the everyday (an everyday not so distanced) as a fearful, life-threatening condition that could ensnare you in its grasp, Holmes connects with everyday life as both relentless routine and the marker of social distinction. In being caught in a process of both estranging the mundane and making banal the strange, Holmes figures a condition that might seem inescapable to the writers of everyday modernity. What this book concerns itself with are not writers who somehow imaginatively escape the dilemma of a Holmes or a Freud, but writers who, in attending to everyday life as a lived experience, embrace more directly the ability to 'make strange'. If the culture of everyday modernity does evidence the process of making the unfamiliar familiar, the group of writers that I am concerned with work to defamiliarize this condition. In attempting to make the everyday vivid, phantasmagoric representation is replaced by practical, poetic and critical operations.

Chapter 2

ARGUMENTS

WHAT FOLLOWS IS NOT an attempt to add detail to this version of everyday modernity. Rather, I want to provide an account of a body of writing that has specifically addressed this everyday modernity as a problem for cultural theory. However, this doesn't mean that we leave behind the ambivalence of the everyday and its contradictory trajectories. The everyday use of the term 'everyday life', a use that evidences an uncertainty about the precise contours of everyday life, points to the same vague and amorphous space that is indicated by the critical tradition that is the subject of this book. This is an everyday life characterized by ambiguities, instabilities and equivocation.

The tradition of theory that I pursue here can best be characterized by a stubborn refusal to underwrite some of the most everyday meanings that are attached to 'the everyday'. So while it is common practice to describe everyday life as a scene of relentless tedium, this tradition has often tried to register the everyday as the marvellous and the extraordinary (or at least to combine dialectically the everyday as both extraordinary and tedious). Similarly, if it is more usual to associate the everyday with the self-evident and the taken-for-granted, this tradition has stressed its opacity and the difficulty of adequately attending to it. This has resulted in a concern with representational forms (montage, for instance) that can seem the very opposite of what might be thought of as an 'everyday' style of presentation. Another example of a general recalcitrance towards more traditional meanings of 'the everyday' is the refusal to reduce everyday life to an arena for the reproduction of dominant social relations. While this is an important focus in some of the theories that I discuss (Lefebvre, for instance), much more stress is placed on the everyday as a site of resistance, revolution and transformation.

The tradition of cultural theory that I'm writing about must be seen as a heterogeneous mix of divergent interests and different positions. These theories of the everyday are not brought together in the hope of establishing identity, or of telling a coherent story of the progressive refinement of an idea. This is instead a story of a range of moments when the idea of the everyday becomes enlivened, when it is set to work and put in crisis, and what links these moments are not shared aims, or similar outcomes, but a comparable set of responses to a dominant understanding of the everyday. The theories and practices that are investigated here offer a fundamental challenge to the idea of everyday life as self-evident, and it is this more than anything that allows me to bring together such a disparate collection of writings. There is a refusal in the work of all the writers that are discussed to see the realm of the everyday as unproblematic. It may be that this is all that unites them. Self-reflexive and struggling with the unmanageability of the everyday, this is a story of various attempts to find approximations of everyday life, to fashion out forms more adequate to the task of attending to the everyday than those that might see it as all too easily knowable.

The works of Georg Simmel, Walter Benjamin, Henri Lefebvre and Michel de Certeau, as well as the cultural formations of Surrealism and Mass-Observation, are the main points of reference for what follows. Between Lefebvre and de Certeau is a gulf that is not easily breached, nor should it be. Between Surrealism and Walter Benjamin lies Benjamin's critique of Surrealism. Yet, for all the arguments and incompatible epistemologies, there seem to be affinities that should be recognized alongside the substantive differences.

Adopting and adapting the title of one of Martin Jay's books would provide an alternative title for this book: *Everyday Life – The Adventures of a Concept from Simmel to de Certeau* (see Jay 1984). The idea that the concept (or problem) has a social life, that it undergoes an adventure, as it is reformulated, re-employed, re-used, in different contexts, under different conditions, is the implicit understanding of my approach. In approaching these varied writers my main concern has been with elucidating the work in relation to a number of questions that I will outline shortly. The central motivating force has been to tackle questions and problems that I see as productive for approaching contemporary everyday life. While my approach insists on the importance of situating theory within specific historical conjunctures and geographical terrains, none of this would be important if I didn't think that such work mattered for an approach to the everyday for the present, and for present-day historical research. The critical rehearsal of Simmel's ideas, for instance, is not a matter of purely historical and academic interest. The Simmel I am interested in is a Simmel who is 'contemporary', who has something to offer the re-imagining of cultural studies and its attention to the everyday.

Animating this account then are three clusters of questions.

Aesthetics

The first series of questions need to be understood as aesthetic ones. At first glance such an orientation might seem slightly at odds with the topic of this book. Isn't the field of aesthetics concerned with the values and practices of high culture, which if not antithetical to the world of the everyday, tend to be removed from it? Our initial move then will have to be to ignore such insistent associations for the moment. If we swap the world of everyday life for the socio-historical terrain of Western fine art (in which aesthetic questions have taken root) what then becomes of aesthetics? Aesthetics, I want to argue, allows us to consider two questions simultaneously. On the one hand, by foregrounding the world as both mental *and sensual* experience it problematically expands the range of meaningful elements attributable to the everyday. If, for instance, boredom is seen as a central experience in everyday life, then it is clearly not limited to the realm of thought (which is usually 'where' meaning is located). Boredom can affect the body and mind as a form of existential and physical tiredness. How should this experience (or these experiences) be understood? How should they be described? This takes us directly to the other central aspect of aesthetics: aesthetics insists on examining the way in which experiences are registered and represented. So aesthetics is concerned with experience and the form such experience takes when it is communicated. Such concerns are clearly crucial for theorizing the everyday. It should also be noted that thinking of aesthetics in this way takes us back to a realm of high culture, though not exclusively. After all, the province of poets, painters, novelists and composers has often been to try and register 'ordinary' experience. The relevance of so-called high culture becomes even more vivid when the formal experimentation of avant-garde artists is taken into account. The attempt to locate and apprehend modern everyday life, and to find forms that are capable of articulating it, might be seen as the overriding ambition of many avant-garde artists of the late nineteenth and early twentieth century. The importance of such an avant-gardist ambition will be central to this book. First though we need to flesh out a notion of aesthetics as it might impact on the theorizing of everyday life.

In his discussion of the term 'everyday life' in his book *Undoing Culture* (1995), Mike Featherstone suggests that 'it appears to be a residual category into which can be jettisoned all the irritating bits and pieces which do not fit into orderly thought'. He goes on to write that 'to venture into this field is to explore an aspect of life whose central features apparently lack methodicalness and are particularly resistant to rational categorization' (Featherstone 1995: 55). This suggests that the everyday cannot be properly accommodated by rationalist thought and that the everyday is precisely what becomes remaindered after rationalist thought has tried to exhaust the world of meaning. It also implies that the concept of everyday life has much in common with the incipient meaning of aesthetics. When the term aesthetics emerged in the work of the German philosopher Alexander Baumgarten at the end of the eighteenth century, it was going to be the 'science of the senses' (Battersby 1991: 35) – a philosophical and scientific attention to sensory, corporeal experience (perhaps the very stuff of the everyday). As Terry Eagleton writes:

> It is as though philosophy suddenly wakes up to find that there is a dense, swarming territory beyond its own mental enclave which threatens to fall utterly outside its sway. That territory is nothing less than the whole of our sensate life together – the business of affections and aversions, of how the world strikes the body on its sensory surfaces, of that which takes root in the gaze and the guts and all that arises from our most banal, biological insertion into the world.
>
> (Eagleton 1990: 13)

The history of attempts to attend to these experiences, like the history of attending to the everyday, is fraught with contradiction. Eagleton suggests that rationalist philosophy's approach to sensory experience operates as a form of colonization: 'the colonization of reason' (1990: 15). What Eagleton points to is the tendency of philosophy to submit sensate experience to the procedures of reason and science without questioning the adequacy of its form of attention. Indeed some philosophers have embraced this colonizing operation with a missionary zeal: 'Science is not to be dragged down to the region of sensibility, but the sensible is to be lifted to the dignity of knowledge' (Baumgarten, quoted in Eagleton 1990: 17).

The example of Baumgarten demonstrates a problematic: to borrow the procedures and materiality of a 'scientific' discourse for attending to everyday life can be seen to remainder precisely that which is the object of study. How often is the particularity of the everyday lost as it is transformed in the process of description and interpretation? As rationalist discourse expands to cover areas of life that are non-rational, that do not follow patterns of logical reasoning, what is lost (as these aspects of life are transformed into suitable objects for attention) is the very 'stuff-ness' that made them urgent problems in the first place. Of course for Baumgarten the intention is precisely to 'rescue' such material from its inchoate state, to transform the material to the point where it transcends its status as 'mere' sensation living in the lowly realms of the everyday. Significantly, much of aesthetics (as a discourse about art) is concerned with the everyday only at the point of such transcendence. Even in the aesthetic discourses that are most concerned with the everyday world of experience, transformation and transcendence are the operative procedures.

At this level of argument the everyday represents an impossibly evasive terrain: to attend to it is to lose it, or as Blanchot writes: 'We cannot help but miss it if we seek it through knowledge, for it belongs to a region where there is still nothing to know' (1987: 15). But this should not be taken to suggest that the everyday is completely unyielding to forms of representation (description or theory); rather it is to suggest that certain forms of discourse (discourses of 'knowledge' in Blanchot's words) are not adequate to their objects and at times fail to accommodate them at all. The other side of this is that there might well be forms of representation that are *more* appropriate, *more* adequate, for attending to the everyday. To suggest that the sensory and the everyday are outside representation, and that they are fundamentally incommensurate with forms of representation, is to miss the fact that sensation and the everyday are already part of a world of representation. To treat everyday life as a realm of experience unavailable for representation or reflection is to condemn it to silence. However, if the sensory and the everyday are seen as already fully colonized by discourse and representation, as if nothing could possibly be outside the forms of representation that are currently in use, then everyday life is neither problematic nor capable of generating counter-discourses. It becomes merely a term used to designate an area already fully represented. An everyday aesthetics would have to negotiate to avoid either one of these endgames.

Tradition might suggest that certain forms of representation are more appropriate for attending to specific aspects of the world. For instance, a poem might be seen as a more fitting form for attending to the world of feelings and emotions than a sociological study; the economic treatise more capable of apprehending capitalism than a novel. Yet in relation to the everyday, all forms of representation are hampered by a similar problem. If, for example, the everyday is seen as a 'flow', then any attempt to arrest it, to apprehend it, to scrutinize it, will be problematic. Simply by extracting some elements from the continuum of the everyday, attention would have transformed the most characteristic aspect of everyday life: its ceaseless-ness. As far as this goes, a good starting point would be to suggest that no form of discourse is ever going to be 'proper' (appropriate) to everyday life. The everyday will necessarily exceed attempts to apprehend it. This would simply mean that the search for the perfect fit between a form of representation and its object (the everyday) needs to be called off. Instead we might say that different forms of representation are going to produce different versions of the everyday. But if what is deemed to be the appropriate form for attending to the everyday (mainstream sociology, say, or novelistic description) has resulted in a lack of attention to certain aspects of the everyday, then the everyday might benefit from the attention of purposefully *inappropriate* forms of representation. Or rather, the everyday might be more productively glimpsed if the propriety of discourses is refused. In the work of Simmel or Benjamin, or in the avant-garde practices of Surrealism or the College of Sociology, or in the 'Anthropology at Home' of Mass-Observation, a form of representation is fashioned that might be seen as *improper*. To use Surrealism to conduct sociological research or to insist on montage as the technique for historical study is to cut across discursive decorum. It is also to test the potential of different forms of representation to apprehend the experience of everyday life.

One of the main arguments of this book is that *something like* an avant-garde sociology is being fashioned when the everyday is taken as the central problematic. A significant concern for theorizing the everyday is the problem of generating a suitable *form* for registering everyday modernity. In other words, all the projects dealt with here can be seen to contribute to the creation of an aesthetics of and for everyday modernity. That the very form of articulating the everyday is seen as a problem, or that describing the everyday might require formal experimentation, implies not only that the everyday has suffered from inattention, but that the kinds of attention that are available are severely out of step with the actuality of the everyday. There is a historical dimension to this that cannot be ignored. The dramatist Bertolt Brecht once suggested that 'new problems appear and demand new methods. Reality changes; in order to represent it, modes of representation must also change' (Brecht 1980: 82). The projects I go on to discuss can all be seen to respond to a sense of everyday modernity as described in the previous chapter. It is this sense of modernity as complex, contradictory (both boredom and mystery) and dynamic that makes traditional forms of representation appear unfit for dealing with modern everyday life. Perhaps the most famous text that deals with the revolutionary aspects of modernization is Marx and Engels' *Manifesto of the Communist Party* [1848]. In this, they treat modernization as an assault on all forms of tradition:

> Constant revolutionising of production, uninterrupted disturbance of all social conditions, everlasting uncertainty and agitation distinguish the bourgeois epoch from all earlier ones. All fixed, fast-frozen relations, with their train of ancient and venerable prejudices and opinions are swept away, all new-formed ones become antiquated before they can ossify. All that is solid melts into air, all that is holy is profaned . . .
>
> (Marx and Engels 1968: 38)

Marx and Engels insist on the everydayness of modernization. As a form of consciousness ('uncertainty and agitation') modernization is unsettling, as an attack on traditional beliefs ('ancient and venerable prejudices and opinions are swept away') it is disorientating, and as an assault on perception ('all that is solid melts into air') it is unnerving. By connecting technological and social changes with changes in everyday experience the *Communist Manifesto* becomes one of the first texts to posit modernity as a revolutionary experience to be located at the level of everyday life.

What then would constitute a suitable aesthetic form for registering daily life in all its newness, uncertainty and lack of tradition? How might such an unsettled form of life register? This might well be the question that the everyday poses to the avant-garde sociologist. The necessity of fashioning new forms (or tools) for apprehending new kinds of experiences (new 'realities') might be seen as the general impetus and problematic attendant on theorizing daily life. What is called the artistic avant-garde seems to offer a repertoire of formal devices for registering a world that appears chaotic, disrupted and radically new. The projects discussed in this book might be seen to exist on the boundaries of art and science, borrowing from the artistic avant-garde (or working in sympathy with them) and yet directing their concerns towards other ends. Here I shall only give a very quick synopsis of some of the formal 'aesthetic' devices that might coexist in both an artistic avant-garde and in a more sociological one.

If everyday life, for the most part, goes by unnoticed (even as it is being revolutionized), then the first task for attending to it will be to make it noticeable. The artistic avant-garde's strategy of 'making strange', of rendering what is most familiar unfamiliar, can provide an essential ingredient for fashioning a sociological aesthetic (to use Simmel's term). Aesthetic techniques, such as the surprising juxtapositions supplied by Surrealism, provide a productive resource for rescuing the everyday from conventional habits of mind. Similarly, if the everyday is conventionally perceived as homogeneous, forms of artistic montage work to disturb such 'smooth surfaces'. But this sociological aesthetic isn't simply designed to 'shock' us out of our established forms of attention; its ambition is to attempt to register the everyday in 'all' its complexities and contradictions. For this montage might be seen as an aesthetic form particularly well suited to the complex and contradictory. Yet if 'everyday life theory' is to promote and practise montage, then, unless it is going to simply register the cacophony of the everyday, it has to find some way of ordering, of organizing the everyday. Here the theoretical is precisely the problem of ordering and arranging, of making some kind of sense of the endless empiricism of the everyday.

The theorists and theories explored in this book (Georg Simmel, Walter Benjamin, Surrealism, Mass-Observation, Lefebvre and de Certeau) can be seen to begin to fabricate an 'alternative' aesthetic for attending to the experience of modern everyday life. It is an alternative to a range of options in regard to the everyday: it is alternative to the instrumentality of governmental attempts to catalogue the everyday; to high culture's propensity towards expressive subjectivism in relation to the everyday; and to science's dour positivism. Theirs is an aesthetic that in negotiating the experience of everyday life never claims to exhaust it. It is an aesthetic of experimentation that recognizes that actuality always outstrips the procedures for registering it. The work of these everyday life theories can be characterized by a hybrid mode of representation. Never simply 'theory' or 'fiction', philosophy or empirical observation, 'everyday life studies' exist on the borders and the gaps between these representational categories. It is an aesthetic that questions the suitability of 'system', 'rigour' and 'logic' for attending to the everyday. As such its theoretical resources emerge from a variety of sources, from writers such as Brecht and Joyce as much as from Marx, from daily observations as much as from intellectual encounters. It is an aesthetic struggling to find a place within a field (social and cultural theory) that is often oblivious to its own aesthetic protocols.

Archives

The second cluster of questions concerns the (related) problem of the archive. At one level this might be thought of as a simple practical question: what would an archive of everyday life include? What could it possibly exclude? For instance, if an archive of the everyday (for example, the one Mass-Observation produced) were to include a potentially infinite number of items (diaries, photographs, observations and so on, compiled by anyone who wants to participate), then how could it be organized? The question of what to include in an everyday life archive raises questions about the appropriate form for collating 'everyday life' material. In the case of Mass-Observation the desire to let the everyday 'speak for itself' resulted in an archive on an unmanageable scale. Two problems immediately become clear. First, if the everyday is going to be represented 'from within', so to speak, then questions emerge about the organization and limits that might be placed on such a necessarily disordered archive. Will everything and anything be included? Will there be any way of organizing this material? A second and related problem becomes evident in any use of this archive. If the archive is made up of a polyphonic everyday, then how is it to be orchestrated into meaningful themes or readable accounts? How can one construct an intelligible articulation from the archive that doesn't submerge the polyphonic beneath the editorial voice at work? In other words the possible use of the archive seems to linger between two extremes: on the one hand an unmanaged accumulation of singularities, and on the other a constrictive order that transforms the wildness of the archive into tamed narratives. The history of Mass-Observation is the history of negotiating this problematic.

So even at the level of collecting and organizing data, more fundamental problems intrude, namely the problem of making the everyday meaningful in a way that doesn't imprison it at the level of the particular, or doesn't eradicate the particularity of the particular by taking off into abstract generalities. This problem can be seen as the dilemma of negotiating between the microscopic levels (most frequently classed as everyday) and macroscopic levels of the totality (culture, society and so on). The issue that this articulates is about the privileging accorded to either one of these perspectives. In recent years (in the wake of certain kinds of arguments associated with accounting for postmodernism) the privilege has tended to fall on the side of the microscopic. Yet, if 'everyday life theory' is a meaningful and historically urgent form of attention, I would want to argue that this is because at some level it simply refuses to remain at the microscopic scale. After all doesn't the notion of *the* everyday suggest a desire for something more than an endless series of singular 'everydays'? Simply put, *everyday life might be the name for the desire of totality in postmodern times.*

However, if the argument that the desire to attend to the 'totality' must be a 'totalitarian' desire is overblown (which it clearly is), then the tendency of 'grand narratives' to erase and ignore vast terrains of experience can't be so easily dismissed. Indeed, as should be becoming clear by now, much everyday life theory is purposefully addressed to responding to the way in which conventional discourse has erased and ignored the everyday. So if general accounts of 'society' or 'culture' are seen as oblivious towards the everyday, then before any general account of these can be proffered the absolute priority is going to be to rescue the everyday from oblivion. If this is the case, the initial move for a cultural theory of the everyday will be to bring to recognition this benighted realm of the everyday – to allow it to become visible in all its particularity. But (and this may be the central dilemma of the everyday archive) if this is the case, might it not become impossible (or at least, less likely) to generate new and better accounts of the social totality as the archive literally submerges this possibility in its exponentially increasing textuality? There is of course no recourse to a solution here. For someone committed to Marxism, such as Lefebvre, without a philosophical (abstract and critical) orientation it made no sense to attend to the empirical. Lefebvre provides a useful approach to this problematic in that he treats everyday life as the *relationships* between different registers of social life. In his *Critique of Everyday Life* he suggests that the singularity of the everyday event (a woman buying sugar, for example) reverberates with social and psychic desire as well as with the structures of national and global exchange (Lefebvre 1991a: 57). The question that this poses for the archive is a massive one. Not only does it suggest the endless proliferation of singular events, but also it demands the relating of these events to economic structures of desire and exchange. The methodological problems this poses for Lefebvre are dealt with in a variety of ways, but as the focus of his work shifts from everyday life in general to the urban everyday, the unmanageability of the everyday archive is increasingly managed by spatializing the interrelations of the everyday.

A more epistemological problem exists in relation to the history of archival practices. For de Certeau, what united the archival practices that emerged in the West as a corollary to colonial expansion (both at 'home' and 'abroad') was a combined operation that both repressed the culture that was supposed to be 'conserved' by the archive, and inscribed there a desire of its own. For de Certeau it is the translation of a lived culture into a *written* culture that marks the taming of the everyday and the inscription of a disciplinary writing. It is clear in de Certeau's work that those discourses (at once archival and scriptural) that might at first glance be seen as attending to the everyday (anthropology, 'official' studies of daily life and so on) work to erase the everyday. Yet it also becomes clear that they are never entirely successful. The everyday exists 'between the lines' (so to speak) of archival practices. So for de Certeau attending to the everyday will also mean attempting to rescue the traces, the remainders of the overflowing unmanageability of the everyday that erupt within representation, and mark the work of repression.

The question of methodology is raised again by the heterogeneity of the material that could be included in an archive of everyday life. While Cultural Studies has developed sophisticated ways of attending to the semiotic material of the visual and verbal, it is massively underdeveloped in relation to the aural, the olfactory and the haptic. An archive of everyday life based on the writings of de Certeau, for instance, might include: walking, talking, cooking, eating, slouching and so on. Both Simmel and Benjamin recognize the everyday of modernity as assaulting the totality of the sensate body. While the theories being considered here don't result in a worked-through approach to the totality of sensory life, they do point to the lack of attention to non-visual and non-scriptural senses. The historicity of everyday sensation might well be a necessary accompaniment to any future theorizing of everyday life. It might also mean that the archive of everyday life includes not only the recording and collection of everyday voices, everyday events, everyday materials and everyday sensations; it should also include a process of everyday-ing archives already in existence. For instance, this might mean attempting to read the haptical (through posture, gait, the sense of a body holding itself) in the negotiated moments of visual description that make up a photographic archive. It might also suggest that the presentation of archival material would benefit from experimental approaches that attempt to articulate the everyday as a sensory realm.

Practices and critiques

The third cluster of questions (again related to the previous ones) circulates around the problem of the everyday as a critical practice and as a form of practical criticism. To put it starkly these questions stress the problem of both description and critique in attending to the everyday. The field of Cultural

Studies (if it is a 'field') has done much to promote the project of critiquing everyday life. But in many ways this critique has been played out as a theoretical endgame. In an article published in 1990, Meaghan Morris characterized a tendency within cultural studies:

> But sometimes, when distractedly reading magazines such as *New Socialist* or *Marxism Today* from the last couple of years, flipping through *Cultural Studies*, or scanning the pop-theory pile in the bookstore, I get a feeling that somewhere in some English publisher's vault there is a master disk from which thousands of versions of the same article about pleasure, resistance, and the politics of consumption are being run off under different names with minor variations.
>
> (Morris 1990: 21)

Morris' complaint is that within Cultural Studies a form of analysis has emerged that privileges an essentially active and resistant subject of everyday culture. From this perspective it doesn't matter what kind of cultural material you look at because potentially it is all open to being used in similarly 'creative' and 'subversive' ways at the point of consumption. While the historical reasons for this approach can partly be explained by seeing it as an over-compensation for a previous formulation that took the subject of everyday culture to be passive and easily manipulated, the result is an endless search for the progressive within the dominant, a search that seems locked into telling the same story time and time again. Whether the everyday is seen as a realm dictated to by overarching structures of power, or as a realm characterized by an endless refusal of such power, the job of critique might seem too easy, too glibly confident of its meaningfulness. Or rather, the practice of critique might simply be *premature*.

If, for many of the cultural projects discussed in this book, the everyday (as a lived actuality) is absent from the professional discourses that might supply critical purchase (philosophy, politics and so on) then, as already suggested, the first priority would be to bring the everyday into the light (so to speak). Until this has happened a critical practice relevant to the everyday will remain undeveloped. Critique, in the sense of mobilizing an available politics, would have to be postponed, because such politics would have already played a part in rendering the everyday mute. In its place a number of other operations would need to be performed. For the likes of Mass-Observation and Michel de Certeau the necessary operation is to reverse the picture we have of the social. Instead of picturing the world as a drama of significant (and exceptional) events and people, set against a backdrop of everyday life, the relation between foreground and background needs to be reversed. For de Certeau this was the necessary prerequisite for a theory of everyday that might begin to sketch the forms that ordinary practice takes. To do this then requires temporarily surrendering the normal codes of political propriety that often drive work seen as critical.

But lest this is seen as some naïve liberal fantasy, it is worth remembering how social forms of critique can emerge. The example of second-wave feminism (briefly discussed in chapter 1) remains pertinent. It was not by setting in motion some abstract political notion of 'equality' and 'liberty' that feminism became such a driving force in the 1970s and 1980s. Rather by first taking on the empirical job of bringing women's lives into discourse (often generating new forms of discourse in the process), a critical account of the psychical depth of patriarchy emerged that simply wouldn't have been possible if the empirical had been approached in the name of previously constituted abstractions such as 'equality'. The very fact that such a broad social and cultural movement immersed itself in the everyday (domestic routines, sexual identity and so on – neatly designated by the slogan the 'personal is political') should alert us to the potential of the everyday to generate new political forms. In other words, the job of description can be the necessary prerequisite for allowing new forms of 'political' critique to emerge. By locating the politics of gender in the everyday, feminism provoked a transformation of politics itself: who could have predicted that politics would come to include the sexual and domestic? If the projects outlined in this book never mutated into immense social movements like second-wave feminism, then their critical potential remains necessarily unknown (or rather, untested). To force them into a political critique based on the kinds of world-pictures that they were experimentally challenging would also have to be seen as premature. Instead, critical evaluation would require a more speculatively sympathetic orientation.

Lefebvre on the other hand employs a more deliberate critique to allow the everyday to come into focus. But it should be noted that the critical procedures that Lefebvre uses (generally Marxist) are not those that are welded to an existent politics. This may seem like a strange thing to say in regard to one of the most insistently political philosophies of the modern age. None the less I would argue that the terms of Lefebvre's Marxism (based as it was on recognizing capitalist society as a radical alienation of men and women's potential humanness) were the very terms that Marxism drops when it is turned into a practical and professional political programme. Indeed the Marxism that Lefebvre privileges for his critique can be seen as oriented more towards anarchism than communism. And perhaps the one explicit principle of anarchism is the forfeiting of a political programme in the name of an experimental orientation that desires to release the unknown (and historically unknowable) potential of human life.

In the work of Lefebvre the residues of rural festivals are seen as offering liberatory potential for everyday life. This privileging of ritualistic material in the everyday suggests the possibility of an attention to the everyday that promotes a cross-cultural perspective (even if the comparative culture is to be found within the culture being examined). The basis for this is an orientation that is necessarily anthropological: it compares and contrasts two or more cultures, not by privileging the one over the other, but by a kind of mutual testing that works to denaturalize both cultures. What is crucial to Lefebvre (and I think to Mass-Observation and de Certeau in some ways) is that this cross-cultural anthropology insists that the *critique* of everyday life can and should be found within the everyday. Thus festival in modern capitalist culture may have become tawdry and commercial, but even in this alienated state it can still point to the possibility of life lived differently (to another tempo, a different logic).

Yet Lefebvre's project was fashioned at a time when the knowledge of Fascism's promotion of ritualistic and irrational material into the everyday was inescapable. The rise of Fascism in the 1930s might be seen to constitute a crisis of critique: it places the terms of critique into doubt at the same time as it makes its deployment terrifyingly urgent. If Fascism does produce some kind of crisis in relation to critical authority, then it does so because it confuses the terms of critique. Fascism might look simply like the outpouring of irrationalism and myth that should be met by a relentless reasoning that would result in the destruction of Fascist myth. Yet it became increasingly clear that the stronger party in this struggle wasn't always (or very often) the 'clear light' of reason. If Fascist myth was to be defeated, how was this to be achieved if not by reason? The alternative was to begin to search out myth and ritual within an everyday culture that might be mobilized against Fascism (a trick learned by propagandists as they promoted the most mythic of irrationalism – nationalism). But Fascism, as well as being a form of irrationalism, can also be seen as a form of ultra-rationalism. Or rather Fascism reveals the ends to which 'reason' (or what has been done in the name of reason) can be put. Thus the link between the racial theory of the nineteenth century and the Jewish Holocaust places an indelible question mark on the innocence and emancipatory potential of reason (see for instance Bauman 1989). For the likes of Mass-Observation (or in another way for Walter Benjamin) Fascism urgently focused attention on to the subject of the everyday.

What all this results in is, I think, a suspicion (sometimes confusingly articulated) about translating everyday life theory and practice into the available language of 'critical' politics. Rather than placing their faith in an emancipatory politics that would be found in the abstractions of philosophy or the pragmatics of politics, writers such as de Certeau seem unerringly to cast their lot with the everyday. It is in the everyday that emancipation might be found (if it is to be found at all); critiques of the everyday will emerge in the practices of everyday life, not in the rarefied or deadeningly 'realist' programmes of political parties. Thus, to return to the problem of Cultural

Studies, 'everyday life theory' holds out an invitation to rethink such dualisms as 'resistance' and 'power'. It does so by re-evaluating the productivity of description (as a foregrounding and recognizing of the everyday) and by re-imaging the practice of critique (by potentially generating new forms of critical practice). As such it is the symptomatic result of a frustration aimed at both politics (as conventionally and endlessly played out) and traditional social and cultural theory (understood as oblivious to the everyday).

Structure

The chapters that follow develop these arguments by focusing on particular theoretical writers or cultural projects. The next three chapters (3, 4 and 5) can be seen as outlining some of the elements of an 'aesthetics' of the everyday (if by this we mean an engagement with both the experience of the everyday and the problem of registering it). These chapters look at the work of Simmel and Benjamin and at various forms of Surrealism. Simmel's methodological approach claims to reveal general qualities of social life by focusing on the incidental and the meagre. For Simmel such work doesn't resolve itself into elaborate theoretical schemas; instead it can be seen to be a sociology of the fragment, where the part is seen as registering the general but is never simply reducible to it. It always remains specific, an unassimilable fragment. Walter Benjamin can be seen as continuing Simmel's project of a sociology of modernity. Benjamin's massive and unfinished *Arcades Project* (unfinishable, I would argue) was to map a prehistory to modernity, to grasp the emergence of modernity in all its contingencies as it hardened into cultural forms. Benjamin's interest is also in the everyday detritus, but there is a reason for this that extends Simmel's approach. For Benjamin the recently outmoded can point us towards a revolutionary contingency, which is capable of demonstrating that 'things could be different'. Between Simmel and Benjamin lies the project of Surrealism, a project whose importance as a resource for attending to the everyday cannot be overstated. It should also be seen as one of the most important aspects of Benjamin's cultural constellation. Surrealism and forms of dissident Surrealism allow the everyday to be 'othered' in a move that forces a denaturalizing of the everyday. It is also in Surrealism that we find two methodological tools for attending to the everyday: the first is the process of montage, seen here as the most crucial representational form for the everyday; the second is a reworking of social anthropology that mobilizes it for attending to the domestic everyday.

The themes of the everyday as modern experience and the difficulty of finding modes of representation that might be used to articulate it are continued in chapter 6 which discusses the work of Mass-Observation. Mass-Observation is a movement that emerged in Britain in the 1930s, partly as a response to the surfacing of ritual and myth within the everyday. Against the view of Mass-Observation as a resolutely positivist project tied to state bureaucracy, I emphasize the aspects of it that can be seen to problematize such a reading. One of the most productive aspects of Mass-Observation has been the unlikely and disquieting marriage of Surrealism and social anthropology. The potential of applying ethnographic protocols to domestic cultures continues the avant-garde practice of making the familiar strange. From this emerged the beginnings of a poetics of the everyday that might, potentially at least, transform the social and cultural realm of the daily by the very act of mobilizing mass attention towards it.

In chapter 7 I review Henri Lefebvre's life-long project of a critique of everyday life. This project extends some of Marx's early writings and applies them to the decades of radical social change that took place during Lefebvre's career. Lefebvre's *Critique of Everyday Life* emerges from a brew of Western Marxism, Surrealism and observations of social transformation. In it he stresses the political imperative of transforming everyday life, and this can be seen as a response to the failure of the Soviet Revolution to change the social and cultural conditions of everyday life in the USSR (or rather, to change them for the better). Lefebvre's continuation of the critique of everyday life focused on the urban environment as a space for the intensification of the alienation of everyday life, as well as a site for its possible transformation.

Chapter 8 focuses on Michel de Certeau's *The Practice of Everyday Life*, and sees it as responding to a very different intellectual and social climate from Lefebvre's project. In its emphasis on the imaginative and inventive practice of everyday life, it is a critique of a theoretical position that sees the social as saturated by the dominance of powerful interests. In his writing on everyday life and popular culture, de Certeau sets up a 'colonial encounter' where the cultures of everyday life are erased by the professional bodies that attend to them. The cultures of everyday life are therefore submerged below the level of a social and textual authority. While they tend to remain invisible and unrepresentable, they perform *something like* a guerrilla war on these authorities (though the limitations of de Certeau's 'war' metaphors will, I hope, become obvious). This position offers a valuable 'view from below', and productively foregrounds a range of practical forms of 'resistance' within everyday life. But at the same time it reworks the very notion of resistance. I argue that de Certeau's poetics problematize cultural theory as a theoretical architecture based on a division between power and resistance. In this his work suggests a productive affinity with the project of psychoanalysis.

In a final and relatively short chapter I speculate on how 'everyday life theory' might be used to re-imagine and relocate Cultural Studies. I also address (all too briefly) some of the more urgent cultural issues that might be seen as missing from such a body of theory, namely some alternative to the European focus of these accounts. What might 'everyday life theory' look like from the perspective of an international frame? Where might 'everyday life theory' (literally) go to consolidate and extend the tradition outlined here? In place of a conclusion, then, chapter 9 simply tries to encourage and expand the broadly experimental project of theorizing everyday life.

'Everyday life' in this account is not a 'given' that cultural theory simply investigates. In some ways it can be seen as the *product* that is generated by the kinds of inquiry that I will be looking at. It is not until we reach the work of Lefebvre and de Certeau that something like 'the everyday' as a specific problematic emerges. The ambitious projects of Simmel and Benjamin (for instance) grapple with the monstrousness of modernity. In their searching for a form of attention that can offer some productive hold on modernity, 'the everyday' begins to emerge as a critical concept and as an *imaginative fiction* for approaching social life. In the cultural theory that such projects generate, the everyday is linked to an experience of modernity that privileges the urban and the unconscious (or the non-conscious). Here and in the cultural formations that follow, the everyday is not something to be condemned or condoned, evaded or embraced. The 'imaginative fiction' of the everyday points to something unavoidable and inescapable, but it also points to something that in crucial ways is *unformed*. Perhaps then the tradition of theory that is the topic of this book evidences an approach to social and cultural life that in both theory and practice is radically (and literally) *reformist*.

Chapter 3

SIMMEL
Fragments of everyday life

I actually consider it a cultural task not unworthy of a philosopher to present
to the broadest possible public a certain intellectual opinion on and absorption in precisely the most superficial and everyday phenomena.

(Simmel, quoted in Rammstedt 1991: 126)

WRITING ACROSS THE END of the nineteenth century and the
start of the twentieth, it is hard to place Georg Simmel's work within
the now established contours of intellectual work. Most famous for his contribution to a nascent sociology, Simmel's writing spans a very broad 'culturalist'
perspective, including philosophical work on aesthetics and the cultural effects
and affects of the 'money economy'. The most vivid assessment of his achievement comes, not from his immediate contemporaries, but from the next
generation of theorists and critics, many of whom were Simmel's students.
A number of writers, either responding directly to Simmel's work or
attempting to register his impact on those critical theorists he taught, have
offered condensed and telling accounts of his work that go to the heart of
the problem of everyday life. For Theodor Adorno, writing (in 1965) about
Simmel's importance for understanding the work of Ernst Bloch (a student
and friend of Simmel), Simmel 'was, for all his psychological idealism, the
first to accomplish the return of philosophy to concrete subjects, a shift that
remained canonical for everyone dissatisfied with the chattering of episte-
mology or intellectual history' (Adorno 1992: 213). For Jack Zipes, writing
again about Bloch, 'Simmel was one of those remarkable intellectuals who
believed that a philosopher must be concerned with everyday occurrences
and small events' (Zipes, in the introduction to Bloch 1989: xiv). Former
students such as Karl Mannheim and Georg Lukács thought Simmel was best

described as a sociological 'impressionist' – a philosophical sociologist who attended to the experience of a fragmented everyday world and the trivial objects it contains in ways analogous to the way in which impressionist painters attended to these same aspects in their paintings. But while these writers are unambiguous about Simmel's achievement, they remain sceptical about its cost. For both Mannheim and Lukács, as well as for Siegfried Kracauer, Simmel stops short of offering any 'workable system' that could make sense of the totality of social experience. Mannheim writes that Simmel's ability 'was not an ability to take a constructive view of the whole of society' (Mannheim, quoted in the introduction to Simmel 1990: 32), while Kracauer writes (in 1920) that 'he never discovered the magic word for the macrocosm that underlies all forms of existence, and he still owes us a far-reaching, all-encompassing notion of the world' (Kracauer 1995: 225). For Lukács (in 1918), Simmel 'was a Monet of philosophy who has not yet been followed by a Cezanne' (Lukács 1991: 147). I will have more to say about Simmel as an impressionist below; for now it is enough to note that, while Simmel's approach to the everyday, and to the experience of modernity, was viewed as innovative and productive, its value has been seen as being seriously undermined by a failure to synthesize his investigations into a philosophical world-view. The complaints that have framed academic contact with Simmel's work have been consistently aimed at an estimation of his work as 'fragmented', 'undisciplined' and 'unscientific' (see Axelrod 1994).

Simmel's own understanding of his sociological project is given in his preface to *The Philosophy of Money* (1900, revised 1907). Simmel notes two central and overlapping directions in his work. On the one hand, 'the unity of these investigations does not lie . . . in an assertion about a particular content of knowledge and its gradually accumulating proofs but rather in the possibility – which must be demonstrated – of finding in each of life's details the totality of its meaning' (1990: 55). On the other hand, his aim was 'to construct a new storey beneath historical materialism such that the explanatory value of the incorporation of economic life into the causes of intellectual culture is preserved, while these economic forms themselves are recognized as the result of more profound valuations and currents of psychological or even metaphysical pre-conditions' (1990: 56). These two directions constitute a move in the field of theory that massively widens the scope for investigating the social. The attention to the details of everyday life (a form of sociological microscopy) means that the experiential, instead of being located in great events, is extended to the non-event-ness of the everyday, while the notion of economics is expanded from a Marxist understanding of economics (a limited economics), to a more general economics that can include an economics of the senses, an economics of nervous energies, an economics of affect.

In investigating the productivity of Simmel's work for theorizing everyday life in modernity, I want to argue that it is precisely in Simmel's use of the fragments of daily life to articulate modern experience that his value lies. Simmel's refusal of the unifying system, the philosophical macroview, is not the result of an inability to connect these fragments; rather it emerges from the attempt to find a form of attention that is adequate (or more adequate) to its object (everyday life in the modern world). To synthesize this into a system would mean erasing not just the singularity of the detail, but the vitality of the relations between details. What has been called Simmel's sociological formalism (an interest in the formal arrangements of social relations) needs to be rethought. Simmel's formalism can be seen as an approach that takes style seriously: the style of living, the style of objects, and the poetics of representing the modern. As another of Simmel's students suggests, Simmel 'conceives of sociology as the study of the forms of sociation. But whoever speaks of forms moves into the field of aesthetics. Society, in the last analysis, is a work of art' (Salz, quoted in Davis 1994: 46).

Impressionism, fragments and totalities

In developing an argument that sees Simmel's project as an 'everyday' aesthetics of the fragment, it is worth exploring Karl Mannheim's description of Simmel as a sociological impressionist. Mannheim suggests that Simmel used

> the same method for the description of everyday life that was previously used to describe pictures or to characterize works of literature. He had an aptitude for describing the simplest everyday experiences with the same precision as is characteristic of a contemporary impressionistic painting which has learned to reflect the previously unobserved shades and values of the atmosphere. He might well be called the 'impressionist' in sociology, because his was not an ability to take a constructive view of the whole of society but to analyse the significance of minor social forces that were previously unobserved.
>
> (Mannheim, quoted in Simmel 1990: 32)

Crucial to this designation of Simmel's work as impressionistic is an understanding of it as being concerned with forms of expression that are associated more with literary and artistic production than with social science. The characterization of Simmel's sociology as impressionism has also been the route for a major reassessment of his thought in recent years. David Frisby, who has energetically re-examined Simmel's work, entitled his first book on Simmel, *Sociological Impressionism: A Reassessment of Georg Simmel's Social Theory* (Frisby 1992b; see also Frisby 1984, 1985, 1992a). Frisby's investigations of Simmel make suggestive connections between Simmel's attitudes and those to be found in the literary and artistic avant-garde in Paris during the Second Empire. Frisby uses the Baudelairian figure of the *flâneur*, the passionate but detached observer of modern life, to elicit crucial similarities and differences between Simmel and the project of the 'Painter of Modern Life' (see Baudelaire 1964; Clark 1985). But while this association with the Parisian avant-garde has provided useful insights, the term 'impressionism' needs to be set in a context closer to Simmel. To pinpoint what impressionism may have meant for Simmel and how it was being used by his students to describe him, we need to look at the particular currency the term had in Germany and especially Berlin at the turn of the century.

In an essay by Lothar Müller called 'The Beauty of the Metropolis: Toward an Aesthetic Urbanism in Turn-of-the-Century Berlin', the term 'impressionism' is examined in the specific context of Berlin, Simmel's home town. Müller suggests that crucial to this context was an understanding of Berlin, not as an artistic capital, but as a technological capital: 'the Berlin of this era, in contrast to Paris, the capital of *aesthetic* modernity in the nineteenth century, was perceived as a centre of a *technological*, civilizing modernity' (Müller 1990: 37–8). It is in relation to this that impressionism was understood not simply as artistic expression but as a *diagnostic* approach to the condition of modernity: 'Impressionism was transformed into a diagnostic category of reflection on the period as a whole, a category in which ultimately the artistic style was only epiphenomenon, a symptom of the underlying style of life' (Müller 1990: 43). Müller draws attention to a book published in Germany in 1907 called *Impressionismus in Leben und Kunst* by Richard Harmann, where impressionism in life was seen as characterized by 'acceleration and transitoriness, hectic activity and mobility, as well as the erosion of all established norms and values'. For Lothar Müller the importance of this book lies in the way it treats impressionism – not simply as an artistic technique but as something that exists both in the lived experience of modern life and across a variety of different cultural expressions:

> In the book's diagnosis of impressionism, the 'impressionist' life-style, as manifested in all social and cultural phenomena, becomes synonymous with the fugitive, with the dissolution of form, with the antiarchitectonic. In philosophy impressionism is evident in the aestheticization of thinking; in ethics it is manifest in the tendency to reject any moral imperative; in drama it is the development of the undramatic; in music, the sublime cultivation of sonority and atmosphere.
>
> (Müller 1990: 44)

A crucial link was made between modern lived experience and cultural expressions in this Berlin context, and this link was most vividly signalled by the figure of the modern everyday as a site of overstimulation and nervousness. In this regard, impressionism, in this expanded sense, was both the name for the neurasthenic experience of everyday life and the cultural form most suited to representing it. As Müller suggests, a 'discursive equation of impressionism and nervousness' (45) emerged at the turn of the century. It is impressionism's adequacy as a form for articulating the discontinuous in the everyday, and for attending to particularly modern forms of experience, that can be seen as the relevant context for situating Simmel's 'impressionistic' approach. This characterization of Simmel's project is useful for understanding his project as a form of sociological microscopy, which employs impressionistic descriptions of everyday life within a philosophical approach where the particularity of the everyday is made to register more general social forces.

Simmel's sociological microscopy should be seen as a response to what he sees as the propensity of sociology to attend to the macroscopic: 'social science generally is still situated in this stage of being able to only consider the very large and clearly visible social structures and of trying to be able to produce insight from these into social life in its totality' (Simmel [1907] 1997: 109). In designating his project as 'microscopy' he suggests a perspective within the social sciences analogous to that produced within the natural sciences by the advent of microscopic investigations. This analogy produces an equivalence between the body as an object of scrutiny for the natural sciences and the social as the object of scrutiny for sociology:

> the life process now revealed itself first in its ties to its smallest elements, the cells, and in its identity with the innumerable and ceaseless interactions between these cells. How they adhere to one another or destroy each other, how they assimilate or chemically influence one another – only this gradually permits one to see how the body shapes, maintains or changes its form.
>
> (Simmel 1997: 109)

Clearly these 'cells' are the everyday for Simmel. Such a microscopic approach figures the encounters of everyday life 'as the genuine and fundamental basis of life' (109). But what is most significant about Simmel's attention to the everyday is that it is in the everyday that he also finds the macroscopic. While the impressionistic description of everyday life can be seen as the basic ingredient for Simmel's sociology, it is not in itself the telos of his project. For Simmel the everyday must be made to reverberate with the interactions, networks and force of social life. The everyday must be made to register vividly the social totality from within. Rather than using the everyday as illustrative of abstract social systems, the everyday must be made to give up its own secrets, the secrets of sociality. In this way the particularity of the everyday isn't reducible to a general theory of society (a system, a world-view); the particularity of the everyday remains unassimilable within such a system. But neither does the everyday fragment remain a singular atom, disconnected from other atoms:

> The fact that people look at and are jealous of one another, that they write each other letters or have lunch together, that they have sympathetic or antipathetic contacts, quite removed from any tangible interests, that one person asks another for directions and that people dress up and adorn themselves for one another – all the thousands of relations from person to person, momentary or enduring, conscious or unconscious, fleeting or momentous, from which the above examples are taken quite at random, continually bind us together. On every day, at every hour, such threads are spun, dropped, picked up again, replaced by others or woven together with them. Herein lie the interactions between atoms of society, accessible only to psychological microscopy, which support the entire tenacity and elasticity, the entire variety and uniformity of this so evident and yet so puzzling life of society.
>
> (Simmel 1997: 109)

Here the everyday is represented as an accumulation of moments. The everyday is a plethora of irreducible particularity, yet across this unmanageable actuality is a language of 'woven' 'threads' that 'bind us together', that point to the possibility of mapping a heterogeneous, diversified and complex totality. While the everyday is unpredictable and indeterminate there is within it the possibility of mapping its equivocality, of situating its ambivalence at the centre of the social. As we shall see, Simmel's diagnosis of modernity is one in which the everyday registers diverse and contrary experiences.

Examples of the way in which everyday materials are made to register more general social forces are numerous in Simmel's work. Essays such as 'The Sociology of the Meal', 'Bridge and Door', 'The Philosophy of Fashion' (collected in Simmel 1997), for example, continually move back and forth between 'impressionistic' descriptions of the everyday event and speculative accounts that treat such material as symptomatic of a dynamic and forceful culture. The process of combining impressionistic particularity with a philosophical form of attention that would extract a dynamic totality from this is summed up in the title of many of his *Jugend* essays: *Momentbilder sub specie aeternitas*. Simmel thought of himself as taking 'snapshots' of everyday life, but 'viewed from the aspect of eternity' (Frisby 1985: 71). Thus the most 'distracted' and impressionistic form of attention (the snapshot) is combined with another form of attention that treats such materials as if they were 'divorced from the contingency of their here and now' (Simmel, quoted in Rammstedt 1991: 139). To treat the everyday in this way can be seen as a form of aesthetics. I would suggest that such an aesthetics should be seen as part of an aesthetic avant-gardism in which the everyday is rendered as vivid, without its everydayness being remaindered in the process.

Simmel announces his project of sociological 'avant-gardism' in his essay 'Sociological Aesthetics' of 1896. This essay presents a sociological aesthetics of the fragment, where the particularity of daily life would reveal funda-mental forces. Thus, 'What is unique emphasizes what is typical, what is accidental appears as normal, and the superficial and fleeting stands for what is essential and basic' (Simmel 1968: 69). In 'Sociological Aesthetics' beauty becomes a form of analysis linked to dialectics, where the everyday is open to aesthetic attention by making it connect with the social totality. In an exuberant passage, Simmel conjures up his avant-garde sociology:

> Even the lowest, intrinsically ugly phenomenon can be dissolved into contexts of color and form, feeling and experience which provide it with significance. To involve ourselves deeply and lovingly with the even most common product, which, would be banal and repulsive in its isolated appearance, enables us to conceive of it, too, as a ray and image of the final unity of all things from which beauty and meaning flow. Every philosophical system, every religion, every moment of our heightened emotional experience searches for symbols which are appro-priate to their expression. If we pursue this possibility of aesthetic appreciation to its final point, we find that there are no essential differ-ences among things. Our world view turns into aesthetic pantheism. Every point contains within itself the potential of being redeemed to absolute aesthetic importance. To the adequately trained eye the totality of beauty, the complete meaning of the world as a whole, radiates from every single point.
>
> (Simmel 1968: 69)

Simmel's aesthetics of the everyday offers a radical programme that takes social interaction as its muse. In this way it doesn't matter what material is scrutinized; all paths lead to the same place – culture writ large. In 1896 such a radical call to register the most marginal, discarded, banal aspects of society must have sounded more like the rhetoric of a bohemian poet than someone setting out the contours of sociology. Here the connoisseur is replaced by the social analyst ('the adequately trained eye') who, steeped in the insignificance of everyday life, finds in it the elementary forces of the social totality. Such an aesthetic, rather than eradicating the everydayness of the everyday, is intended to reveal the everydayness at its core. Such a socially aesthetic programme, for Simmel, is mobilized, not just for social analysis, but also for social change: 'The more we learn to appreciate composite forms, the more readily we will extend aesthetic categories to forms of society as a whole' (Simmel 1968: 74). As an example, he offers a reading of the aesthetic basis of socialism: 'that society as a whole should become a work of art in which every single element attains its meaning by virtue of its contribution to the whole' (74).

Where Simmel's attention to the everyday most explicitly evidences the productivity of his analysis is when it attends to the historicity of the experience of the everyday, nowhere more so than when he diagnoses the modern everyday as a neurasthenic experience.

Diagnosing the modern everyday

At the end of his essay 'Sociological Aesthetics' Simmel writes: 'Exhausted nerves which are drifting between hypersensitivity and lack of sensitivity can be excited only by the most opaque forms and rudely accurate details, or else by the most tender and starkest stimuli' (Simmel 1968: 80). For Simmel, the modern everyday evidences a continual assault on the nervous system but the effect of such an assault is radically ambivalent: 'drifting between hypersensitivity and lack of sensitivity'. In the same year that he wrote 'Sociological Aesthetics' he attended the Berlin Trade Exhibition and wrote an analysis of it for the Viennese newspaper *Die Zeit*. His description of the exhibition reads like an allegory of the commodification of the urban everyday: 'The way in which the most heterogeneous industrial products are crowded together in close proximity paralyses the senses', while 'every few steps a small entry fee is charged for each special display' (Simmel [1896] 1991: 119). The exhibition, like the metropolis he will write about, is both a continual assault on the nerves and the form most suited to those whose nerves are shattered. The urban everyday is a form of desensitization that also provides the sensory material that is 'loud' enough to affect tired and battered nerves. At the Berlin Trade Exhibition,

> Every fine and sensitive feeling, however, is violated and seems deranged by the mass effect of the merchandise offered, while on the other hand it cannot be denied that the richness and variety of fleeting impressions is well suited to the need for excitement for overstimulated and tired nerves.
>
> (Simmel 1991: 119)

Simmel's review of this event figures an ambivalent relationship between the almost shell-shocked visitor to the exhibition and the mass of different commodities on display. But what is even more striking is that he makes the relationship *between* commodities themselves register the ambiguous situation of the modern individual:

Indeed it strikes one as curious that the separate objects in an exhibition show the same relationships and modifications that are made by the individual within society. On the one side, the depreciation of an otherwise qualified neighbour, on the other, accentuation at the expense of the same; on the one side, the levelling and uniformity due to an environment of the same, on the other, the individual is even more accentuated through the summation of many impressions; on the one side, the individual is only an element of the whole, only a member of a higher unity, on the other, the claim that the same individual is a whole and a unity.

(Simmel 1991: 122)

Simmel, it would seem, is an analyst of the phantasmagoria of modernity, lived out as the contradictory experience of individuality in everyday life. For Simmel, individuality is the dominant mode of experience in a money economy and it is essentially ambivalent. It is lived as atomized, alienated, uniqueness at the same time as it is experienced as uniformity and monotony. The individual and the commodity share a similar fate, and for the purpose of analysis can be used to highlight each other's condition. In his most famous essay, 'The Metropolis and Mental Life', Simmel gives his most succinct account of the effects and affects of the modern everyday on consciousness.

It is worth noting that between the years 1871 (when it became the capital city of a united Germany) and 1919, 'the population of Greater Berlin quadrupled, from 915,000 to 3.7 million' (Haxthausen and Suhr 1990: xv). When the editors of a recent volume of essays about Berlin culture during these years state that Berlin was experiencing a 'period of runaway growth, intense social flux, and industrial expansion' (Haxthausen and Suhr 1990: xv) they are clearly not overstating their case. Berlin was a city 'honeycombed by the notorious tenement blocks into which the majority of the population – primarily the office and factory workers who by now [around 1900] represented more than half of the city's inhabitants – were penned' (Brodersen 1996: 2–3). Lothar Müller points out that Berlin at this time was a city of intense contrasts between wealth and poverty, decay and modernization, a city of 'tensions between traditional and modern rhythms of life'. Berlin, 'with its factories, its dense traffic, its advanced technology, its expansive dynamism' (Müller 1990: 38), was a border-town of advancing modernity (figure 3). It is a fitting production site for Simmel's 1903 essay 'The Metropolis and Mental Life'.

Simmel's essay figures the metropolis as a sensory situation that generates a psychological condition: 'The psychological foundation, upon which the metropolitan individuality is erected, is the intensification of emotional life due to the swift and continuous shift of external and internal stimuli' (Simmel 1971: 325).

Figure 3   Berlin, Friedrichstrasse, at the turn of the century

To the extent that the metropolis creates these psychological conditions – with every crossing of the street, with the tempo and multiplicity
of economic, occupational and social life – it creates in the sensory
foundations of mental life . . . a deep contrast with the slower, more
habitual, more smoothly flowing rhythm of the sensory-mental phase
of small town and rural existence.

(325)

Against this experiential residue of a rural everyday that exists as a shared cultural memory, the everyday life of the metropolis is experienced as disorientating, aggressive – a continual barrage of shocks. Rather than the entrepreneurial asceticism that Weber diagnoses, Simmel finds sensory bombardment: a helter-skelter rather than an 'iron-cage'. For Simmel the city is a space of over-stimulation, where stimuli 'force the nerves to make such violent responses, tear them about so brutally that they exhaust their last reserves of strength' (1971: 329). On the one hand this produces the neurasthenic and the agoraphobic (Simmel 1991: 474–6; Vidler 1991), but on the other it produces a new type of indifference:

> There is perhaps no psychic phenomenon which is so unconditionally reserved to the city as the blasé outlook. It is at first the consequence of those rapidly shifting stimulations of the nerves which are thrown together in all their contrasts and from which it seems to us the intensification of metropolitan intellectuality seems to be derived.
>
> (Simmel 1971: 329)

The sensory condition of the metropolis (sensory bombardment) will disrupt the subject's capacity to negotiate everyday life. But this will also provide the conditions for the metropolitan type to function in spite of this. What Simmel is keen to register is the cost involved in adapting (or not) to this sensory environment. At one extreme lies the neurasthenic fate of a pathological response, at the other lies the total indifference 'toward the distinction between things' (Simmel 1971: 329). If the metropolis is the expressive environment of the money economy, the cost in terms of social interaction and experience is a decrease in emotional responses, a general transformation from qualities to quantities: 'It has been money economy which has thus filled the daily life of so many people with weighing, calculating, enumerating and the reduction of qualitative values to quantitative terms' (327–8).

Simmel's approach to everyday life continually moves from impressionistic detail to abstraction and back again. In an attempt to capture the everydayness of everyday life, Simmel works to hold on to the experience of everyday life without erasing it under the auspices of an abstract philosophical system. But while the impressionistic details puncture any claim to homogeneity, the aesthetic field that they present is one of a generalized experience of modernity. This is partly due to the practice of 'philosophical' impressionism that in its very form tends towards the general. For Simmel this is the value of sociological work, but it is not a generalized view from above; rather it works to 'construct a new storey beneath historical materialism'. Simmel's sociology is a form of base materialism that seeks to diagnose fundamental forces by treating the everyday as the most significant material for analysis. As a form of attention to the everyday, such impressionism was both complemented and disrupted by the practice of 'montage' that would emerge as the predominant avant-garde technique of the twentieth century. It is significant that Walter Benjamin followed the path laid down by Simmel in his attention to the urban everyday of modernity, but insisted on the practice of montage as his basic methodology. For Benjamin to travel from Simmel to montage he had to pass through Surrealism.

Chapter 4

SURREALISM
The marvellous in the everyday

Any serious exploration of occult, surrealistic, phantasmagoric gifts and phenomena presupposes a dialectical intertwinement to which a romantic turn of
mind is impervious. For histrionic or fanatical stress on the mysterious side of
the mysterious takes us no further; we penetrate the mystery only to the degree
that we recognize it in the everyday world, by virtue of a dialectical optic that
perceives the everyday as impenetrable, the impenetrable as everyday.

(Benjamin [1929] 1985: 237)

How long shall I retain this sense of the marvellous suffusing everyday existence?
(Aragon [1926] 1987: 24)

Surrealism and the everyday

THERE IS A DANGER THAT Surrealism's attempt to make the
familiar (the everyday) unfamiliar has itself become all too familiar. The
term 'surreal' has become part of a general social currency to be used in
reference to everything from advertising to talking about personal experience – it has become everyday. The art historian Thomas Crow has written
of the fate of the artistic avant-garde 'as a kind of research and development
arm of the culture industry' (Crow 1985: 257). For Crow,

> The case of Surrealism is perhaps the most notorious instance of this
> process. Breton and his companions had discovered in the sedimentary
> layers of earlier capitalist forms of life in Paris something like the
> material unconscious of the city, the residue of earlier repressions. But

in retrieving marginal forms of consumption, in making that latent text manifest, they provided modern advertising with one of its most powerful visual tools – that now familiar terrain in which commodities behave autonomously and create an alluring dreamscape of their own.

(Crow 1985: 257)

Worn thin by over-use and ambivalently linked to processes of commodification, Surrealism is reduced to a set of formal techniques exemplified by 'the chance encounter on a dissecting table of a sewing-machine and an umbrella' (Lautréamont, quoted in Ades 1986: 115). To recover Surrealism's potential for attending to the everyday we need to return to moments when the Surrealist project refused either to inhabit the separate realm of 'art and design' or to be reduced to supplying it with innovative techniques.

Peter Bürger's *Theory of the Avant-Garde* also privileges Surrealism. His account sees Surrealism as an attempted 'sublation of art in the praxis of life' (Bürger 1984: 51). Terry Eagleton has explained this as an impulse 'to dismantle the institutional autonomy of art, erase the frontiers between culture and political society and return aesthetic production to its humble, unprivileged place within social practices as a whole' (Eagleton 1986: 131). In essence then, Surrealism would have to become everyday; it would have to be of the everyday. While the history of Surrealism (see Gersham 1974; Lewis 1988; Nadeau 1987) has evidenced the difficulty of maintaining such an impulse, the task here is to recover something of its possibility. To do so will require a tactical refusal to treat Surrealism as an 'art form'. Instead I want to see it as a continuation of avant-gardism in general, an avant-gardism that belongs to sociology as much or as little as it does to art.

I want to read Surrealism as a form of social research into everyday life (Surrealism as ethnography, sociological Surrealism, Surrealistic cultural studies and so on), to see its products not as works of art but as documents of this social research. In this way artistic techniques such as collage become methodologies for attending to the social. Collage (or montage) provides a persistent methodology for attending to everyday life in Surrealism. In its juxtaposing of disparate elements (umbrellas, sewing machines, etc.) it generates a defamiliarizing of the everyday. If everyday life is what continually threatens to drop below a level of visibility, collage practices allow the everyday to become vivid again by making the ordinary strange through transferring it to surprising contexts and placing it in unusual combinations. But Surrealism is not just a technique for making the ordinary extraordinary; the everyday in Surrealism is *already strange* (it is collage-like). In Surrealism the everyday is not the familiar and banal realm that it seems to be; only our drab habits of mind understand it in this way. Instead the everyday is where the marvellous exists. As such, collage is both a way of breaking habits of mind that would submit the everyday to normalizing impulses and a suitable form for representing the everyday. It is in the actuality of the everyday, when passing a second-hand shop, for instance, where umbrellas and sewing-machines find themselves collaged together on a dissecting table. Surrealism is about an effort, an energy, to find the marvellous in the everyday, to recognize the everyday as a dynamic montage of elements, to make it strange so that its strangeness can be recognized. The classic Surrealist can be seen as Sherlock Holmes-like: faced with the deadly boredom of the everyday, the Surrealist takes to the street, working to find and create the marvel-lousness of the everyday.

If Surrealism's impulse is to overcome the separate spheres of knowing, so as to achieve practical operations in everyday life, then our first task will be to see how it negotiates its way out of the enclave 'art'. Ironically, it is the rhetoric of 'science' that provides the possibility. By dressing the move-ment in the garb of science, Surrealism effected a refusal of both art and science; or rather it rendered both terms inoperable within conventional use. The kind of avant-garde aesthetic-science that Surrealism proposed would make it incompatible with either the doctrine of autonomous aesthetic activity or the beliefs of a positivist empiricist science. This was a 'science' that threw scientificity into crisis. As we will see in other contexts (Mass-Observation, Michel de Certeau), such a tactical use of 'science' provided avant-garde theorists of the everyday with a powerful resource, a resource that coun-tered the 'rationalism' of science with the possibility of a science of everyday life that would operate in the murky waters of myth and ritual.

It is enough here to provide just a couple of examples. The first journal of Surrealism, *La Révolution Surréaliste* (1924–9), edited initially by Pierre Naville and Benjamin Péret, was designed to mimic the popular scientific journal *La Nature*. As Dawn Ades suggests:

> Naville chose *La Nature* as his model partly to distance the new review deliberately from other art and literary magazines, but also to suggest a commitment to 'research,' the gathering of evidence – although it was evidence of a kind meant to subvert or question the 'scientific' certainties of a 'reign of logic.'
>
> (Ades 1986a: 159)

At the same time the main participants in the Surrealist project opened a 'Bureau of Surrealist Research' (*Bureau de Recherches Surréalistes*) at 15 rue de Grenelle in Paris and advertised for revolutionary research participants (Lewis 1988: 20; Nadeau 1987: 91–3). As if the refusal of art-ness was not evident enough, the Bureau of Surrealist Research published a declaration in January 1925 in which they state: 'We have nothing to do with literature; but we are quite capable, when necessary, of making use of it like anyone else. *Surrealism* is not a new means of expression, or an easier one, nor a metaphysics of poetry' (quoted in Nadeau 1987: 240–1). Surrealism continually employed a scientific language, writing of 'research', 'exploratory investigations' and 'laboratory work'. The authentic feel of much of this is provided by the fact that a good proportion of first-wave Surrealists, including André Breton, came from medical backgrounds (see the biographies in Krauss and Livingston 1986: 193–237).

As well as embracing a certain discourse of science, Surrealism worked to refuse the material trappings of 'art and design'. As we will see, the 'literary' practices of Breton and Aragon work against the conditions of literary narrative. But perhaps the most productive refusal of the trappings of 'art and design' comes from Pierre Naville in the third issue of *La Révolution Surréaliste*:

> I have no taste except distaste. Masters, master crooks, smear your canvases. Everyone knows there is no *surrealist painting*. Neither the marks of a pencil abandoned to the accident of gesture, nor the image retracing the forms of the dream, nor the imaginative fantasies, of course can be described.
>
> But there are *spectacles* . . . The cinema, not because it is life, but the marvellous, the agency of chance elements. The street, kiosks, automobiles, screaming doors, lamps bursting in the sky. Photographs: *Eusebius, Le Matin, Excelsior, La Nature* – the smallest ampoule in the world, followed by a murderer. The circulation of blood in the thickness of a membrane.
>
> (Naville, quoted in Ades 1986a: 160)

The fact that Pierre Naville was very quickly ousted from his editorial role in the journal to be replaced by Breton, who was at the same time writing a number of essays on painting (which would make up *Surrealism and Painting* [Breton 1972b]) shows the difficulty of providing any definitive account of Surrealism (Krauss 1987: 98–9; Krauss and Livingston 1986: 19–20). Our task is not, however, to account for internecine struggles, but to try and recover the possibilities Surrealism offers for an approach to everyday life; as such the Naville quote is exceptionally useful. In this polemic Naville condemns painting and drawing as unserviceable for Surrealism, but at the same time he suggests a number of places where the Surrealist everyday will be found. In Naville's text Surrealism has no need of invention; the surreal is already there in the everyday: in 'the street, kiosks, automobiles, screaming doors, lamps bursting in the sky'. Alongside this, the surreal everyday exists in popular magazines: in scientific journalism where microscopic photography renders the body 'strange', or in the 'sensationalist' press where images of crime scenes exist side by side with pictures of celebrities. The Surrealist sociologists of the everyday have no recourse to the studio; it is in the street and the kiosk that materials will be found. The everyday (encounters, happenings, suggestive juxtapositions), and the representational realm that inhabits it, not only provides the material for Surrealist investigation, it also provides the form: montage.

Later I will consider two Surrealist documents of everyday life: Louis Aragon's *Paris Peasant* and André Breton's *Nadja*. But first a brief word on Surrealism's methodology.

Marvellous montage

> Philippe Soupault, looking somewhat haggard, would ring the doorbells and ask the concierges 'if Philippe Soupault did not live there'. Benjamin Péret would insult priests on the street . . . Robert Desnos went into trances at Breton's house. Georges Limbour, famished and simulating Desnos's trance, would get down on all fours, bark, and eat the dog's food. Louis Aragon sang softly: 'No, I won't go home.' Jacques Prévert, at night dressed as a hooligan, would lead astray the innocent passer-by in the bourgeois quarters. Tanguy captured spiders, which he ate alive to terrify the neighbourhood. Dali . . . gave lectures at the Sorbonne with his bare right foot soaking in a pan of milk.
>
> (Waldberg 1997: 34–5)

About thirty-five years later Guy Debord would call these types of operations 'conscious alterations in everyday life' (Debord [1961] 1981b: 68–75). Surrealism's attention to everyday life stands the everyday on its head. If the everyday was to be perceived as the marvellous, against common understanding of the everyday as ordinary and drab, then an alteration was necessary. A Surrealist politics of the everyday always included a dual perspective: ' "Transform the world," Marx said; "change life," Rimbaud said. These two watchwords are one for us' (Breton [1935] 1972a: 241). The capitalist everyday was impoverished and alienated, and required social revolution to transform it. But rationalist consciousness was also impoverished and this required Rimbaud's 'long, boundless, and reasoned disordering of all the senses' (Ross 1988: 102). Surrealism's commitment to the Communist Party was as vociferous as it was unorthodox, and it's hard not to feel that Rimbaud figured ahead of Marx in the pantheon of Surrealist heroes. For Surrealism, contemporary social organization (capitalism) hadn't eradicated the marvellous in the everyday, even if it had sidelined it to marginal pockets. More importantly, the existence of the marvellous in the everyday was alienated from consciousness by forms of *mental organization*. What was needed was a systematic attack on such mental bureaucracy.

Breton's definition of Surrealism provided the terms for such systematic disorganization:

> SURREALISM, *n*. Psychic automatism in its pure state, by which one proposes to express – verbally, by means of the written word, or in any other manner – the actual functioning of thought. Dictated by thought, in the absence of any control exercised by reason, exempt from any aesthetic or moral concern.
>
> (Breton 1924: 26)

Psychic automatism was the name given to the processes of surrealistic production that tried deliberately to negate the control of reason. If states of mind could be found that would make the subject more responsive to chance encounters, hypnotic trances for instance, then there were also operations within representation that could capitalize on chance.

> When the conversation – on the day's events or proposals of amusing or scandalous interventions in the life of the times – began to pall, we would turn to games; written games at first, contrived so that elements of language attacked each other in the most paradoxical manner possible, and so that human communication, misled from the start, was thrown into the mood most amenable to adventure. From then on no unfavourable prejudice (in fact, quite the contrary) was shown against childhood games, for which we were rediscovering the old enthusiasm, although considerably amplified.
>
> (Breton, quoted in Waldberg 1997: 93)

One such game was *Exquisite Corpse*, described as a 'Game of folded paper played by several people, who compose a sentence or drawing without anyone seeing the preceding collaboration' (Waldberg 1997: 93–4). The name itself comes from the results obtained the first time Surrealists played it: 'The exquisite corpse will drink the new wine' (94). Other practices included seances, forms of automatic writing deliberately designed to privilege unconscious associations and visual forms of automatic production that 'find' images in the abstract landscapes of paint surfaces (Lewis 1988: 18–20).

For this study it is a moot point whether such production becomes an end in itself, or if it is used as a 'training ground' for altering consciousness in everyday life. No doubt it was at times both. What is more important are the operations themselves and the values they are predicated on. Crucial to all Surrealist practice is the production of juxtaposition. As such, all forms of practice can be seen as collage practices even if they don't follow the 'cutting and sticking' implied by the term. For Breton there was a way of evaluating such juxtapositions:

> It is, as it were, from the fortuitous juxtaposition of the two terms that a particular light has sprung, the light of the image, to which we

are infinitely sensitive. The value of the image depends upon the beauty of the spark obtained; it is, consequently, a function of the difference of potential between two conductors.

(Breton 1924: 37)

What is at stake here is the production of the 'spark', generated by the juxtaposition of different materials, juxtapositions possible in a range of spheres: in poems and paintings, in everyday encounters in the street or in the 'everynight' encounters of the dream. The more difference there is between the two (or more) ingredients, the greater the spark. Slight differences remain within a familiar world; massive differences produce shocks and sparks that jolt us out of the familiar. As such it becomes the perfect foil for habits of mind that have become blinkered by routinized thought. The privileging of consciousness over social relations has resulted in Surrealism being designated as a form of idealism. This is not without its truth, though the weight of such an 'insult' seems to have lessened in recent years. On the other hand, 'idealism' doesn't come close to the materiality of Surrealist practice, both on the page and in the actuality of everyday life. If there is one material site for studying the everyday for Surrealism it must be the streets of Paris (the city that exemplifies the birth of urban modernity). Such pedestrian production is exemplified by *Nadja* and *Paris Peasant*.

Nadja and *Paris Peasant*

Breton's *Nadja* ([1928] 1960) is made up of a number of elements that mark it out as distinct from mainstream novelistic narration. Composed of: a contemplative 'preface' where a number of anecdotes of coincidence are recounted and reflected upon; the story of Breton's various encounters with a woman called Nadja; photographs that relate to this story and to other parts of the text; drawings and other 'evidence' related to the text; and a final afterword – *Nadja* doesn't add up to a novel. Maurice Blanchot suggests that the main text of *Nadja* should be seen as a *récit*, a tale that tells of a singular and exceptional event. In relating this to other *récits*, such as *The Odyssey*, Blanchot claims:

> Something has happened, something which someone has experienced who tells about it afterwards, in the same way that Ulysses needed to experience the event and survive it in order to become Homer, who told about it. Of course the tale (*récit*) is usually about an exceptional event, one which eludes the form of everyday time and the world of the usual sort of truth, perhaps any truth. This is why it so insistently rejects everything which could connect it with the frivolity of a fiction

(the novel, on the other hand, contains only what is believable and familiar and yet is very anxious to pass for fiction).

(Blanchot 1981: 109)

He adds: 'The tale is not the narration of an event, but that event itself, the approach to that event, the place where that event is made to happen' (109). If, for Blanchot, the novel deals in the everyday, it does so in a way that evades the everyday. On the other hand the tale is the everyday when the everyday is exceptional or marvellous. In its refusal to exercise the rhetorical tropes of the novel and persuade us we are entering a 'world', *Nadja* offers us the marvellous everyday stripped of description. Here places are actual. As a tale, *Nadja* is a chronicle of Breton's relationship (sexual, financial, poetic) with a woman he meets by chance. The tale chronicles the various meetings he has with her and the walks they take around the city and outskirts of Paris. Nadja herself is both *femme fatale* and a 'helpless' woman in need of Breton's care. The ambivalent representation of Nadja's relationship to the everyday is exemplary of the Surrealist conception of everyday life: she is seen as having escaped the everydayness of the everyday, at the same time as being in danger of falling back into its routines. The gendering of the everyday is ambivalent but powerful – the marvellous everyday is made vivid by a femininity out of control; at the same time, another feminine everydayness threatens to engulf Nadja in the domestic. We will return to this shortly.

One of the elements that mark the actuality of *Nadja*'s surrealistic everyday, are the photographs by Jacques-André Boiffard. Boiffard's photographs punctuate the tale of *Nadja* as a form of evidence, not of the event but of the place of the event. The photographs are empty of episode. Here is Michel Beaujour describing Boiffard's photographs in *Nadja*:

> What we are shown is nothing: not only have the places defended themselves against the photographer, but those that have allowed themselves to be captured . . . are quite dumb: nothing is suggested in these banal photographs. These photographs almost empty of human presence, proceed from a zero ground of representation: they never move away from the amateur's snapshot or out-of-date picture postcard.
>
> (Beaujour, quoted in Ades 1986a: 163)

In an apparent condemnation of Boiffard's photographs Beaujour finds the most adequate terms to attend to them: 'amateur snapshots' and 'out-of-date picture postcards' (figure 4). The scene of *Nadja* is an artless and outmoded presentation of places that themselves refer to another time than the actuality of the tale. While Nadja and Breton traverse Paris and its environs, the everyday spaces that they encounter echo with the ghosts of the past, but

Figure 4 'And the dead, the dead' – photograph by Jacques-André Boiffard (1928) of the Place Dauphine for *Nadja*

these ghosts can only signify as an absence. This is the heroic everyday of popular struggles that never found a place in the monuments of official history.

In a recent rereading of *Nadja*, Margaret Cohen takes seriously Benjamin's claim that *Nadja* effects a 'substitution of a political for a historical view of the past' (Benjamin, quoted in Cohen 1993: 80). The sites of meetings and wanderings become an index of a repressed history of struggles, revolutions and betrayals. Thus the Place Vendôme is remembered not for its column and statue, but for the toppling of this column during the Commune of 1871 (an act organized by Courbet). *Nadja* is a tour and a detour of the non-monumental history of repressed popular struggles, struggles that can be seen as the eruption of everydayness in the everyday. As Blanchot suggests, everyday life becomes vivid 'in moments of effervescence – those we call revolution – when existence is public through and through' (Blanchot 1987: 12). When Breton and Nadja reach the Place Dauphine (figure 4), Breton writes: 'Where only two or three couples are at this moment fading into the darkness, she seems to see a crowd. "And the dead, the dead!"' (Breton 1960: 83). Such a space as this reveals, as Cohen suggests, 'traces of the insurrectional past in the uncanny present': 'Multiple ghosts of revolutionary violence moreover descend on the place Dauphine from all sides, from the Pont-Neuf, where "the Revolution tore down the bronze statue of King Henri IV" to the Palais de Justice burned down by the Commune' (Cohen 1993: 100–1). Thus, in the everyday environment of Parisian streets lies a history of insurrection and struggles, struggles that Breton uses as a ghostly presence and a reminder. These were attempts to transform not the 'means of production', but the fabric of everyday life.

And it is this fabric that Breton's writing ambiguously articulates, for it is Nadja herself who Breton recognizes as having transformed her everyday life (a transformation that Breton is often deeply resistant to), but it is also everyday life that is the threat that will possibly normalize her. In this Breton plays the part of the paternalistic artist, who alone can save his muse from a fate she doesn't recognize:

> Astonished as I continued to be by her behaviour, based as it was on the purest of intuition alone and ceaselessly relying on miracle, I was also increasingly alarmed to feel that, when even [ever] I left her, she was sucked back into that whirlwind of ordinary life continuing around her and eager to force her, among other concessions, to eat, to sleep.
> (Breton 1960: 114–15)

Nadja's behaviour as a fatale femininity transcends the humdrum everyday at the same time as the domestic (managed femininity) continually threatens to bring her down to earth so that she can live (eat, sleep). Where is Breton in all this? Where is his everyday? Does he sleep and eat? And does this force him back into the everyday? In many ways *Nadja* demonstrates Surrealism's tendency to depict a radically ambivalent everyday (that is both marvellous and stultifying) and figure it through femininity. Breton figures the everyday from outside: if he is absent from the domestic everyday he is also excluded (or excludes himself) from the everyday as marvellous. The marvellous is always elsewhere along with the feminine; Breton remains a tourist in the everyday as both marvellous and mundane.

Similar ambiguities of everyday life can be seen to be in operation in Louis Aragon's *Paris Peasant* (Aragon [1926] 1987). The first half of the book offers a tour through the Passage de l'Opéra. This seems to provide Aragon with a mnemonic device as he recounts reminiscences of past encounters in the various bars and shops in the Passage. *Paris Peasant* is made up of a variety of types of representation (including a mini-play) as well as a typographically varied text where textual bits of actuality find their way on to the page in the shape of labels from bottles, newspaper articles, shop signs and so on. But what gives the Passage its ambivalent everydayness is its historicity. *Paris Peasant* offers an evocation of the everyday as marvellous in an actuality that places it on the brink of destruction.

Aragon's text is dated 1924 and was published in 1926; between these dates the Passage was 'sacrificed to the extension of the Boulevard Haussmann' (Geist 1983: 476). The destruction of the Passage had been threatened since 1860 and in 1873 the arcade's *raison d'être*, the opera house, was burnt down: 'the arcade was left as a fragment of a no longer existing architectural ensemble' (476). If the arcade lost 'its power of attraction' for the rich and powerful, it, in turn, became host to a variety of social types including the various Dada and Surrealist groups that met in the Bar Certa. The faded grandeur is, of course, what attracts them, as well as the possibilities of sexual and alcoholic intoxicants. The Passage presents a 'geography' of everyday pleasure, the best antidote to the everyday as mundane. In the sensual realm of the hairdressers, Aragon contemplates the teaching of a bodily geography:

> As far as I know, the geography of pleasure has never been taught, although proficiency in this subject would constitute an effective weapon against life's tediums. No one has assumed the responsibility of assigning its limits to the frisson, of drawing the boundaries of the caress, of charting the territory of ecstasy.
>
> (Aragon 1987: 57–8)

Other shops offer opportunities to remember: the stamp shop, for instance, offers Aragon reminiscences of childhood. But if this is the everyday as marvellous, then the easy nostalgia this affords is continually undercut by the social actuality of the planned destruction.

Aragon's text details, through newspaper clippings and the posters displayed by shops in the arcade, the struggle of the arcade. The shopkeepers have formed themselves into a collective to try and fight the BD Haussmann Building Society. At the same time newspapers are revealing a conspiracy that shows the building society (a supposedly civic department) as involved financially with the massive department store, Galeries Lafayette. With hindsight, but also plainly visible at the time, the battle has already been lost. If this is a site of the everyday as marvellous, then its destruction is already guaranteed. Against the forces of big business what political will can the marvellous muster? A handful of shopkeepers and a few bohemian types. *Paris Peasant* is politically and surrealistically pessimistic; it holds little hope for the everyday, in terms of both the actuality of everyday and the effort of will needed to find the marvellous in the everyday.

Reading the preface of *Paris Peasant* you can hear the voice of someone who recognizes the impossibility of the Surrealist project:

> Each day the modern sense of existence becomes subtly altered. A mythology ravels and unravels. It is a knowledge, a science which begets itself and makes away with itself. I am already twenty-six years old, am I still privileged to take part in this miracle? How long shall I retain this sense of the marvellous suffusing everyday existence? I see it fade away in every man who advances into his own life as though along an always smoother road, who advances into the world's habits with an increasing ease, who rids himself progressively of the taste and texture of the unwonted, the unthought of. To my great despair, this is what I shall never know.
>
> (Aragon 1987: 24)

The historicity of the everyday and the marvellous is stressed, but it's a losing battle. The question of the marvellous in the everyday can only solicit anxiety.

The sacred in the everyday

If, in the dialectic between finding the Surreal in everyday life and manufacturing it in artistic products, a history of 'mainstream' Surrealism privileges the latter over the former, then there are pockets of dissident Surrealism that redress this balance. The potential of Surrealism as a sociology of everyday life is perhaps most fully realized in the poet-ethnologists who gather around the journal *Documents* (1929–30) (see Bataille *et al.* 1995) and the Collège de Sociologie (1937–9) (see Hollier 1988). In the pages of *Documents*, the editors Georges Bataille and Michel Leiris brought together a heterogeneous range of materials (body parts, old coins, new movies, festive rituals) in an onslaught against conventional ascriptions of aesthetic value. By combining Western fine art with ethnographic and archaeological studies, *Documents* ruptured the domain of aesthetic value; as Denis Hollier suggests, 'ethnography exceeds the auspices of the fine arts geographically, as archeology exceeds it historically' (Hollier 1992: 5). In juxtaposing cultural materials from a range of societies (societies ideologically represented as structurally exclusive – the West versus the rest), a radical cultural relativism was produced that combined 'the corrosive analysis of a reality now identified as local and artificial' with 'the supplying of exotic alternatives' (Clifford 1988: 130). By drawing connections across cultures as well as privileging 'other' cultures, *Documents* used ethnography to perform 'a radical questioning of norms' as well as 'a levelling and a reclassification of familiar categories' (129). What this suggests is the possibility of rethinking and re-imagining Western everyday modernity by juxtaposing it with 'other' cultures – by a global cross-cultural perspective.

In the Collège de Sociologie such a perspective was taken as the basis for a research group dedicated to the 'Sacred Sociology of the Contemporary World' (Hollier 1988: 157–8). The term 'sacred' is a reference to Durkheim's sociology, particularly *The Elementary Forms of Religious Life*, where indigenous Australian society is examined as structured across two worlds – the sacred and the profane (Durkheim [1912] 1995: 216–25). Such a division is easily translated into the non-everyday and the everyday, and Durkheim's work reveals the structural reliance these two worlds have on each other. Of course Durkheim is looking at what he sees as an 'elementary' culture, not a modern Western culture that might be considered as 'post-sacred'. The radical nature of the Collège is exemplified by its refusal to buy into this myth of rationalist post-sacred modernity, and instead to pursue the possibilities offered by ethnography for finding the sacred in the heart of the modern Western everyday. For Michel Leiris such a project results in a self-ethnography – an othering of the self and the everyday world it inhabits, that focuses on the 'sacred' not as a separate realm, but as a realm that lies at the centre of the everyday.

Between the demise of *Documents* and the emergence of the Collège, Leiris joined Marcel Griaule's Mission Dakar–Djibouti (1931–3), an ethnographic 'mission' that crossed 'Africa from the Atlantic to the Red Sea along the lower rim of the Sahara' (Clifford 1988: 55). From this emerged his *L'Afrique fantôme* (1934) – a text composed of dreams, fragments of observation, and a consistent self-analysis of his fears and desires (see Clifford 1988: 165–74; Torgovnick 1990: 105–18). If this is ethnographic 'fieldwork', it is never clear who or what the object of study could be aside from Leiris himself. Such a work can be seen as a prologue to the sustained autobiographical project that continued during Leiris' life. Starting with *Manhood* and culminating in his four-volume *Rules of the Game* (see the two volumes so far translated into English: Leiris [1948] 1991, [1955] 1997), the subject, Michel Leiris, is subjected to an ordeal analogous to the bullfight: 'The Autobiographer as Torero' as Leiris titles his 'Afterword' to *Manhood* (Leiris [1939] 1992).

In January 1938, Leiris gave a lecture to the Collège de Sociologie called 'The Sacred in Everyday Life' (which was published in July in the *Nouvelle*

Revue Français, along with texts by Bataille and Roger Caillois that together constituted 'For a College of Sociology' [Hollier 1988: 7, 24–31, 98–102]). The text, which maps out his autobiographical project, begins with a question, the answer to which is the everyday:

> What, for me, is the *sacred*? To be more exact: what does my sacred consist of? What objects, places, or occasions awake in me that mixture of fear and attachment, that ambiguous attitude caused by the approach of something simultaneously attractive and dangerous, prestigious and outcast – that combination of respect, desire, and terror that we take as the psychological sign of the sacred? . . . It is a matter of searching through some of the humblest things, taken from everyday life and located outside of what today makes up the officially sacred (religion, fatherland, morals).
>
> (Hollier 1988: 24)

The everyday that is the site for Leiris' sacred is the stove in his family's house, his parents' bedroom, the bathroom toilet, the racecourse, his father's gun, and various words and names. The details need not concern us. Here is the material geography of Freud's *The Psychopathology of Everyday Life*, and like Freud's book, here the modern everyday is removed from 'the Iron Cage' of reason and is recognized as a world of myth, superstition and the sacred. In an assessment of Leiris' contribution to the Collège, Denis Hollier writes:

> The College of Sociology cast its lot against life that would be exclusively quotidian. It was imperative to escape. The exception, that which eluded dailiness, was deemed sacred. The strength of Leiris's contribution, indicating how much he has to offer, is summed up in the wording of his title: 'The Sacred in Everyday Life' replaces simple antagonism by polemical inclusion.
>
> (Hollier 1997: 122)

Whether it was necessary to travel to Africa to realize the possibilities that Surrealism offered for an ethnography of everyday life in Western modernity is hard to say. It does seem clear, though, that cultural differences had to collide in a way that couldn't be managed by the dominant accounts of 'civilization' for everyday life to become both vivid and 'other'. At the same time that Leiris was publishing 'The Sacred in Everyday Life' the seeds had already been sown for an 'Anthropology at Home' in England. Such a project (the subject of chapter 6 on Mass-Observation) contained the same constellation of ingredients (a Surrealist poetics coupled with an application of ethnographic perspectives on Western culture) while directing them (as we will see) to quite different ends. Before looking at Mass-Observation, we need to follow the deployment of Surrealist poetics as Walter Benjamin critically negotiated them. Benjamin's approach to Surrealism makes vivid the themes around everyday life that we will need to insist upon again and again: the privileging of a specifically urban everyday and the investigation of the everyday as a non-conscious realm.

Chapter 5

BENJAMIN'S TRASH AESTHETICS

Method of this project: literary montage. I need say nothing. Only exhibit (*zeigen*). I won't filch anything of value or appropriate any ingenious turns of phrase. Only the trivia, the trash – which I don't want to inventory, but simply allow it to come into its own in the only way possible: by putting it to use. (Benjamin 1989 [N1a, 8])[1]

SITUATING THE WORK of Walter Benjamin in a tradition for theorizing the everyday is not without its problems. As the editors of a collection of writings on Benjamin suggest, 'if we are to search for the actuality of Walter Benjamin, perhaps it is to be found in his quietly determined failure to belong – to a speciality, to an institution, to an easily specifiable tradition of thought' (Marcus and Nead 1993: v). Such a 'failure' is clearly productive and has generated a secondary literature that is overwhelming in its scale. As well as being an indication of the work's range and productivity, it is also a sign of the work's ambiguities. Commentary on Benjamin's work is always answerable to the charge that in privileging one aspect of the work it fails to attend to another: a Marxist Benjamin ignoring a Benjamin informed by Jewish mysticism; a Benjamin interested in the possibilities of new technologies neglecting a Benjamin fascinated by historical remains. Yet the very fact that Benjamin is not easily assimilated within definable categories should signal the potential of the everyday as a useful 'non-category' for attending to his work. When Peter Osborne comments that 'everyday life flows through the whole of Benjamin's later writings', he also warns that 'it is rarely to be found reflectively, as the object of an explicit theorization' (Osborne 1995: 180). To fashion Benjamin into a theorist of the everyday requires privileging certain moments across a body of work and forging the

links between them. While this might obscure some of the tensions operating in any single text, it has the advantage of bringing together aspects of
the work that might otherwise seem irreconcilable. From the point of view
of the everyday, Benjamin's interest in the epic theatre of Brecht (for instance)
is not a rejection of his commitment to a messianic belief in redemption.
Instead they both become part of a heterogeneous project for rescuing the
everyday life of modernity from silence.

The theme of everyday life as a problematic is central to Benjamin's
work. His approach echoes Simmel's interest in the microscopic and the
unassimilable particularity of the material world. When Benjamin describes
his project as being '[T]o detect the crystal of the total event in the analysis
of the small, individual moment' [N 2, 6] he could almost be quoting from
Simmel. In comparison with Simmel though, Benjamin seems less certain
about the possibility of uncovering a 'base' that might make sense of the
modern everyday. To bring everyday material together in a productive juxtaposition seems to look more like a chance encounter than a methodological
procedure, a daring wager rather than a 'sure thing'. Such differences produce
telling contrasts between the two writers while at the same time pointing
to historical changes in the perception and condition of everyday life.

Benjamin's approach to history is through 'trash' – through the spent
and discarded materials that crowd the everyday. In this everyday material
world different temporalities exist side by side: the latest version alongside
last year's model. Everyday life registers the process of modernization as an
incessant accumulation of debris: modernity produces obsolescence as part
of its continual demand for the new (the latest version becomes last year's
model with increasing frequency). But for Benjamin the modern everyday is
not to be found just in material objects; the world of affects, of sensation
is equally important. Benjamin's project charts a time of both increased accumulation and intensified sensation. In Benjamin's unfinished *Arcades Project*
(Benjamin 1999) nineteenth-century Paris is the scene for tracing the modern
everyday. Here the city is orchestrated by the flow of commodities and their
apparitions (advertising, cinema and so on). The Paris of the *Arcades Project*
teems with bodies, images, signs, stimulants, movement, and is experienced
as a perpetual assault on both tradition and the human sensorium alike. But
if modernity evidences a wealth of material goods and an intensification of
sensation, for Benjamin it paradoxically displays a paucity of communicable
experience.

Benjamin's importance as a theorist of the everyday is most evident in
his attention to the everyday experiences of modernity. Evident throughout
Benjamin's later work are the interlinked themes of the decrease in communicable experience and the problem of finding a poetics that is capable of
articulating the actuality of modern life. If traditional narrative forms are no
longer adequate for representing the modern everyday, it is not because they

have become shop-worn, but because the transformation of everyday life itself has meant that everyday experience is no longer available to this form of representation. As his friend Brecht put it, and as we have already quoted, 'Reality changes; in order to represent it, modes of representation must also change' (Brecht 1980: 82). For Benjamin the historicity of experience needs to be recognized, apprehended and made available for criticism. To a certain degree Benjamin finds a poetics for apprehending the modern everyday in Surrealism, but Benjamin's take on Surrealism is a dissident one. If Surrealism finds the right field for attending to the modern (everyday life) and performs the poetic operations necessary for apprehending it (montage), it fails to mobilize its tools in a resolutely critical way. While Surrealism finds the mythic in the everyday, it also falls under its spell. Surrealism has the tools to puncture the dream of modernity, but fails to cash in. Thus, Benjamin describes his *Arcades Project* in relation to the failure of Surrealism:

> Setting off the slant of this work against Aragon: whereas Aragon persistently remains in the realm of dreams, here it is a question of finding the constellation of awakening. While an impressionistic element lingers on in Aragon ('mythology') – and this impressionism should be held responsible for the many nebulous philosophemes of his book – what matters here is the dissolution of 'mythology' into the space of history. [N1, 9]

If Surrealism fails (and in practice it clearly does for Benjamin), then it is due to a lack of attention to the historicity of modern experience. Benjamin's theoretical attention to the historicity of the everyday is inscribed in his writings in the idea of the 'dialectical image': these are specific constellations that can awaken thought and history from its slumber in the mythic realm of the 'dream'. Dialectical images operate for Benjamin as 'dialectics [history] at a standstill' [N 2a, 3]. What this requires is the arrest of the flow of history (particularly its representation as the march of progress) so that it can be recognized as a specific experience of a moment. Benjamin's thought is historical, but it does not set out to weave a convincing narrative of the past: 'For every image of the past that is not recognized by the present as one of its own concerns threatens to disappear irretrievably' (Benjamin 1982: 257). Surrealism must be put at the service of making the historicity of the modern recognizable, and for this it can't be treated as part of an unfolding story or remain within the charm of the dream: 'Can it be that awakening is the synthesis whose thesis is dream consciousness and whose antithesis is consciousness? Then the moment of awakening would be identical with the "Now of recognizability", in which things put on their true – surrealistic – face' [N 3a, 3].

Suggestive as such ideas are they are hard to pin down to a practice. Benjamin's *Arcades Project* was part homage and part antidote to Aragon's book and it grew to gargantuan proportions. By the time Benjamin died (overtaken by the historicity of his moment[2]) the project was a collection of quotes, ideas and historical fragments. To see how Benjamin's thinking and his concept of the 'dialectical image' might impact on a theory of everyday life, we need to see it in operation, to sèe it put to use. As well as the theo- retical fragments, Benjamin has left us a series of 'snapshots' of the *Arcades Project* in his 1935 Arcades Exposé, 'Paris – the Capital of the Nineteenth Century' (Benjamin 1983a: 155–76). These will provide the material for the final section on Benjamin.

Ragpicking

In the mass of commentary that has attended Benjamin's work, particularly his monumental *Arcades Project*, the most vivid characterization of his approach to the everyday is to be found in the title of an essay by Irving Wohlfarth: 'The Historian as *Chiffonnier* [ragpicker]' (Wohlfarth 1986). This description of a methodological approach to culture, analogous to ragpicking, is first offered by Benjamin himself to describe the work of his friend Siegfried Kracauer: 'And if we want to visualize him just for himself, in the solitude of his craft and his endeavour, we see: a ragpicker at daybreak, lancing with his stick scraps of language and tatters of speech in order to throw them in his cart, grumbling, stubbornly, somewhat the worse for drink' (Benjamin 1998: 114). The words *chiffonnier* and ragpicker, or the German term *Lumpenhändler*, designate a practice and a person with an uneasy relationship to the everyday life of modernity. Ragpicking is the 'career' of those who have been remaindered by capitalist modernization (figure 5); for instance, the one-time craft worker made redundant by industrialization, or impover- ished aristocrats, or the present-day homeless. In *The Eighteenth Brumaire of Louis Bonaparte*, Marx refers to these members of the lumpenproletariat as 'the whole indefinite, disintegrated mass, thrown hither and thither' (Marx [1852] 1968: 137). Ragpickers, outmoded by modernization, struggle to get by, by finding value in what has been devalued, outmoded. The detritus of modernity is scoured for its use-value. It is here that the analogy between the ragpicker and the cultural historian has importance for theorizing everyday life. Benjamin, like Simmel, will look to the meagre materials of everyday life in his attempt to apprehend actuality. As Richard Wolin suggests, Benjamin's project is to extract the noumenal from within the phenomenal realm: 'to reverse the terms of Western metaphysics by ceding pride of place in the field of philosophical inquiry to what had previously been merely derided and scorned: the ephemeral and transient aspects of the phenomenal world' (Wolin 1989: 210). Such a description echoes forcefully with the words of Charles Baudelaire, Benjamin's literary guide to the everyday life

Figure 5   Ragpicker (1899–1900) – photograph by Eugène Atget. Albumen-silver print, 9 3/8 x 7" (24 x 18 cm). The Museum of Modern Art, New York. Abbott-Levy Collection. Partial gift of Shirley C. Burden. Copy Print © 2001 The Museum of Modern Art, New York

of modernity: 'By "modernity" [*modernité*] I mean the ephemeral, the fugitive, the contingent' (Baudelaire 1964: 13). But Benjamin's project isn't just about attending to the 'infinitesimal, the overlooked' (Sieburth 1989: 14); its material objects must also signal a different temporality, another time (or rather they must live in two times). Crucially, they must be out of fashion. The 'object' of fascination that animates Benjamin's later work is the Parisian arcade, not in its heyday but as a 'ruin' existing in a time when it has been superseded, outmoded. The ragpicker deals in the second-hand, in the dreams of the past for a future that was never realized. The modern-day ragpicker treads a fine line between a sentimental attitude towards the past and a revolutionary nostalgia for the future. When the latter takes precedence over the former, the ragpicker's radical task becomes one of cataloguing the broken promises that have been abandoned in the everyday trash of history.

The focus on 'trash', on the detritus of modernity as it exists in the actuality of everyday life, allows Benjamin to perform a double operation. On the one hand it allows his account of modernity to refuse the lure of celebrating the new, of eulogizing progress. On the other hand it also prevents a sentimentalizing of the past. For Benjamin these two would only get in the way of recognizing the now-ness of everyday life: 'Overcoming the concept of "progress" and the concept of "period of decline" are two sides of the same thing' [N 2, 5]. Debris allows for a radical refusal of progress; it allows for a vision of history that is nothing if not attentive to its unreason. In one of his most poetic utterances, Benjamin figures history as nothing but detritus:

> His eyes are staring, his mouth is open, his wings are spread. This is how one pictures the angel of history. His face is turned toward the past. Where we perceive a chain of events, he sees one single catastrophe which keeps piling wreckage upon wreckage and hurls it in front of his feet. The angel would like to stay, awaken the dead, and make whole what has been smashed. But a storm is blowing from Paradise; it has got caught in his wings with such violence that the angel can no longer close them. This storm irresistibly propels him into the future to which his back is turned, while the pile of debris before him grows skyward. This storm is what we call progress.
>
> (Benjamin 1982: 259–60)

But Benjamin doesn't remain within the melancholy realm often ascribed to him. His project is an attempt to redeem the everyday experience of modernity from silence. In the face of the endless proliferation of trash, Benjamin potentially suggests a 'trash aesthetics' that could be used radically and critically to attend to the everyday. The method might be thought of in terms of 'recycling' – an ecology of everyday experience.

Articulating the experience of the everyday

The most sustained reflection on the experience of the modern everyday occurs in Benjamin's essay of 1939, 'Some Motifs in Baudelaire'. But to reach this essay we need to turn to an earlier essay, 'The Storyteller: Reflections on the Works of Nikolai Leskov' (1936). In this earlier essay Benjamin vividly conjures an image of modern experience as devalued:

> It is as if something that seemed inalienable to us, the securest among our possessions, were taken from us: the ability to exchange experiences.
> One reason for this phenomenon is obvious: experience has fallen in value. And it looks as if it is continuing to fall into bottomlessness . . . With the [First] World War a process began to become apparent which has not halted since then. Was it not noticeable at the end of the war that men returned from the battlefield grown silent – not richer, but poorer in communicable experience? . . . For never has experience been contradicted more thoroughly than strategic experience by tactical warfare, economic experience by inflation, bodily experience by mechanical warfare, moral experience by those in power. A generation that has gone to school on a horse-drawn streetcar now stood under the open sky in a countryside in which nothing remained unchanged but the clouds, and beneath these clouds, in a field of force of destructive torrents and explosions, was the tiny, fragile human body.
> (Benjamin 1982: 83–4)

The juxtaposition of the 'fragile human body' with a landscape destroyed by modern industrial warfare vividly figures a world that has been utterly changed by modernization (all that was solid has melted into air – so to speak). Everything has been transformed: the tempo of everyday life and the landscape the body exists in. The loss of experience that the passage articulates is to do not with a lessening of the 'event-ness' or 'episode' of the everyday, but with the meaningfulness and communicability of its modern form. We may experience more in a quantitative manner but we cannot make more of it. It cannot be incorporated into the meaningfulness of life. The modern experience of the everyday leaves us silent. It is this silence that needs to be challenged, not so as to provide coherence or amelioration, but so that it can be recognized, criticized and changed. Finding forms for articulating the everyday is for Benjamin a politics of everyday life.

The question that everyday modernity poses for Benjamin (and is answered to some degree by the work of Baudelaire) concerns the way that the experience of modern life might find a communicable form. As for many German writers, for Benjamin the investigation of experience plays on the nuanced distinction between experience as that which is simply lived-through

(*Erlebnis*) and experience as something that can be accumulated, reflected upon and communicated (*Erfahrung*). If *Erlebnis* is immediate it also tends towards being inchoate (it is pre-language, pre-reflection). *Erfahrung* on the other hand is what makes *Erlebnis* socially meaningful; it is the point at which experience is examined and evaluated. In English this distinction is made through context rather than by use of a different word. For instance, to talk about an 'experienced' mechanic or cook suggests a world of experience that accumulates into a form of knowledge and know-how that can be communicated to an apprentice. This is the world of *Erfahrung*. *Erlebnis* on the other hand is in English signalled by the same word, but now it means simply the sensate registering of the world: *Erlebnis* is what we do moment by moment. For Benjamin everyday modernity evidences a major trauma: modern *Erlebnis* is no longer registered as *Erfahrung*. The 'fragile human body' that has been bombarded on the battlefield and whose senses have been daily assaulted in the modern city has had a glut of *Erlebnis*. What has been blocked is the sense-making that would give account of this within a collective culture. And this is because those forms of communication, consciousness and representation simply haven't been revolutionized in the way that daily experience has. What we are left with is 'experience' that doesn't enter into meaningfulness, can't be reflected on, and so is unavailable for criticism.

In Benjamin's essay 'Some Motifs in Baudelaire' modern everyday life is characterized by 'shock' and any theory of modern experience has to confront this historically specific quality of experience. It is the modern everyday as 'shock' experience that needs addressing, and to attend to it only within the terms of the authentic moment of *Erlebnis* is to condemn it to silence, and to lose it for a political struggle of the everyday. Benjamin writes about Baudelaire as a poet of modern everyday 'shock' experience: 'Of all the experiences which made life what it was, Baudelaire singled out his having been jostled by the crowd as the decisive, unique experience' (Benjamin 1982: 154). For Benjamin the experience of shock is to be found in the metropolitan crowd, in the industrial mode of production, in traffic and advertising. For Benjamin, 'Moving through this traffic involves the individual in a series of shocks and collisions. At dangerous crossings, nervous impulses flow through him in rapid succession, like the energy from a battery' (Benjamin 1982: 132). These moments of 'shock experience' (*Erlebnis*) fail to enter into the shared discourse of experience (*Erfahrung*) that could give the modern everyday a voice that would allow for both critical attention and critical practice. In exemplifying the difference between *Erlebnis* and *Erfahrung*, Benjamin cites the unskilled factory worker: 'The unskilled worker is the one most deeply degraded by the drill of the machines. His work has been sealed off from experience [*Erfahrung*]; practice counts for nothing there' (Benjamin 1982: 133). The experience of factory work (which, Benjamin suggests, corresponds to the experience of a passer-by in a crowd) remains at the level of *Erlebnis* precisely because 'practice counts for nothing'. Experience in this sense can't accumulate, because the nature of this experience is not available for attention. To privilege the moment of experience (*Erlebnis*) over the possibility of *Erfahrung* (experience as accumulated and communicable knowledge) is to remain locked into an eternal repetition of the same.

But how could *Erfahrung* be reconfigured so that it could communicate modern everyday experience? How could it redeem the silence of modernity? Isn't it the very nature of modern shock experience that makes it unavailable for communicable experience? This is where Benjamin's dialectics of experience and expression are most valuable and most optimistic for attending to modern everyday life. On the one hand it becomes clear that the reason for giving such weight to Baudelaire is precisely because Benjamin sees Baudelaire as a poet who can give *Erfahrung* to the shock experience (*Erlebnis*) of modern life. As Andrew Benjamin writes:

> The importance of Baudelaire's poetry is that it has allowed *Erlebnis* to be enframed by *Erfahrung*. For Benjamin, Baudelaire's battling crowd 'is the nature of something lived through (*Erlebnis*) to which Baudelaire has given the weight of experience (*Erfahrung*).' Baudelaire turned *Erlebnis* into *Erfahrung*. Perhaps this is Benjamin's final conclusion.
> (Benjamin 1989: 133)

On the other hand Benjamin will find the possibilities of *Erfahrung* in the actuality of modern shock experience itself: a poetics of distraction is imagined emerging from an everyday 'shock' life. If Baudelaire offers a form for articulating the modern everyday experience that doesn't render it dumb, so too do a number of other representational forms. Indeed a central concern of Benjamin's work can be seen as promoting forms of representation that offer (potentially) a political articulation of modern experience. Benjamin's interest in montage in film, his promotion of Surrealism, his continued dialogue with the work of Bertolt Brecht, can all be seen as an attempt to find cultural forms that could give voice to the experience of everyday life.

Benjamin is a dialectical thinker, and modern cultural forms and modern experience are not autonomous (and discrete) realms. Margaret Cohen suggests that 'Benjamin concludes *One-Way Street* by dissolving the text's opposition between proto-Chock [shock] and *Erfahrung*, asking whether violent contemporary contact with external reality may in fact be the precursor of *Erfahrung* not yet recognized as such' (Cohen 1993: 185). Benjamin's task is not simply to find suitably modernized forms for *Erfahrung*, but to suggest that *Erfahrung* has itself changed. Thus for Benjamin the theme of distraction becomes something that might characterize both the lived experience of everyday modernity (the multifarious pulls on attention) and the forms most productively able to articulate it (hence Benjamin's optimistic view of popular cultural forms).

If the experience of modern life can be seen as characterized by the pene-tration of technological and industrial forms into everyday life, then this works as both 'poison and cure' – i.e. it is what casts experience into oblivion, at the same time as it offers the resources for a 'new' *Erfahrung* ('not yet recognized as such') that can rescue experience and open it to critical atten-tion. The relationship between technological experience (the factory, say) and technological forms of representation is recognized. Both can be seen as the cause of alienation while potentially being analytic tools for dealing with such alienation (again we are within a stone's throw of Simmel):

> Whereas Poe's passers-by cast glances in all directions which still appeared to be aimless, today's pedestrians are obliged to do so in order to keep abreast of traffic signals. Thus technology has subjected the human sensorium to a complex kind of training. There came a day when a new and urgent need for stimuli was met by the film. In a film, perception in the form of shocks was established as a formal principle.
> (Benjamin 1982: 132)

The modern everyday shock experience is the training ground for being able to articulate it. So too is modernity's most celebrated representational device – cinema. In one of his most famous essays, 'The Work of Art in the Age of Mechanical (Technological) Reproduction' (1936) Benjamin offers a vision of the technical device of cinema as the most capable technology for rec-ognizing the *Erlebnis* of everyday life in the *Erfahrung* of communicable form:

> Our taverns and our metropolitan streets, our offices and furnished rooms, our railroad stations and our factories appeared to have us locked up hopelessly. Then came the film and burst this prison-world asunder by the dynamite of the tenth of a second, so that now, in the midst of its far-flung ruins and debris, we calmly and adventurously go travelling. With the close-up, space expands; with slow motion, movement is extended.
> (Benjamin 1982: 238)

The cinema that Benjamin imagines is a cinema of the everyday, founded on principles of montage. It offers itself not in the form of traditional narrative, but as an analysis of everyday experience. In some ways it is a cinema of experience that is never limited to the purely optical:

> Even if one has a general knowledge of the way people walk, one knows nothing of a person's posture during the fractional second of a stride. The act of reaching for a lighter or a spoon is familiar routine, yet we

hardly know what really goes on between hand and metal, not to mention how this fluctuates with our moods. Here the camera intervenes with the resources of its lowerings and liftings, its interruptions and isolations, its extensions and accelerations, its enlargements and reductions.

(Benjamin 1982: 239)

Here is imagined a cinema that evades the phantasmagoria of modernity by invoking the haptical as much as the optical, where the embodied experience of navigating modernity is open to representation. It is also a cinema that turns the distraction of everyday life back on itself. A poetics of distraction is seen as the potential that cinema (as a montage practice) promises. Benjamin's project is focused on the search for new forms that might allow distracted experience to become meaningfully articulated. The influence of his friend Siegfried Kracauer is crucial here. In a number of essays in the mid-1920s Kracauer diagnoses 'distraction' in cinematic experience as both a symptom and a (potential) cure (Kracauer 1995). It is a symptom of an alienated and modern form of life, where tradition is continually blasted by modernity. Cinema reproduces this through the spectacle of the phantasmagoria. But cinema also allows for a new form of seeing that might be characterized as distracted; this form of attention (or non-attention) not only is appropriate to the modern everyday but might also provide for potentially critical articulations of it.

In Benjamin a poetics of cinematic distraction is only hinted at:

Reception in a state of distraction, which is increasing noticeably in all fields of art and symptomatic of profound changes in apperception, finds in the film its true means of exercise. The film with its shock effect meets this mode of reception halfway. The film makes the cult value recede into the background not only by putting the public in the position of the critic, but also by the fact that at the movies this position requires no attention. The public is an examiner, but an absent-minded one.

(Benjamin 1982: 242–3)

What this might mean in terms of the viewing practices of audiences or in terms of the kind of films that might mobilize distraction for the political aims that Benjamin has in mind isn't made clear. In putting forward 'an absent-minded' critical examination, which might be able to articulate aspects of modern everyday life, Benjamin is positing the everyday as something that can't be approached as a fully conscious experience. This is experience that is partly inchoate, and it will need to generate poetic forms that allow this to be articulated. It is only in this way that the modern form of *Erlebnis* can become a new *Erfahrung*. The key to this is montage (this is what seems to be suggested by a distracted poetics or a poetics of distraction). While Benjamin is keen to promote a range of sites for the transformation of the modern *Erlebnis* into *Erfahrung*, the place where we should most expect to find a new articulation of everyday life is in Benjamin's own practice.

Dialectical images of everyday life

> What differentiates images from the 'essences' of phenomenology is their historic index . . . These images must be thoroughly marked off from 'humanistic' categories, such as so-called habitus, style, etc. For the historical index of the images doesn't simply say that they belong to a specific time, it says above all that they only enter into legibility at a specific time. And indeed, this 'entering into legibility' constitutes a specific critical point of the movement inside them. Every Now is determined by those images that are synchronic with it: every Now is the Now of a specific recognizability . . . It isn't that the past casts its light on what is present or that what is present casts its light on what is past; rather an image is that in which the Then and the Now come together into a constellation like a flash of lightning. In other words: an image is dialectics at a standstill. [N3, 1]

Nowhere is Benjamin's thinking more suggestive for a theory of everyday life than in his notion of the dialectical image. Here the historicity of the everyday enters into legibility. The dialectical image is a constellation (a montage) of elements that, in combination, produce a 'spark' that allows for recognition, for legibility, for communication and critique. What Benjamin is aiming at is a collage practice that can arrange the materiality of modernity into a design that awakens it from its dreamscape and opens it out on to history (the awakening that he finds missing in Surrealism in general). For this Benjamin was explicit: he would intervene as little as possible, merely orchestrate: 'I need say nothing. Only exhibit.' For his friend Adorno this practice was open to the critique that it lacked a theory of mediation: 'Materialist determination of cultural traits is only possible if it is mediated through the *total social process*' (Adorno 1980: 129, emphasis in original). He continues: 'calling things by their names tends to turn into a wide-eyed presentation of mere facts. If one wished to put it very drastically, one could say that your study is located at the crossroads of magic and positivism. That spot is bewitched. Only theory could break the spell' (129).

For Adorno, in a critique that echoes Benjamin's own critique of Surrealism, Benjamin is seen as remaining within the 'bewitched spot' of

Surrealism (magic and positivism) and in desperate need of theoretical rigour. But for Benjamin the explicit historicity of everyday life is the only 'theory' that could break the spell of the dream. But if this mixture of 'magic and positivism' could operate to concoct constellations that would throw the experience of everyday life into recognizability, how was this going to work in practice? What were the conditions of Benjamin's dialectical image that could puncture the dream of modernity and spill out its contents into the realm of legibility? A section ('Louis-Philippe or the Interior') from the 'Arcades Exposé' (1935) will serve as an example.

The 'Exposé' consists of micro-chapters that offer a truncated version of the *Arcades Project* (or what the *Arcades Project* might have been). All follow the same title format: a proper name followed by a social phenomenon; either one or the other – the two become equivalent. The 'Exposé' is made up of six such chapters and apart from the one on the interior includes 'Fourier or the Arcades', 'Daguerre or the Dioramas', 'Grandville or the World Exhibitions', 'Baudelaire or the Streets of Paris' and 'Haussmann or the Barricades'. Benjamin begins the 'Louis-Philippe or the Interior' chapter by invoking a moment for the lived and 'private' experience of the interior: 'Under Louis-Philippe, the private citizen entered upon the historical scene' (Benjamin 1983a: 167). This historical moment emerges as a separation of the 'private' and the 'public' as a structural division of everyday life: 'For the private citizen, for the first time the living-space became distinguished from the place of work. The former constituted itself as the interior. The office was its complement' (167). As such the private realm became the privileged site of fantasy: 'His drawing-room was a box in the world-theatre.' This box was operated on by all sorts of phantasmagoric practices, particularly Art Nouveau. But it was also a site for the transformatory practices of the inhabitant as collector:

> The collector was the true inhabitant of the interior. He made the glorification of things his concern. To him fell the task of Sisyphus which consisted of stripping things of their commodity character by means of his possession of them. But he conferred upon them only a fancier's value, rather than use-value. The collector dreamed that he was in a world which was not only far-off in distance and in time, but which was also a better one, in which to be sure people were just as poorly provided with what they needed as in the world of everyday, but in which things were free from the bondage of being useful.
>
> (Benjamin 1983a: 168–9)

If the interior offered the chance to transform (magically) the lived commodity relationship, it also opened itself to a form of investigation that treated material goods with the forensic gaze of the detective:

Living means leaving traces. In the interior, these were stressed. Coverings and antimacassars, boxes and casings, were devised in abundance, in which the traces of everyday objects were moulded. The resident's own traces were also moulded in the interior. The detective story appeared, which investigated these traces.

(Benjamin 1983a: 169)

The materiality of the interior and the experience of those who use it come together in the historicity of the moment. In radically synoptic details a constellation is generated that takes the reader from the emergence of a specific private realm, through the interior design practices of the time, to the psychology of collecting and its employment of the commodity against itself, to the emergence of the detective novel as the form for linking the traces of experience to the notion of crime. If Benjamin is operating at the crossroads of magic and positivism such a bewitched spot might be the very site of everyday life. But reading through Benjamin's notes about the *Arcades Project* and the singular importance given to montage as an organizing principle, the 'Exposé' disappoints. You can't help but imagine that Benjamin envisaged a much more radical formal presentation of these 'facts'. The small book he published as *One-Way Street*, with its photomontaged cover and its juxtapositions of different elements, is probably much closer to how he would have wanted to present the *Arcades* material. Of this though we will never know. What Benjamin leaves is an 'architectural' theory for attending to the modern everyday.

In chapters 3 to 5 a theory of the everyday is presented that is both emergent and protean. In the very different practices that I've considered, 'the everyday' is not something that has become a galvanizing 'object' for consideration. But what is being generated is a range of approaches that are crucial for theorizing everyday life. In the work of Simmel, Surrealism and Benjamin an approach is being forged that attempts to attend to a side of life that is not simply contained (or containable) by consciousness. Without employing a fully psychoanalytic framework, both Simmel and Benjamin can be seen as treating the ephemera of the everyday as symptoms of much larger forces. How they go about this is very different: Simmel's 'impressionism' is directed at philosophical insights, while Benjamin's 'montage' practice is dedicated to a critical history of the present. Surrealism, of course, was much more insistent on a psychoanalytic framework, and yet for Benjamin it could never achieve a critical distance from phantasmagoric representation. The everyday as nonconscious experience is a thread that I will pick up in the chapters that follow; here it is enough to say that a nascent theory of the everyday offers an approach to experience that treats the everyday as a demand for inventive forms for attending to it. An approach that favours distraction and montage is arrived at, not through abstract thought, but by foregrounding experience as modern, urban and everyday.

In the work of Simmel, Surrealism and Benjamin, the sphere of everyday life is seen as quintessentially urban. The modern metropolis is seen as a realm where the problem of the everyday is unavoidable. Partly this is due to the spectacular technological changes brought about by modernity; partly it is due to a romanticism of the city. At this point we should look to see what is being excluded from this approach to everyday life. How would the everyday lives of women feature in this project? For the most part women are absent. Part of the project of developing 'theories of the everyday' is going to be rescuing pre-feminist theory from its gendered orientation. There is much here that might be useful: Simmel's emphasis on spheres of sociability (the meal, for instance) might be reworked in a way that articulates the gendering of the everyday; Benjamin's work on interiors might similarly be explored.

In approaching the everyday, the work of Simmel, Surrealism and Benjamin has begun to explore the possibilities of forms of representation that move away from realism and naturalism. Most significant has been the engagement with avant-garde forms. The radical practices of montage offer a vivid way of making the familiar strange, and it is this as much as anything that will offer something like a methodological base to this tradition of 'everyday life studies'. To what ends such montage practices are employed (in the name of the everyday) is not determined in advance, and we have little idea of how Benjamin might have brought together his massive *Arcades Project*. Benjamin's suggestive hints about a poetics based around distraction and awakening remain abstract.

In chapter 6 I will look at a project that combines the legacy of Surrealism with an ethnographic approach to everyday life. As we will see aspects of the radical formal potential of montage are accompanied by an equivocal desire to awaken consciousness from its dream world. In Mass-Observation the theoretical density of a Benjamin or a Simmel is missing, but instead there is a practical density that points to a theory 'not yet recognized as such'.

Notes

1   Walter Benjamin's 'Konvolut N: Re the theory of knowledge, theory of progress' is part of Benjamin's *Arcades Project* that has now been translated in its entirety (Benjamin 1999). 'Konvolut N' is the metacritical heart of the *Arcades Project* and central to my reading of it. Further reference to this 'Konvolut' will simply be signalled by Benjamin's numbering system in square brackets.

2   Benjamin committed suicide while fleeing from the Nazis in 1940.

Chapter 6

MASS-OBSERVATION
A science of everyday life

We shall collaborate in building up museums of sound, smell, foods, clothes, domestic objects, advertisements, newspapers, etc.

(Mass-Observation 1937a: 35)

Ethnography cut with surrealism emerges as the theory and practice of juxtaposition.

(Clifford 1988: 147)

IN OVER A THOUSAND FILE reports and a similar number of boxes of raw materials can be found the strangely ordinary documents of everyday life. Accounts of nightmares; meticulously detailed records of drinking habits in Bolton pubs (timed to the second with a stopwatch); pages and pages of diary records; thoughts on margarine – such items make up just part of the archive of everyday life generated by Mass-Observation. At one and the same time mundane and poetic, Mass-Observation offers an interminable attention to the daily. In the years leading up to and during the Second World War, Mass-Observation sought out the ordinariness of extraordinary times. Yet if the extraordinary could also show an ordinary face (a face that was extraordinary in a different way), the very banality of the daily could reveal a poetics that was saturated with myth. The status of the mythologies of daily life was the problem that Mass-Observation faced.

In the winter of 1936, at the time of the Abdication crisis of Edward VIII, a group of people living in Blackheath in London 'discussed the possibility of enlisting volunteers for the observation both of social happenings like the Abdication and also of "everyday life", as lived by themselves and those around them' (Madge 1976: 1395). This group consisted of Charles

Madge (a poet and reporter for the *Daily Mirror*), Kathleen Raine (a poet and critic), Humphrey Jennings (a painter, writer and documentary film-maker), David Gascoyne (a poet and a painter), Stuart Legg (who, with Jennings, was working with the GPO Film Unit in Blackheath), and various friends. In January 1937, in a letter to the *New Statesman and Nation*, Charles Madge, writing on behalf of the group, invites voluntary observers to write to 6 Grotes Buildings, Blackheath (the home of Madge and Raine) to co-operate in this project of collecting 'mass observations'. In the letter Madge suggests that a combination of psychoanalysis and anthropology is needed 'to deal with elements so repressed that only what is admitted to be a first-class upheaval brings them to the surface' (Madge 1937a: 12). At the same time Tom Harrisson, a self-taught anthropologist, is applying the methodology of partic-ipant observation to 'the wilds of Lancashire', in an attempt to bring anthropology 'home' and to understand the everyday life of his native culture (Tom Harrisson, quoted in Jeffery 1978: 20). Just back from Malekula in what was then called the New Hebrides (now Vanuatu), he takes a variety of manual jobs (mill worker, lorry driver, ice-cream vendor) in 'preparing himself to become the ethnographer of Bolton' (Madge 1976: 1395). By a strange coincidence a poem Harrisson wrote about his experience in Malekula (*Coconut Moon: A Philosophy of Cannibalism, in the New Hebrides*) is published by the *New Statesman and Nation* and is printed directly below Madge's letter. Recognizing similarities between his Bolton project and the interests of the Blackheath group, Harrisson suggests a collaboration, and together with Madge and Jennings a further letter is written, a letter that has all the hall-marks of a manifesto (Harrisson *et al.* 1937).

In the attempt to establish a national panel of part-time observers who will provide accounts of their everyday life, further invitations are made through the pages of the *Daily Express*, the *Daily Herald*, the *News Chronicle* and *Left Review*, and within a couple of months about a thousand offers of participation are received (not all of which will materialize). One significant feature of this drive was the large number of women recruited, partly due to the inclusion of an account by a 'housewife' of the details of her everyday life in some of the adverts. In Bolton Tom Harrisson manages to persuade a number of people (including unemployed workers, a 'tramp preacher' called 'Brother Joe' Willcock, as well as a variety of students, artists and writers) to become full-time observers for the 'Worktown' project. By the end of 1937 Mass-Observation has published a booklet outlining the project (Mass-Observation 1937a) and a collection of observations by the national panel in response to 'day-survey' directives (Mass-Observation 1937b), and is preparing a book of its first year of work (Mass-Observation 1938). After the publication of the day-surveys Humphrey Jennings distances himself from the project ('he shied away from what he felt to be a banal streak in Tom's expressionist quasi-anthropology' [Madge 1976: 1395]). The two sides of

Mass-Observation's operation, the part-time national panel (providing a cross-section of accounts of daily life as well as responding to other directives) and the work of full-time observers (focusing on the observation of others in geographically specific regions such as Bolton, Blackpool and London), are organized and co-ordinated by Madge and Harrisson. In 1940, Madge (who had swapped roles with Harrisson in 1938, and was conducting a survey on economic attitudes in Bolton) leaves Mass-Observation on account of Harrisson's decision to affiliate the project with the Home Intelligence Department of the Ministry of Information. In this chapter I will focus on this initial stage, the first few years of Mass-Observation, before it is tied to a government body and while Madge is still part of the equation.[1] It is during this period that the questions of everyday life (What are the particular experiences and activities that characterize everyday life in the modern world? How do different social groups experience everyday life? How can these experiences and activities be attended to and represented?) are at their most productively problematic. It is the unresolved and experimental side of Mass-Observation that I take as being of most interest for theorizing everyday life.

Tensions in Mass-Observation

From the start, Mass-Observation can be seen as characterized by tensions and conflicts, both across its various practices and between the perspectives of those involved in the project. Most of these tensions are not only productive for the project, but an inevitable and a necessary response to its initial conception. Emerging, as it does, on the fault-line between science and art, objectivity and subjectivity, rationalism and irrationalism, there is something necessarily unstable about the project. While attempts at accounting for Mass-Observation often end up privileging one side of this divide at the expense of the other, the difficulty of maintaining the precarious balance of its conflicting aims is often evidenced in the work of those who participated in it. The association of Madge and Harrisson, the two main protagonists, each with one side of this divide has worked to compound the perceived division of Mass-Observation into two distinct spheres. Even in Mass-Observation's own work, Madge and Harrisson continually mark out their differences: 'Charles [Madge] is a poet . . . he is interested in feelings . . . My interest was to describe as exactly as possible how people behave' (Mass-Observation 1983: A26, 2). Such distinctions seem to fit the stereotypes of 'dreamy poet' versus 'hard empiricist', but they are never static in Mass-Observation literature and don't stand up to prolonged scrutiny. Take, for instance, this attempt at differentiation at an earlier point:

> Tom Harrisson believes that Mass-Observation, by laying open to doubt all existing philosophies of life as possibly incomplete, yet by refusing

> to neglect the significance of any of them, may make a new synthesis
> . . . In the other author's [Madge's] opinion, Mass-Observation is an
> instrument for collecting facts, not a means for producing a synthetic
> philosophy, a super-science or super-politics. The availability of the
> facts will liberate certain tendencies in science, art, and politics, because
> it will add to the social consciousness of the time.
>
> (Mass-Observation 1937a: 47)

Here, there is no simple recourse to positivist empiricism on either side.
The use of the word 'facts' does not denote a belief in a scientific objectivity that sees the representational world as transparent; rather the facticity
of an observer's account resides in its ability to 'tell us not what society is
like, but what it looks like to them' (Mass-Observation 1938: 66).

The critical attention that Mass-Observation has received over recent
years has tended to reinforce and fix one side of the dynamic that the project
tried to negotiate. Most frequently asserted is the idea that Mass-Observation
continues the kind of social exploration practised in the nineteenth century,
where the 'scientific' objectifying gaze, which had been aimed at colonized
cultures, was turned towards the bodies and everyday life of the poor and
marginalized who live in the physical centre of Western metropolitan society.
This argument has seen Mass-Observation as a symptom of the dominance
of white bourgeois masculinity, which fashions and fixes its identity by copi-
ously describing another group (another class, another 'race') as exotic,
uncivilized and barbaric in relation to itself, which is taken as the norm.
Writing about the Mass-Observation photographs of Humphrey Spender[2] (but
by implication, applicable to their other observational activities), Jessica Evans
comments on the dominant trend of characterizing the project:

> much has been written of the way . . . [they] reproduced the structure
> of a colonial-bourgeois gaze on to the anthropological other. The very
> presumption of realism in these photographs effaced the position of
> knower and thus rendered 'the other' as a savage yet paradoxically
> impoverished threat.
>
> (Evans 1997: 145)

Such a reading seems to me, not only negligent of the variations in Mass-
Observation activity, but to be deploying a methodological instrument that
is historically blunt and can't differentiate between cultural practices in the
1930s and those in the 1830s. It de-differentiates by imposing overarching
meanings on the social function of technologies such as photography and jour-
nalistic reportage. Such a position towards Mass-Observation has often taken
the Bolton project (Worktown) as embodying Mass-Observation, and has
treated Tom Harrisson as its main and sometimes only voice. While such an

approach necessarily has to edit out the heterogeneity of Mass-Observation practices, it has provided much damning evidence to bolster its account. In establishing Mass-Observation as enacting a colonial gaze on to the exoticized bodies of the working class, the words of Tom Harrisson seem to provide all the ammunition the historian could need. When Harrisson moves from the New Hebrides to Lancashire his intention is to employ the same ethnographic approach to the inhabitants of Bolton as had been used on the 'natives' of Malekula. Steve Edwards makes the point by using a quotation from Tom Harrisson:

> 'The wilds of Lancashire or the mysteries of the East End were as little explored as the cannibal interior of the New Hebrides, or the head hunter hinterland of Borneo . . . In particular, my experience living among cannibals in the New Hebrides . . . taught me the many points in common between these wild looking, fuzzy haired, black smelly people and our own, so when I came home from that expedition I determined to apply the same methods here in Britain.' As the site of the expedition shifted from the New Hebrides to Bolton, scrutiny was transferred directly from the 'black smelly savages' with their fuzzy hair to the dirty working class with their flat caps or curlers.
>
> (Edwards 1984: 18)

Tom Harrisson's words invoke a world formed by colonial relations. His words echo those of social explorers such as William Booth, who in his crusading pamphlet *In Darkest England and the Way Out* asks: 'May we not find a parallel at our own doors and discover within a stone's throw of our cathedrals and palaces similar horror to those which Stanley has found existing in the great Equatorial forest?' (quoted in Jackson 1992: 90). Published in 1890, the pamphlet's very title was meant to indicate an immediate connection between colonial Africa ('darkest Africa') and the East End of London. But while the analogy that Harrisson makes between 'fuzzy haired, black smelly people' and the inhabitants of the East End and Lancashire seems to concur with a colonial attitude to working-class life, such analogies were used by Harrisson to refer to a much wider range of classes in Britain. While the quote that Edwards uses is from a piece of writing produced in 1947,[3] eight years earlier Harrisson was accentuating the analogy in a very different direction:

> Well at the age of 22 I went to an island in the pacific called Malekula and spent three years living among cannibals, whom I found were neither better nor worse than old Harrovians [Harrow is where Harrisson went to school]. I tried to get an inside picture of their customs and ways of thinking, and for this I found it essential to live as they live. Then I came back to England and went to live in an

industrial town, trying to apply the same principles of observation to our own civilization.

(Mass-Observation 1983: A26, 2)

Here any indication of class specificity for 'cannibals' is aimed at the privileged ex-pupils of a public school (which significantly includes Harrisson himself) and the application of an ethnographic approach in Bolton suggests a wider purview than simply working-class culture. The use of the term 'cannibals' in Harrisson's writing is clearly designed to be polemical: it is used in a classic avant-gardist attempt to de-naturalize cultures perceived as self-evident, 'normal'. Of course, when used in relation to working-class culture, what Harrisson 'forgets' is the way that such a 'primitivist' term can simply be seen to continue an established practice of 'racing' the working class.

The reading of Mass-Observation as enacting a 'colonial-bourgeois gaze' is further extended by John Taylor, by reading the Bolton project in relation to the work of the national panel (Taylor 1994: 152–81). The split between observational activities in Bolton and the observational activities of the national panel is read as a division of intellectual labour that reflects and intensifies class divisions. Thus the observation of working-class Boltonians is seen as a mainly visual scrutinizing gaze: 'the ideal instrument for the job is an ear plug. *See* what people are doing. *Afterwards*, ask them what they think they are doing, if you like' (Harrisson, quoted in Picton 1978: 2). Such a form of attention enacts a 'dumbing' of the working-class 'objects' of investigation, fetishizing and 'othering' them. The national panel, however, works in reverse in that it enables 'volunteer diarists . . . coming mostly from the middle and lower-middle classes . . . the newly voluble classes of non-professional writers or speakers to be read and heard, to signify at some higher "national" level in the publication of books' (Taylor 1994: 158).

This argument, that Mass-Observation works to intensify class differences by giving a voice to the middle classes while simultaneously 'dumbing' the working classes, is at first glance compelling. However, this is not something borne out by a detailed historical inquiry into a movement that in actuality was much more complex and contradictory. In a number of ways Mass-Observation can be seen to work across this divide: for instance, in the panel surveys emphasis is given to accounts by people precisely because they are underrepresented by the panel as a whole. An example of this is in the book *May 12th Mass-Observation Day Surveys*, where accounts by the unemployed and manual workers are given more space because they were comparatively rare (Mass-Observation 1937b). This follows the scientific principle of the 'cross-section', as Mass-Observation makes clear: 'It is essential that Mass-Observation should recruit from all classes, from all localities and from every shade of opinion' (Mass-Observation 1937a: 32). Similarly, in a Mass-Observation radio broadcast the voices that were heard were not those of the southern middle class, but the accents of northern working-class men and women. It also would appear that, in criticisms such as the ones I have outlined, Bolton itself is not allowed to have any class complexity, being seen as made up entirely of workers with their 'flat caps or curlers'. I will return to some of these criticisms when I consider the particularity of the Bolton project and I will also look more closely at the ethnographic approach that was being employed there. In arguing against such accounts of Mass-Observation I am not arguing against the partial truths that they contain, merely calling for an account more attentive to the complexity of the project.

In this account I want to keep the tensions within Mass-Observation alive, and to try and maintain the precarious balance in their attention to everyday life. Writing about the cultural politics of the period in a review of Humphrey Jennings' *Pandaemonium*, E. P. Thompson's suggestion is that writers 'take the pulse of the time itself' (Thompson 1985: 165). Such a view might reveal a moment of political and intellectual eclecticism, where the boundaries of knowledges and methodologies weren't completely fixed by institutional and academic professionalism, where what would now be called a 'left liberal humanism' could accommodate both a Marxist-Leninist notion of the vanguard leading the masses and radical ideas of democracy, and where intellectual interest in popular culture and everyday life could include talk 'about such a shabby, old fashioned, suspect, uncerebral thing as the imagination' (Thompson 1985: 165). This was a moment when the amateur and the specialist could participate in a social experiment such as Mass-Observation. Perhaps the best way of describing the moment of Mass-Observation's attention to the everyday is to suggest that it was characterized by an attitude that Kathleen Raine describes as 'at once irrational and objective' (Raine 1967: 47). To understand Mass-Observation's articulation of this moment, it is necessary to look at the social and cultural materials that allowed it to emerge.

Surrealist ethnography

In an essay exploring the relationship between ethnography and Surrealism in France between the wars, James Clifford suggests that a tradition of ethnographic surrealism characterizes the work of dissident Surrealists such as George Bataille. While he focuses on the influence of ethnography on Surrealist activity, he comments that a converse tradition, where Surrealism has been a resource for ethnography, could also be delineated. In a footnote he points to the work of Mass-Observation as an example of this Surrealist ethnography (Clifford 1988: 142–3). If Surrealism included a vague adherence to the work of psychoanalysis joined with an aesthetic practice based on the principle of montage, and an anthropological approach (ethnography) focuses on the macro-analysis of the meanings and experience of a culture, then their combination could be characterized as a practice of understanding society as a *totality of fragments*: the montage of incidents seen as symptomatic of repressed forces. In this characterization of Mass-Observation the admix of Surrealism and anthropology forms the vital core. By employing Surrealism for an ethnographic project, the 'will to order' of anthropology is seriously undermined, while at the same time Surrealism's tendency to revel in mythic individualism is effectively countered.

The year of those initial conversations about the possibility of Mass-Observation, 1936, was also the year of the first International Surrealist Exhibition in London. This huge and chaotic exhibition at the New Burlington Galleries, curated by a committee that included both Humphrey Jennings and David Gascoyne, contained works by 'every prominent Paris surrealist', and also featured Jennings' and Gascoyne's paintings (Ray 1971: 136). Charles Madge was also instrumental in promoting Surrealism in Britain, writing 'one of the earliest essays [in Britain] devoted to literary surrealism', in 1933 (Madge 1933). What is so striking about Madge and Jennings' relationship to Surrealism is their critical attitude towards what they see as a tendency for aestheticism within Surrealism. For Madge, writing in 1934, this was caused by a failure to recognize the radical interdisciplinarity of Surrealism as a project. Quoting George Hugnet he insists that 'surrealism is not a literary school' but 'a laboratory of studies, of experimentation, that rejects all inclinations of individualism', and goes on to write that 'this should act as a warning to readers who are too apt . . . [to] treat surrealist poetry separately from the other activities of the surrealist laboratory' (Madge 1934: 13). In Britain this tendency of containment was seen as being exemplified by Herbert Read who promoted Surrealism as a new form of romanticism, rather than as a revolutionary attempt to overcome the separation of art and everyday life. It was in a review of Read's collection *Surrealism* ('so expensive, so *well* produced') that Humphrey Jennings draws connections between Surrealism as romanticism, as a *style*, and the functional use of surrealism for capitalism. In response to Read's critique of classicism as a 'tool of a classical-military-capitalist-ecclesiastical racket', Jennings writes:

> Is it possible that in place of a classical-military-capitalist-ecclesiastical racket there has come into being a romantic-cultural-*soi-dissant* co-operative-new uplift racket ready and delighted to use the 'universal truths of romanticism – co-eval with the evolving consciousness of mankind' as symbols and tools for its own ends? Our 'advanced' poster designers and 'emancipated' business men – what a gift Surrealism is to them when it is presented in the auras of 'necessity', 'culture' and 'truth' with which Read and Sykes Davies invest it.
>
> (Jennings in Jackson 1993: 220)

The limitations of Surrealism as an aesthetic style, narrowly defined as the province of professional cultural producers ('to be already a "painter", a "writer", an "artist", a "surrealist", what a handicap' [Jennings 1993: 221]) is set against Surrealist 'coincidences' in everyday life:

> 'Coincidences' have the infinite freedom of appearing anywhere, anytime, to anyone: in broad daylight to those whom we most despise in places we have most loathed: not even to us at all: probably least to petty seekers after mystery and poetry on deserted sea-shores and in misty junk-shops.
>
> (Jennings 1993: 220)

The Surreal poetry of everyday life would be found in everyday life by those unconnected to specialized aesthetic movements. Mass-Observation, which was going to be 'the observation by everyone of everyone, including them-selves' (Mass-Observation 1937a: 10), would find Surrealist material within the everyday world. Such critiques parallel those of Walter Benjamin: it is not Surrealism as a revolutionary project that is being critiqued, but its failure to distance itself from the phantasmagoria of modernity (advertising, aestheti-cism and the like). As we shall see, the project imagined by Mass-Observation fits much more closely with the early potential of Surrealism as a hetero-logical research activity. It also (in the work of Humphrey Jennings) evidences an interest in 'dialectical images'. Where Mass-Observation seems to differ is in the participants' insistence on attending to the everyday as a mass project of collecting 'facts'. The radical positivism of Mass-Observation suggests (potentially) a project so vast that, rather than commenting on the everyday, it would become conterminous with it.

As in early Surrealism, Mass-Observation employed a range of tropes associated with science (terms such as 'research data' and 'laboratory', as well as the continual use of 'science' and 'scientific') in a struggle to distance itself from the aestheticizing tendency in Surrealism. The use of the term 'science' in Mass-Observation is insistent, but it is also precarious and open to a wide range of meanings. The use of such tropes, while dialogically opposed to aestheticism, wasn't merely a tactical use of science rhetoric, meaningless in itself. But neither did it mean buying into the dominant scien-tific paradigm of the time. The 'sciences' that Mass-Observation references are precisely those whose status as science was open to question: psychology, anthropology and sociology. Science as objectivity is asserted at the same time as its possibility is put in crisis. In Mass-Observation's initial 'manifesto' a list is given of the various topics that it will focus on. In the list 'science' and everyday life are negotiated in a Surrealist montage:

Behaviour at war memorials.
Shouts and gestures of motorists.

The aspidistra cult.
Anthropology of football pools.
Bathroom behaviour.
Beards, armpits, eyebrows.
Anti-semitism.
Distribution, diffusion and significance of the dirty joke.
Funerals and undertakers.
Female taboos about eating.
The private lives of midwives.

(Harrisson *et al.* 1937: 155)

Most items on the list could be imagined to 'fit' a social scientific investigation (though a couple seem altogether too wayward – 'Beards, armpits, eyebrows', 'The private lives of midwives', for instance). But taken together the effect is of a random selection of topics from the margins of social life, an obsession with the oddities of everyday life. While the use of a list might suggest a 'scientific' desire for exhaustive and rigorous investigation, the actuality of this particular list seems to be a studied attempt at being systematically unsystematic.

Elsewhere the reference to 'science' is used by Mass-Observation for political purposes; the deployment of a scientific approach in the use of social anthropology and psychoanalysis is a weapon that will counter contemporary tendencies such as the 'outbursts' of atavism and 'racial superstition' in Germany (Mass-Observation 1937a: 11). Mass-Observation's 'science' is aimed at the emergence and circulation of an affective economy of representations, a social imaginary made up of mass images that can be treated as dream elements and wish fulfilments of a social unconscious. By treating modern forms of ideology as a continuation of sympathetic magic, ritual and superstition, a scientific ethnography can reveal the emotional depth of the political in everyday life (Mass-Observation 1937a: 14). Such a science can also be seen to offer a resistance to the lure of these affective economies, particularly the racist economy of Nazi culture. The problem that Mass-Observation poses, but never resolves, is the question of critical distance in relation to myth: can science offer a form of analysis that can simply point out the error of myth and read it as ideology? Or, if this position is unavailable, should it set itself the task of privileging counter-myths that offer more liberatory potential? Given the political situations of the time – economic depressions, the rise of Nazism and other Fascist formations (one of the first file reports for Mass-Observation is a detailed observation of Mosley's march through Bermondsey [Mass-Observation 1983: A3]) and the emergence of a Popular Front against Fascism – the function of political symbolism in everyday life had a terrible urgency. In attending to the circulation and consumption of such symbolism it was perhaps inevitable that Mass-

Observation would evidence a particularly forceful engagement with the mass media.

While both Jennings and Madge continued to produce Surrealist poetry in the mid-1930s (a poetry marked by the collaging of the 'actuality' of everyday life (Chaney and Pickering 1986: 39; Raine 1967: 50–1)), both were moving in a direction that brought them into a productive contact with the social practice of the mass media: Madge by becoming a journalist for the *Daily Mirror* and Jennings by joining John Grierson at the GPO Film Unit in 1934. This involvement in the mass media signals a number of important elements for the emergence of Mass-Observation and for understanding its approach for attending to everyday life. On the one hand newspapers, magazines, the radio and cinema articulated a fantasy world of superstition and ritual (advertising and horoscopes, for example) which increasingly penetrated daily life. On the other hand media representations of contemporary events and their impact on daily life were being produced by an elite who continually manufactured an idea of 'the people' to legitimate their own interests. What was needed was a mechanism for non-elite voices to be heard that would give accounts of everyday life and everyday responses to social and political events. Rather than offering a simple split between mass-media representation (false) and everyday life experience (true), Mass-Observation can be seen to be working with an understanding of everyday life that is inseparable from the mass media, while clearly not being reducible to the image it presents. As well as focusing on the 'ephemera' of everyday life, Mass-Observation sought to attend to politically important events, where the penetration of the mass media was inescapable, and where the non-fit between a representation of 'the people' and the heterogeneous actuality of people could be most vividly articulated. As has already been noted, the event that provoked the formation of Mass-Observation was the 1936 Abdication crisis.

The relationship between events of national and international significance and the world of everyday life needs some explanation. Firstly, events such as the Abdication crisis are seen as moments when 'mythic' and 'ritualistic' elements of a culture come to the surface. Thus the marital status of the king and the woman he wants to marry is seen as providing materials for an anthropology of sexual taboo, mythic rituals of crowning and uncrowning, superstition and so on. This suggests that the everyday (its social 'rules') is seen most vividly at points of crisis, moments when everyday life becomes public. Secondly, the investigation of everyday life at the point of political crises might reveal gaps between 'mass' representation (in the media) and the lived experience of the 'masses' at such moments. By collecting accounts of everyday experience at times of crises, Mass-Observation can be seen to be set up in response and antagonism to the machinery of the mass media, its interests and its forms of (mis)representation. Mass-Observation's publications often begin with a montage of newspaper headlines and editorials, which produce a sharp contrast with the everyday accounts that follow. Thirdly, and related to this second point, is the distinction between a mediatic representation that promotes an idea of consensual meaning to the event and the everyday world which is demonstrated as being radically heterogeneous and where such events are met with unanticipated responses and indifference. In some ways this can be seen as a relationship between a media technology which had come to saturate the everyday to the point where nearly everyone was living in relation to the same world of representation (everyday life as homogeneity), and the active and lived experience of people which not only couldn't be reduced to this representation, but in many ways was radically removed from it (everyday life as heterogeneity). By engaging with forms of communication distinct from state and commercial media, Mass-Observation can be seen as privileging an alternative mass media, made up of networks of communication based in pubs and clubs and in the 'gossip' networks of local communities. Alongside this, Mass-Observation's production, its attempt to produce collective newspapers, can be seen as galvanizing some of these networks into a potential counter 'mass' media (where mass points to the side of production rather than consumption).

While the Abdication crisis (because it was seen as making socially repressed material apparent) was the event that first interested Mass-Observation, other similar events were used as subjects for investigation. The coronation of George VI became the putative event for the publication of a collection of day-surveys made by the national panel (Mass-Observation 1937b), and the 'Munich crisis' is the event that kicks off the 1939 book *Britain*. This last example offers a typical instance of Mass-Observation's perspective. Starting with a quote from a newspaper – 'While Europe was tensely watching the crisis over Czechoslovakia . . .' – it continues by asking who exactly is 'tensely watching'? 'How many more were more tensely watching the racing news and daily horoscope?' (Mass-Observation 1939: 7). It was in this way that a mass-media representation could be countered by an everyday representation where the observers who made up Mass-Observation 'will be the meteorological stations from whose reports a weather-map of popular feeling can be compiled' (Mass-Observation 1937a: 30).

It was the assembling of a body of observers (both the panel and the 'investigators') that constituted the explicitly ethnographic aspect of Mass-Observation and established it as a form of social movement. As has already been mentioned, the observers in Mass-Observation were split between the national panel of part-time unpaid observers (who either volunteered after reading about Mass-Observation or found out about it by word of mouth, often from other observers) and the full-time paid observers. The split is more than a question of time and money. While the full-time 'trained' observer (often paid only a pittance, and then only when funds allowed) was 'ideally a camera with no distortion' and spent most of their time watching and listening to others, the part-time untrained observer, who would send in accounts (day-surveys) of themselves and their immediate group, 'would be *subjective* cameras, each with his or her own individual distortion' (Mass-Observation 1938: 66). While this seems to demarcate knowledge between the objectivity of scientific training (such as it was) and the subjectivity of lived experience, the line between the two was much more blurred than this suggests. For instance in the forward to *Mass-Observation*, Julian Huxley could write: 'In fact, some of the "day-surveys" I have seen, made by observers with no scientific training, would put many orthodox scientists to shame in their simplicity, clearness and objectivity' (Mass-Observation 1937a: 6). It would also seem that if these were 'subjective' accounts, then they would require some form of 'objective' *interpretation* from the ethnographer to make them usable for scientific analysis. In practice, however, such observations were used in a way that allowed them 'to speak for themselves' (as much as this is ever possible). Similarly, the full-time observers (who certainly didn't receive much training that could count as 'scientific') filed observations of activities in pubs and on beaches without recourse to a set of criteria, often giving very vivid accounts that include their own responses (see the various examples in Calder and Sheridan 1985).

This blurring between what an anthropologist at the time would call 'native informants' and 'participant observer', which has often been taken as evidence of Mass-Observation's unscientific confusion,[4] needs to be understood as a practical and ethical response to the project of applying anthropology to 'ourselves' by refusing the interpretative authority of specialist ethnographers. I would argue that Mass-Observation is most productive, as an approach to everyday life, when it treats 'natives' as the ethnographers. In doing so (particularly through the structure of the national panel), Mass-Observation can be seen as generating a radically democratic project. It is here that Mass-Observation can be seen to fulfil the promise of Surrealist ethnography: the potential for everyone (academic ethnographers, capitalist industrialists, working men and women, and so on) to become 'natives'.

The move towards ethnography by 'Surrealists' like Madge and Jennings can be explained with recourse to their critiques of the aestheticizing tendencies within Surrealism and their understanding of Surrealism as a *social* involvement in everyday life. What also needs understanding is the 'surreal' potential of ethnography as a practice for attending to everyday life at 'home'. In this, ethnography and Surrealism share a number of common features: both abandon the 'distinction between high and low culture' (Clifford 1988: 130); both can be seen as ways of defamiliarizing the everydayness of the everyday; and both question the 'taken-for-granted-ness' of everyday activities. It is when ethnography is practised 'at home' that its most surreal and critical possibilities are revealed. Most important here is the way in which the taken-for-granted aspects of daily life can be questioned by treating them in the same way *as if* they were part of a totally unfamiliar culture. In this single move the question of which activities contain meaning, which practices are most important, is left open, and investigation into the significant aspects of a culture should have no recourse to pre-established hierarchies of taste and import.[5] In bringing 'anthropology home', everyday life becomes the privileged scene for ethnographic investigation. That which might have become invisible through over-familiarity is re-invested with the potential for surprise and meaning. Here the ritual elements that make up the everyday are taken as the culturally significant, but the significance is seen as neither self-evident nor easily available for interpretation.

Ethnography practised at home meant that the most 'banal' of everyday activities could have the potential for revealing cultural meanings; at the same time, the most exceptional events are studied not in terms of their 'declared' significance, but in terms of the activities and practices they engender. In this way an understanding of the way a vague concept like 'class' operates in a culture must be seen in the everyday practices and preferences of people in their responses towards margarine and butter (Mass-Observation 1983: A9). Similarly the everyday activities of smoking (Mass-Observation 1938: 8–24) and drinking (Mass-Observation 1938: 24–31; 1943) are seen as potential material for understanding the cultural meanings of everyday life within everyday life. The activities of observers charting drinking and smoking habits with stopwatches and notebooks have been seen by a number of historians and critics as proof of the 'fact that the kind of knowledge Mass-Observation was to gather was positivistic' (Evans 1997: 146). In this way Mass-Observation is seen as the 'ghosts of those earnest Victorians collecting butterflies, classifying fossils, pressing botanical specimens into their note-books, but without any theories to tie all the information together' (Picton 1978: 2). In a particularly telling phrase Tom Picton suggests that in Mass-Observation 'time and motion study was confused with documentary' (Picton 1978: 2). From the point of view of Surrealist ethnography such practices are the very opposite of the instrumental rationality of scientific management. The utilitarian positivism of 'time and motion' is a world away from treating activities as if they were magical rituals. For some of those involved in Mass-Observation it was not the trappings of scientific rationality that caused problems, but the perceived tendency to see ritual everywhere in the everyday:

> I think Tom [Harrisson], having worked a lot in remote parts of the world, was perhaps too anxious to find parallels in the life of this country. And so having observed ritualistic dancing, and the masks, the costumes and other art connected with it, he would constantly be on the lookout for the same sort of thing in Bolton. For example, at every possible opportunity the children used to put on paper hats and dance

Figure 6 'Children in paper hats, Bolton' – photograph by Humphrey Spender (1937). Courtesy of Bolton Museum and Art Gallery

> about [see figure 6]: these were quite innocent, childish affairs, but Tom was inclined to put rather mysterious interpretations on them.
>
> (Spender 1982: 16)

For the Surrealist ethnographer of everyday life everything is potentially mysterious, nothing is innocent of meaning.

Poetry of everyday life

While a small panel had been organized before Mass-Observation was 'officially' formed, its expansion in response to the publicity generated by the formation of Mass-Observation was massive and at times overwhelming. This growing national panel wrote reports in response to a number of different directives concerning specific areas of investigation: reading choices, reactions to advertising, smoking habits, social attitudes to margarine, newspaper reading, bad dreams and nightmares, personal appearance and clothes (Mass-Observation 1983). These directives required the panel members to gather opinions of friends and acquaintances as well as voicing their own views and experiences. Alongside this, Mass-Observation asked the panel to record their everyday life in a loosely directed diary form. These day-surveys (as they were known) took place on the twelfth day of each month and panelists were asked to report on conversations they had had, on their dreams, local events, feelings, the weather and so on. The fourth day-survey fell on the day of the coronation of George VI (12 May 1937) and would make up the bulk of Mass-Observation's first book-length publication (Mass-Observation 1937b). By the end of the first year, Mass-Observation had collected a total of 1,730 reports from the national panel, consisting of about 2,300,000 words (Mass-Observation 1938: 47). Given the scale of the material and the difficulty of dealing with such an exponentially expanding archive, they decided temporarily to suspend the day-surveys (which made up the majority of the material), concentrating instead on surveys of special days (holidays, etc.) and topic-based research (pursued through 'directives' by the national panel).

The formation of a national panel and the amassing of observational material seemed to be relatively easy compared with the problem of knowing what to do with the collected material. Given that Mass-Observation had 'not set out in quest of truth or facts for their own sake, or for the sake of an intellectual minority, but aims at exposing them in simple terms to all observers, so that their environment may be understood, and thus constantly transformed' (Harrisson et al. 1937: 155), it was crucial that the material was published. The methodological and theoretical approaches to the collecting and organizing of this material for publication are of crucial signif-icance for understanding Mass-Observation's attention to everyday life.

Looking at the very first directive, the importance of psychoanalysis is immediately evident. This initial directive, written in December 1936 (prob-ably by Madge in consultation with Jennings, Raine and others), was sent out to about twenty people, who were required to ask a number of ques-tions of as many people as they could. The directive stated: 'Answers should be obtained from the person questioned at a speed which will prevent him [sic] from taking refuge in a merely conventional and socially correct response' (Mass-Observation 1983: A 4). This form of questioning was designed to encourage 'free association' and discourage forms of normative self-regula-tion, in relation to both social conventions and the 'policing' activity of the super-ego. One noticeable element of this is a tactic of surprise, where a seemingly straightforward question is followed by a more bizarre one, for instance, after being asked about the importance of religion, the interviewee is asked, 'Do you welcome or shrink from the contact by touch or smell of your fellow men?' The ordering of questions points to a specific montage practice:

Name
Address
1.   Age
2.   Married or unmarried
3.   What are your superstitions, in order of importance?
4.   Do you pay attention to coincidences?

5.   What is your class?
6.   What is your Father's profession, and your own?
7.   Do you or did you hate your Father, and if so, why?
8.   Do you or did you hate your Mother, and if so, why?
9.   Do you or did you want to get away from home, and if so, why?
10. Do you want to have a son, or a daughter, or both?
11. Do you hate your boss; do you hate your job?
12. What is your greatest ambition?
13. Did you want the King to marry Mrs. Simpson, and if so, why?
14. Were you glad or sorry when the Crystal Palace was burnt down and if so, why?
15. Do you approve of the institution of marriage as it exists in this country at present? If not, how would you wish it changed?
16. Are you in favour of the disestablishment of the Church of England?
17. Are you religious? If so, in what form?
18. Do you welcome or shrink from the contact by touch or smell of your fellow men?
19. Can you believe you are going to die?
20. How do you want to die?
21. What are you most frightened of?
22. What do you mean by freedom?

(Mass-Observation 1983: A 4)

What is at stake here is a use of psychoanalysis aimed at revealing more than the repressed prehistory of the individual. The movement from questions concerning a subject's affective relationship with their parents to questions about feelings towards their boss suggests that purposeful connections were being made between social structures and personal life in relation to the workings of the unconscious. Similarly, responses to questions concerning the destruction of the Crystal Palace are followed by a consideration of the subject's own mortality, again making connections between the personal and the social which suggests that material in the everyday public world can be invested with unconscious meanings. There is no need to assume that Madge and others are expecting to find or interested in finding Jungian symbolic archetypes of the collective unconscious, or for that matter, the common outpourings of a national psyche (such approaches might simply figure the social unconscious as too unified). What they are interested in, as an experimental approach, is the possibility of using psychoanalysis for looking at everyday life. This unsystematic use of psychoanalysis should come as no surprise given their involvement in Surrealism, but it does suggest a rather different use of psychoanalysis. Rather than providing an interpretive frame, or a mechanism for producing works of art (automatic writing and the like), psychoanalysis is a tool (or set of tools) that is being used to encourage the emergence of unconscious material in the everyday world. The importance of the unconscious in everyday life (and everynight life) is continually asserted, as panel members are asked to record their dreams for day-surveys, and are asked to make reports of 'Bad Dreams and Nightmares' for a special survey on anxiety dreams and their relationship to the social anxieties on the eve of war (Mass-Observation 1983: A 20).

If these 'special directives' allowed a number of particular issues to be investigated, they didn't offer the range of materials that the day-surveys produced. By taking one specific day, and seeing how it is being lived and dreamed across the country, by people unknown to each other, the full 'totality of fragments' of the everyday could be envisaged. These day-surveys took the basis of commonality (everyone experienced the same day, the same coronation) to emphasize the diversity of the lives being lived. It is the mixture of diversity and commonality (diversity as commonality) that I think is particularly important to Mass-Observation, and crucial to its understanding of everyday life. What continually needs asserting is the historical context of these experiments – crucially, their critically dialogic response to the image of a society where diversity was being brutally and systematically eradicated (Nazi Germany), in comparison to their political support for the Popular Front and the possibilities of a consensus of radically different political positions against a common enemy. How Mass-Observation translates this is in the practice of promoting a 'totality of fragments', of a society 'united' by a heterogeneous everyday, a commonality of diversity. What remained was how to find a form for producing such an image of society.

For Humphrey Jennings the idea of the 'image' was of crucial significance. As Kathleen Raine remembers, 'he spoke always of "the image" never of "the symbol"' (Raine 1967: 49). Using an example from Jennings' collection of images, *Pandaemonium: The Coming of the Machine as seen by Contemporary Observers* (Jennings 1995), Charles Madge explains the particularity of the image for Jennings. Referring to an extract from the diary of Michael Faraday, where Faraday observes a balloon dropping ballast over Vauxhall on a sunny day, producing the effect of a stationary cloud of golden particles, he writes:

> The 'image' here consists not only of the balloon, the golden cloud of dust particles, Vauxhall, the date, Faraday watching and Faraday's physical discoveries, but of the relations between these elements and other elements, all ordered into a larger universe of imagery. The individual image, and the imaginative eye that seizes it, is a point of *ordonnance* in such a universe. It is not only verbal, or visual, or emotional, although it is all these. It is not in the elements, but in their coming together at a particular moment, that the magical potency lies.
>
> (Madge 1982: 47)

Such an understanding of 'the image' connects powerfully with Benjamin's notion of the 'dialectical image' as a dynamic moment capable of interrupting historical narratives of progress. The material of the day-surveys would together constitute such an image, an image where the fragments of daily life could come into meaningful relationship.

Charles Madge and Humphrey Jennings decided that the day-surveys of the coronation could be edited together to make an image of 'an extraordinary picture of England – extraordinary, though the material they report is completely ordinary' (Mass-Observation 1937a: 31). In practice the editing of the manuscript that would become *May 12th: Mass-Observation Day-Surveys* involved a complex montage, where the two hundred or so observations could be disassembled into 'moments' or themes, so that they could be reassembled in a way that allowed the reader to move through the day continually immersed in a mesh of different experiences rather than presented with consecutive accounts of the day. They needed to present the material in such a way as to avoid imposing overarching patterns of interpretation on to it ('Our first concern is to collect data, not to interpret them' [Mass-Observation 1937a: 34]). The practice of montage signals not only the importance of Surrealism (the 'umbrella and a sewing machine lying together on a dissecting table'), but also the filmic montage practices of the Soviet avant-garde (theorized and exemplified by Eisenstein and Vertov), a practice that would have been familiar to Jennings and Stuart Legg as well as practically engaged with at the GPO Film Unit at Blackheath. Collage and montage are the materials of Mass-Observation's practice and it is worth returning to montage theory (as discussed in chapter 4) to explain in more detail why it was so important and what it allowed them to do.

In a number of ways montage is the most appropriate form for representing everyday life as the pell-mell of different worlds colliding. Firstly, collage can be seen as a theory of shock. Important for Surrealism and Soviet film-makers is the idea that the collaged fragment has some kind of 'charge' that is released when it is brought into contact with a different kind of element: thus one charged fragment detonates another, which in turn produces a reaction. In the heterogeneous world of everyday life, such collisions are inevitable. The collaging of day-surveys could bring an account of a day in the life of a wealthy suburban woman (entirely 'ordinary' in itself), into collision with the same day as experienced by a working woman in Glasgow to produce a shocking contrast, which not only vivifies both accounts, but allows them both to be defamiliarized, made strange. Clearly, there is a huge potential for montage to generate critical forms of reading, by making contradictions and antagonisms explicit within the social realm.

> My brother took a little brandy as we sat down in the drawing room and played a quiet game of chess. I turned on the radio and so listened

to the descriptive account of the Coronation being broadcast at the moment. We seem fated to hear the actual crowning ceremony, which we intended to ignore when we set out to play tennis.

I laid in bed till 6.15 a.m. and got up, washed and shaved. I ate my breakfast and read the paper. On leaving the house I encountered a tramp who asked if I could make him some tea. He looked a pitiable creature and held out two half-pennies in a grimy hand as if to offer payment for the service.

(Mass-Observation 1937b: 322)

But while this collage practice could articulate social differences, it could also be a space that allows for unexpected contacts to be made, and unantici-pated coincidences to be found; montage is capable of revealing 'explosive' links where they are least expected.

Secondly, montage allows for the *simultaneity* of difference within the everyday to be represented. The effects of the uneven and unequal devel-opment of a capitalist society produce a range of temporalities that exist at the same time. Rather than seeing a culture as at a particular stage of devel-opment, society is best thought of in terms of a non-synchronic simultaneity, whereby groups of people are living across different temporalities. So, for instance, expressions such as 'still living in the 60s' can have more than metaphoric meaning. Similarly, unequal access to new technologies and emerging lifestyles produces different temporal consciousnesses. Collage, then, is a synchronic representation of non-synchronic simultaneity.

10.30 a.m. Arrive at S– Theatre to connect up radio set to talkie equip-ment in order to relay the King's speech at 8 p.m. This is being done in 15 shows in town. Many adjustments required to get satisfactory performance.

(Mass-Observation 1937b: 271)

Out they came from the cart – off came harness, and for ten or fifteen minutes each horse was gone over. 'He'll be dangling his ticket round Ilkla on his round tomorra.' Butcher's cart with pastoral group of very dead skinned sheep in red white and blue bows.

(Mass-Observation 1937b: 329)

Thirdly, and associated with this, is the refusal of montage to subsume these diverse elements into a homogeneous whole. Instead of accumulating these elements into a resolved and meaningful unity, collage offers a bombard-ment of materials that resist narrative resolution. Rather than placing events and images into a seemingly natural order (the linearity of progressive sequence), collage allows its condition as an articulation to be made evident: the relationships between elements are denaturalized, suggesting that they can always be re-articulated in different arrangements. Similarly, because the elements of a collage often utilize different representational modes (in *May 12th* these would include different vernaculars, different ways of writing), there is the possibility of disarticulation, where the disruption of one element by another challenges the authority of any one representational mode and allows the problematizing of representation itself. Lastly, and again related to the previous points, the potential of montage is the production of a representation where the fragments of everyday life aren't welded together in the service of an overarching framework, but neither is the idea of 'totality' abandoned in favour of endless fragments. Rather a critical totality of fragments is possible that attempts to see the world as a network of uneven, conflicting, unassimilable but relating elements:

> Its [collage's] heterogeneity, even if it is reduced by every operation of composition, imposes itself on the reading as stimulation to produce a signification which could be neither univocal nor stable. Each cited element breaks the continuity or the linearity of the discourse and leads necessarily to a double reading: that of the fragment as perceived in relation to its text of origin; that of the same fragment as incorporated into a new whole, a different totality. The trick of collage consists also of never entirely suppressing the alterity of these elements reunited in a temporary composition. Thus the art of collage proves to be one of the most effective strategies in the putting into question of all the illusions of representation.
>
> (Group Mu, quoted in Ulmer 1985: 88)

These aspects of montage are only potential qualities rather than necessary characteristics of the practice. It should be remembered that daily newspapers practise a form of montage, but to very different ends. The radicality of Mass-Observation's montage technique in *May 12th* should be seen as a critical response to the techniques of newspapers, as well as to the institutionalized forms of social criticism to be found in government agencies. By using montage in this way *May 12th* also suggests a different relationship between reader and text: rather than being the recipient of knowledge, the reader is left to make their own connections within a work that appears to have no ordering principle apart from disorder.

In one way, though, *May 12th* was a significant failure for Mass-Observation: it was a large hardback book (over 400 pages), very expensive (12s 6d) and sold only about 800 copies (Calder and Sheridan 1985: 62). The price was a particularly sore point given Mass-Observation's stress on the importance of feeding back information for a non-elite public, and is in striking contrast to the availability of a monthly book from the Left Book Club for only 2s 6d. A number of attempts were made to rectify the situation by trying to persuade local libraries to buy it and by offering it for hire through the mail. What was most awkward was the antagonism it raised amongst the national panel who were in fact the authors of the book, but couldn't afford a copy. Whatever the shortcomings of the experiment (and these lessons would be taken to heart) it can be seen as a significant moment for Mass-Observation in generating a form for the articulation of everyday life. If Mass-Observation publications after *May 12th* can be seen to dilute the radicality of this technique, offering more editorial comment, framing and ordering material in less polyphonic ways, they should still be understood as continuing the practice of montage. Perhaps, though, the practice of montage (as an epistemological and practical orientation) is least evident in the more conventionally anthropological work of Mass-Observation in 'Worktown'.

Worktown: cannibals in Bolton

The image that most often accompanies mention of Mass-Observation in recent critical accounts is an image of the educated middle-class English southerner 'observing' (or spying, tracking and so on) the impoverished working-class northerner (Edwards 1984: 19; Picton 1978: 2). This image of intrusive voyeurism is partly a product of self-representation by Mass-Observation. Writing an article for the *Daily Mirror* about a piece of research on razor slashing in Halifax, Harrisson had himself photographed, notebook and pencil in hand, crouched and peering through a key-hole. The title of the piece, 'Public Busybody No.1' (*Daily Mirror* 6 Dec 1938: 14), alongside the staged photo of Harrisson, suggests a range of meanings. Harrisson appears as the hybrid detective, somewhere between an American private eye and the more scientifically minded Sherlock Holmes (the trope of detection was already in use in the first booklet – 'not for nothing has the detective become a figure of popular admiration' [Mass-Observation 1937a: 30]). But Harrisson's image also suggests the voyeur or Peeping Tom (playing of course on his first name and his 'dirty Mac' coat) and brings to mind the sexual connotations of 'through the key-hole films', which is also reinforced through the content of the accompanying article about 'slashers' and their female victims. Lastly (and least evident) is the meaning of social anthropologist in 'the field', notebook at the ready. The voyeuristic aspect of Mass-Observation was also something that contemporary criticism focused on with accusations of 'interfering', 'Mass-eavesdropping', 'Busybodies of the left', and producing a 'psychoanthroposociological Nosey Parker Bill' (quoted in Mass-Observation 1938: 58–9). Such attacks, however, were at the time aimed

Figure 7 'Tom Harrisson with Mass-Observers, Bolton' (Harrisson is the one standing) – photograph by Humphrey Spender (1937). Courtesy of Bolton Museum and Art Gallery

not at the Bolton project, but at the first two publications: the Mass-Observation booklet and *May 12th*. The move in recent years has been to make the Bolton project stand in for Mass-Observation in general and for Mass-Observation to be seen as part of a general documentary project of the 1930s, a project seen as unified by the trope of the Oxbridge intellectual making his (the gender here is of course intentional) expedition to the North.[6] The most famous example of this is George Orwell's *The Road to Wigan Pier* (1937), with its excessive commentary on the smell and the bodies of the working class of Wigan.[7] The class-racism that is implied in such accounts has rightly been a subject for critique, but in the case of Mass-Observation it has unproductively closed off inquiry into the particularity of the Bolton project.

Writing in 1970 for a republication of *The Pub and the People*, Tom Harrisson is keen to distance himself from projects like George Orwell's:

> It is difficult to remember how in those far-off days, nearly everybody who was not born into the working-class regarded them almost a race apart. Even good books like George Orwell's *Road to Wigan Pier*, which really tried to get under the surface, started out from this underlying and sociologically miserable premise. The biggest thrill which this

> lately initiated 'cannibal' experienced was finding it no more difficult to be accepted as an equal in a cotton mill, as a lorry driver or ice-cream man.
>
> (Harrisson 1970: 6)

This claim of social ease fits easily within the domain of 'the anthropologist as hero' and should be treated sceptically. Of more interest is Harrisson's identification of himself as a 'cannibal'. I have already shown how Harrisson uses this term for characterizing (by analogy) the general population of Britain, as well as more specifically the pupils at the public school he attended (Harrow). That this is also a term of self-identification suggests that Harrisson is using it to insist on a version of cultural relativism that, potentially, has the power to destabilize and problematize 'ethnographic authority', as well as to counter notions of cultural superiority. I want to suggest that the Bolton project drew on a loose paradigm of British social anthropology and tried to apply it to British society, and that in doing so it partly undid the contradictory strands that were holding such a paradigm together. In looking at the intellectual materials that Harrisson and others were employing in Bolton and in other towns in Lancashire, what becomes evident is the 'strangeness' that results from deploying them within a 'domestic' context. Thus in bringing anthropology 'home', anthropology itself became significantly altered. My argument is that in transforming these materials, Mass-Observation put them in crisis and, up to a point, made them unusable as instruments for producing *conclusions* about cultures. One of the most striking features of the Bolton project, and an ironic fact considering the privileged position it has in the representation of Mass-Observation, must be the lack of published results that it generated. Considering that Mass-Observation was committed to 'turning around' research by putting it back into the public realm, and had managed to produce three books within a year using the meagre resources of the Blackheath group, it is surprising that only one publication resulted from the Bolton project, and this came out several years after the project finished. Given that the Bolton project had a large number of full-time observers, that it was relatively well funded and had been given (generous) advances by Victor Gollancz for the publication of four books (Jeffery 1978: 26), the 'failure' of this part of the project must be seen as an important question in attending to it. To treat the Bolton project as a 'failure' is not to dismiss it but to open it up to questions that are generally productive for theorizing everyday life.

Towards the end of the Mass-Observation booklet, Harrisson and Madge point to the intellectual materials that they will be using for research. They mention a book by the Lynds called *Middletown* (1929), a book which, if nothing else, accounts for the decision to refer to Bolton as 'Worktown', or 'Northtown' as it was originally called. But most significantly they stress the importance of British social anthropology. Readers of *Mass-Observation* are encouraged to buy *Notes and Queries on Anthropology*, a general guide-book to anthropological research methods drawn up by a committee that includes nearly every significant anthropologist working from Britain at the time (Seligman, Haddon, Malinowski and so on). Madge and Harrisson point to the section on sociology (social anthropology rather than physical anthropology) as the basis for Mass-Observation research: 'Such a framework as this will be most useful as a starting point' (Mass-Observation 1937a: 58). But they go on to insist 'it will be developed, modified and supplemented until it becomes unrecognisable'. The social anthropology on which they are basing their work needs investigating, partly to reveal the theoretical basis for the investigation of everyday life in Bolton, and partly to demonstrate how this basis became 'unrecognizable' in the actuality of 'observation'.

When Harrisson started the Bolton project in 1936, he had completed three years' fieldwork in Malekula, which had resulted in the book *Savage Civilisation* (1937) – the title of which suggests that the dominant distinctions between 'primitive' culture and 'civilized' culture were already being purposefully problematized. During the 1910s to 1930s, Malekula and its surrounding islands had been the site and subject of a number of intensive anthropological studies by anthropologists such as W. H. R. Rivers, T. T. Barnard, John Layard and Bernard Deacon (Stocking 1996: 300–4). Writing 'Components of the National Culture' in 1968, Perry Anderson could compare the relative lack of sociological work in twentieth-century Britain with the vibrancy of its anthropological intellectual culture. Anderson writes, 'the failure of a body of classical sociology to emerge in England, and its consequence, the withered half-life of the subject to this day, were of large intellectual moment' (Anderson 1992b: 52). However, Anderson suggests that, 'If modern British society was distinguished by its failure to produce any classical sociology, there was no less arresting obverse of this phenomenon. For the same society produced a brilliant and flourishing anthropology' (92). The reason for this, in Anderson's view, was that the question of the social totality of British culture 'remained unposed' – 'because British society was never challenged as a whole from within' (92). However, because of Britain's imperialist project it '*exported* its totalizations onto its subject people' (93). What Anderson's characterization of British social anthropology leaves out (it is specifically a synoptic overview of a national culture) are the differences within anthropology, and the critique of colonialism that emerged (albeit in a piecemeal and inconsistent fashion) in the practice of cultural relativism.

The period between the wars can be seen as a moment within British social anthropology of concentrated critical debate, a period when a number of different theories and methods for ethnographic fieldwork were being proposed and challenged. Significantly the debates not only concerned how to attend to a 'culture' (the meanings and beliefs of everyday life), but included questions of what a 'culture' was. The focus for debate ranged across a number of issues. The question of whether a genealogical perspective should be adopted (Rivers' 'historical reconstruction' [Stocking 1996: 236]) was pitted against a proto-structuralist approach (Malinowski's interests in the relation between beliefs and actions within a synchronic view of culture). Similarly the importance of Freudian psychoanalysis for anthropology was a subject fraught with debate (Frazer's 'that creature Freud' versus Rivers' 'myth reveals the unconscious history of the race just as the dream reveals the unconscious history of the individual' [Rivers, quoted in Stocking 1996: 242]). Perhaps most important was the question of whether a 'culture' should be understood as a unity in the Durkheimian sense of 'collective representation' or whether conflict and contradictions are essential ingredients of a culture. Such issues would clearly impact on any attempt to write the everyday culture of Bolton.

The negotiation of these questions in the work of Bronislaw Malinowski (who became a member of Mass-Observation's funding committee, and their most critical and enthusiastic supporter) should be seen as the single most influential version of social anthropology available during this period, and a significant point of reference for the Bolton project. Malinowski took a permanent position at the London School of Economics in 1922, and immediately began publishing the results of fieldwork conducted in the Trobriand Islands during the First World War. His *Argonauts of the Western Pacific* appeared in 1922 followed by *The Sexual Life of Savages* in 1929. In these and other books Malinowski outlined a methodology of 'participant observation'. Participant observation required that an ethnographer, so as to understand the unfamiliar 'host' culture, 'has to attune himself as far as possible to the strange mode of behaviour of his human material' (Malinowski in Mass-Observation 1938: 98). To do this requires anthropologists immersing themselves in the culture, empathizing with the 'natives' and sympathetically following their cultural practices. For Malinowski, ethnography meant 'going native' in an attempt 'to grasp the native's point of view, his relation to life, to realise his vision of his world' (Malinowski 1922: 25). While (for Malinowski) this is what allows access to a culture, it is not what guarantees scientific knowledge, as James Clifford explains: 'the ethnographer's personal experiences, especially those of participation and empathy, are recognized as central to the research process, but they are firmly restrained by the impersonal standards of observation and "objective" distance' (Clifford 1986: 13).

In this way it becomes clear that the Trobriand Islander's account of Trobriand society is necessarily insufficient (for social anthropology), and that the anthropologist's account of the institutions of kinship or whatever is a ('scientific') form of attention 'not available to the untutored awareness of the native informant' (MacIntyre 1984: 214). The relationship between this position and colonial domination is founded on the assumption that what is 'objective' is the meta-language of the ethnographer, a thinly disguised variant of the ethnographer's own cultural language, and it is in this way that cultural superiority is written into the activity of ethnography. The work of Tom Harrisson in Malekula can be seen as immersed in the practice of participant observations. As Charles Madge notes:

> Tom Harrisson had recently returned from Malekula, in the New Hebrides. His book about it, *Savage Civilization*, could be read as a manifesto for the view that the only way to understand and enter into the Malekulan way of life was by living among them, eating their food, drinking kava and taking part in Malekulan rituals and activities. Tom followed this up by taking a job in a Lancashire mill and preparing himself to become the ethnographer of Bolton.
>
> (Madge 1976: 1396)

The methodology of participant observation is a vague and open one, but if it exists in the work of Malinowski as structured on the superior inter-pretative knowledge of the scientific observer over the un-knowledge of the native informant, then in the work of Mass-Observation in general this para-digm is significantly problematized. For one thing, in the work of the national panel the 'native informants' are also the 'scientific observers' in that they are given the platform to speak. If 'proper' anthropological participant obser-vation necessarily relies on a cultural separation between the observer and the observed, then any cultural identity between the two is likely to undo participant observation from the start. In the Bolton project, where partici-pant observation is more fully embraced, the interpretative framework that Malinowski would insist on seems to work to frustrate the production of Mass-Observation material. Now while it is clear that the Bolton arm of Mass-Observation (under the jurisdiction of Harrisson) was more straight-forwardly anthropological in its outlook, I want to argue that the general problematic of Mass-Observation can be seen in evidence here too. To put it more categorically: if the Bolton project was dedicated not simply to collecting ethnographic material but also to making anthropologically coherent interpretations of this material then it failed to achieve this. My argument, however, would be that 'anthropologically coherent interpretation' is precisely not the operative basis of Mass-Observation, and that participant observation (much like psychoanalysis) is best seen as an investigative tool rather than an interpretative position. If the Bolton project at times tends towards conventional anthropology it never really attains it, and this is because Mass-Observation is dedicated to an understanding of everyday culture as contradictory and resolutely heterogeneous.

The adoption of a specifically Malinowskian framework can be seen in Harrisson's timetable for the Bolton 'pub' project:

Main stages in the Worktown survey were thus:

a. Public house reconnaissance and description; preliminary penetration. 3 months.
b. Penetration by observers into all parts of Worktown pub life. 2 months.
c. Observation without being observed. 10 months.
d. Work conducted more openly; active co-operation with all sorts of people in all spheres of local life. The study of individuals, letters, diaries, documents. 3 months.
e. Data from important people. 2 months.
f. Studies of statistics, organizations and published sources. 3 months.
(Mass-Observation 1943: 11)

Malinowski's approach to fieldwork can be seen as a three-stage practice: participation, observation, 'interrogation'. This approach is clearly what is being enacted in the Bolton timetable, where participation and observation make up the bedrock of research, to be supplemented by interviews and 'formal' research at the end. Of course, participant observation also includes conversation and involvement, rather than simply 'invisible' observation. In the above timetable, what is being investigated by Mass-Observation in Bolton isn't limited to northern working-class everyday life (though this is part of the reason for choosing Bolton), but includes the investigation of class in general (relations between classes, class aspirations and so on) as well as economic and cultural institutions and forms of authority. So, as well as spending a good deal of time in pubs, the full-time observers spent a lot of time attending religious services and getting involved in 'cult' religions that were popular in Bolton, such as the Mazdaznans (Calder and Sheridan 1985: 30–9). Attending football matches was accompanied by involvement in every political meeting and political party in Bolton.

The four books that Gollancz was expecting to publish were *The Pub and the People*, by John Sommerfield and Bruce Watkin; *Politics and the Non-Voter*, by Walter Hood and Frank Cawson; *How Religion Works*, by J. L. Wilcock and others; and *Blackpool: One Week a Year*, by Herbert Howarth and Richard Glew (Mass-Observation 1939: 227). The only book that actually got to press was *The Pub and the People* in 1943. Of course a number of reasons can be given as to why these books never saw the light of day (as well as the hundreds of photographs that were taken and paintings that were painted): the ambitiousness of the project, the disruption of war and the unsystematic collection of materials are all probable causes. But while the outbreak of war might be seen as an unforeseen contingency (though this is doubtful given Mass-Observation's continual concern with the rise of Fascism), they can all be seen as symptoms of the difficulty or impossibility of applying a Malinowskian framework to the Bolton research. My speculative understanding of the relative failure of the Bolton project is that it constituted an implicit and necessary critique of the 'scientificity' of a Malinowskian framework that never found its way to explicit critique.

The difficulty that Mass-Observation had in producing an account of Worktown society within the scientific paradigm of social anthropology can be seen in its account of class. Class was a major orientation for Mass-Observation, but although Madge was a member of the Communist Party, their approach to class can be seen to be significantly different from a traditional Marxist one. Rather than working with an abstract assumption that society was organized by the conflict of two main classes, their research allowed a notion of class to emerge from everyday life that can be seen as much more mutable, heterogeneous and performative. For instance, in a directive to panel members in 1939 on the subject of class, one woman offered an analysis of class that included twenty-eight different categories, from 1. Royalty, to 28.: 'people who are crude, dirty and irresponsible. Have no community feeling outside their own grade and 27. Quite content to live and produce children on the dole. Of their circumstances they would say "It's good enough for the likes of us". It seems they know their own value' (Calder and Sheridan 1985: 159). The writer who invented this range of classes was someone who was born into category 28, but who lived in grade 19, although her husband was from grade 10. The importance of such a system of classification is not that it offers a coherent understanding of class, but that it shows what the experience of class 'feels like' to someone. In this case it is not just something complexly stratified, but something that is malleable and ranges across economic and cultural categories organized around the poles of historical memory and social desire. What becomes clear is that class as a meaningful distinction within everyday life is open to any number of eccentric readings which can't be subsumed into overarching interpretations.

The idea of class as something to be looked at from the position of everyday life is evident in Tom Harrisson's account of it in an essay of 1942, significantly titled 'Notes on Class Consciousness and Class Unconsciousness':

> The idea of looking upwards and working upwards in a clear-cut form first impressed itself on me at my public school, where there was an elaborate system of privilege and caste, mainly based on the length of time you had been there, but also on how good you were at games. The speed at which you could move down stairs, which waistcoat button could be undone, which hand you could put in your pocket, what cereals could be eaten at breakfast, where you could walk, a hundred habits, were determined entirely in this way.
>
> (Harrisson 1942: 152)

Class has become something much more complexly 'open' to both the inves-
tigator and the 'classed' actor even if its forms of operation appear to be
obsessively fixed. Seen in more nuanced forms, it is understood as complex
identification that includes not just economics, but also emotional invest-
ment, social aspiration, as well as a malleability that allows for a certain
amount of play between the categories. The malleability and performativity
of class can be seen in the emphasis on social signification, clothing, movement and speech – the symbolic gestures or semiotics of everyday life. In
the work conducted on pubs Harrisson suggests that the class that is enacted
is something that takes significantly different forms across the week:

> Broadly, we found the whole of Worktown went up the social scale
> at the weekend. On a weekday, anybody in Worktown wearing a
> bowler hat was either B class or a mourner. At the weekend, anybody
> could and did wear a bowler, and the visible class distinctions of Tuesday
> became inextricably confused on Saturday afternoon. Weekend
> Worktown was a place superficially populated by well-to-do middle-
> classites – on an ordinary weekday, a city of wooden clogs, grimy faces,
> manual workers.
>
> (Harrisson 1942: 156)

This is a performative understanding of class that can speculate about the
unconscious articulations of class, without being in any position to 'fix' it
into a coherent pattern. The understanding of class is as something that
doesn't take coherent and systematic forms, and in many ways can't be
exhaustively recorded and analysed. In stressing that 'class' operates uncon-
sciously and is not available for conscious scrutiny, Harrisson might be seen
as challenging the empiricist basis of much of the Worktown project.

In treating Worktown as a 'failure' (in terms of its productivity) I want
to suggest that the anticipated transformation of social anthropology (social
anthropology becoming 'unrecognizable') was in practice replaced by a recognition of such a framework as unwieldy and in the end unusable. The potential
critique of social anthropology and its authoritative forms of cultural knowledge and narration are only present as an absence in the Bolton project (the
unwritten books). The material that was published doesn't challenge the
authoritative power of ethnography. Perhaps if it had, other, more productive forms of presenting the material might have emerged. Perhaps a
continuation of a montage practice might have produced a different practice
and alleviated the protracted struggle to write an authoritative ethnography
of the culture of Bolton. In many ways Tom Harrisson's book *Savage
Civilisation* offers evidence of an experimental ethnography (it is a hybrid
practice of auto-ethnography, historical ethnography and poetry) that is
missing in the Bolton project. If the Bolton project failed, it failed as Surrealist

ethnography and showed evidence of Mass-Observation's move towards more conventional attention to everyday life.

A politics of everyday life

Mass-Observation's methodological and theoretical approach to the everyday was contradictory, confused and emphatically unsystematic. But this confusion and contradiction needs to be seen as offering productive responses to an everyday world that could itself be seen as contradictory and unsystematic. If Mass-Observation is seen as a response to everyday life at a particular historical conjuncture, then the conflicts it evidences can be much more clearly understood. The historical moment of Mass-Observation is dominated by anticipation of war, a war that by 1936 could be seen as being generated by the mass mystificatory powers of Fascism throughout Europe (including Britain). This would be a war that would not just require physical force, but necessarily entail 'weapons' that could defeat what was clearly a spectacular and seductive enemy. Looking back on Mass-Observation, in 1976 Tom Harrisson could sum up its emergence 'as a several-pronged reaction to the disturbed condition of western Europe under the growing threat of Fascism' (Harrisson 1976: 11).

It is worth emphasizing Mass-Observation's 'several-pronged-ness', as this suggests an awareness of a heterological approach to the problem of the everyday. There are a number of themes around which this contradictory approach is evident. To start with Mass-Observation continually vacillates between claiming that 'the people' lack political agency, and championing a 'grass-roots' politics that is simply marginalized (or more usually ignored) by those who represent them (particularly the mass media). At issue as well is the question of whether social transformation will come from a vanguard movement by an elite, or will be generated from within everyday life. Similarly problematic is how to respond to the affective power of Fascism: should Fascism be countered through 'scientific' de-mystification, or through the promotion of an affective economy of a different order – an alternative system of myths?

The 'several-pronged reaction' to the threat of Fascism found Mass-Observation pursuing conflicting aims. Again it is tempting to see this in relation to the personalities involved. For instance, writing in 1940, Tom Harrisson could defend, in the name of science, a certain approach to 'doorstep surveys' on behalf of Mass-Observation, the Ministry of Information and corporate capitalism (Harrisson 1940b: 31). Writing in 1937 as a communist, Charles Madge would critique the capitalist press and call for a popular poetry for mass circulation. His example of what a popular poetry could be is a story from the *Daily Mirror* about a 'Human Mole' who lived in a potting

shed in a public park in the heart of Nottingham (Madge 1937b). Such contradictions are not unique to Mass-Observation, but it would be hard to imagine
a more vivid picture of contradiction than a group of avant-garde Surrealist
ethnographers working for the government.

The moment of Mass-Observation coincided with the high point of the
Popular Front: a united front against the threat of Fascism, which produced
surprising coalitions and victorious Popular Front governments in France and
Spain. The Communist Party (of which Charles Madge was a member) had been
encouraging Popular Frontism since 1933. But while the Popular Front produced a necessary sense of optimism, to take a Popular Frontist position in the
late 1930s would mean having to hold intellectually contradictory positions.
For one thing the Popular Front was geared to producing images of unity, of
trying to find ways of getting people to come together *en masse*. At the same time
the danger of Fascism could be seen precisely in the spectacular lure of the
'mass' coming together in an erasure of difference. Similarly, Popular Frontism
might mean holding on to a belief in a 'popular' and stubborn refusal of Fascism
in everyday life (a 'common sense' anti-Fascism and anti-anti-Semitism), while
at the same time recognizing the power of 'superstition' and 'myth' to hypno-
tize the 'mass' into holding racist 'superstitions'. Popular Frontism as a contradictory orientation was Mass-Observation's position in the late 1930s.

By way of example, on the subject of the agency of the 'mass', Mass-
Observation could characterize 'the people' as passive and obedient, sleep-
walking automata. In describing the effects of the Abdication crisis,
Mass-Observation wrote, 'at last England had to face a situation to which there
was no stock response. Millions of people who passed their lives as the obedient automata of a system now had to make a personal choice, almost for the
first time since birth' (Mass-Observation 1937a: 9). Or a little later in the same
booklet it could make the following claim for the practice of observation:

> It will encourage people to look more closely at their social environ-
> ment than ever before and will place before them facts about other
> social environments of which they know little or nothing. This will
> effectively contribute to an increase in the general social consciousness.
> It will counteract the tendency so universal in modern life to perform
> all our actions through sheer habit, with as little consciousness of our
> surroundings as though we were walking in our sleep.
>
> (Mass-Observation 1937a: 9)

This understanding of people as 'living in a dream' should be seen as one
'prong' of Mass-Observation's approach to everyday life, an approach that
demands a reflexive consciousness in attending to the details of everyday life
and the political events that impinge on it. It is also this prong that can be seen
to promote 'science' in the face of 'superstitious' and 'mythic' belief (the very

breeding ground of Fascism). But another prong is also clearly visible and can be seen as the obverse of this, stressing instead the creativity and agency of the 'mass' within the everyday. For instance, rather than seeing people as passively led by the mass media, Mass-Observation instead sees a huge gulf between mass media representations and the experience and understanding of the world in everyday life. Mass-Observation continually juxtaposes newspaper by-lines on current events with the heteroglossia of everyday life, where responses vary from antagonism to cynicism, from outrage to bewilderment, from refusals to acquiescence. Mass-Observation's 1939 publication *Britain* provides a vivid example of the 'several-pronged' approach.

Britain should probably be seen as the most successful working through of some of the problems evidenced by the Bolton project and the radical experimentation of *May 12th*. While *Britain* doesn't have the radical formal (dis)order of the *May 12th* experiment, or the exhaustive scope of the Bolton project, it can be seen as a reconciliation between the two projects. *Britain* came out as a Penguin Special and is said to have sold about 50,000 copies within 24 hours of publication (Jeffery 1978: 34). While this book was framed by an organizing editorial voice, the sections it contained were made up of quotes that were not merely supportive of this editorial voice. In some ways the editing voice has the effect of a 'chorus' that doesn't so much interpret as question the possibility of interpretation. Reading through the sections that make up the book, the reader is not being guided towards 'conclusions'; rather the book evidences a continuation of the destabilizing effects of collage. If the title of *Britain* might suggest totalizing accounts of the 'State of the Nation' kind, a glance at the contents page alerts the reader to other aims. The book includes a chapter on popular attitudes towards science, a section on the Munich crisis, accounts and discussions of wrestling, and detailed investigation of the popular dance craze 'the Lambeth Walk'. The discontinuities between the sections suggest the kind of approach that will become familiar in the work of someone like Roland Barthes in his *Mythologies* (Barthes [1957] 1973), or the uneven attention to the everyday by British cultural studies in the 1970s and 1980s.

A comparison between the chapter on the Munich crisis and the one on the Lambeth Walk highlights the difficult productivity of Mass-Observation's approach. The chapter on the Munich crisis analyses media representations of 'popular opinion' of Chamberlain's policy of appeasement towards Nazi Germany, and contrasts them with views and opinions gathered from a random selection of people. The result is a stark contrast between media representation (a continually changing representation that works by speaking 'in the name of the people') and the dissent and outright hostility towards Chamberlain in the quoted *vox populi*. A version of the Munich crisis chapter was broadcast on the BBC in June 1939, and as Paddy Scannell suggests, it 'was the only piece of broadcasting that gave a dissenting voice to appeasement' (Scannell and Cardiff 1991: 101). This wasn't to suggest that a public was untouched by the creation of 'public opinion' in the media (how else did people know about such events?); rather it suggested an active process of reading these represented events. Similarly, the Lambeth Walk isn't a piece of popular culture exempt from the processes of the mass media; rather its popularity is partly a result of mass media forms. What connects the Lambeth Walk and the Munich crisis is a much-expanded notion of 'politics and culture' that is articulated in everyday life:

> What people feel about the war danger is an obviously serious subject, but it is less obvious why the popularity of a dance is anything more than a frivolous interest. But if we can get at the reason for the fashion, and see it in its setting, it may help us to understand the way in which the mass is tending. We may learn something about the future of democracy if we take a closer look at the Lambeth Walk.
>
> (Mass-Observation 1939: 140)

The Lambeth Walk is shown as evidencing a number of features: it is a mass participatory spectacle (in August 1938, 3,000 dancers took part in an outdoor Lambeth Walk in Camberwell [177]); it is not dogmatic and allows for all sorts of improvisations; and it can be seen as a continuation of festival culture and 'the world turned upside down' ('Men dress up as women or pretend to be animals' [145]). The craze for the dance also evidences the way that 'popular' culture doesn't solicit a consensual response, but generates a whole host of different attitudes towards it. The heterogeneity to be found within this one form is evidenced internally – in the various versions of the song that accompanied the dance. Perhaps surprisingly some versions of the song included self-reflection about the nature of the dance: whether it is an 'escapist response' to the anxieties of war, or an affective opposition to war. The idea of the dance functioning in democratic struggle is evidenced in the example of 'the Anti-Fascists who broke up a Mosleyite [the British Fascist leader] demonstration in the East End by "doing the Lambeth Walk"' (175). Such uses of the dance can be seen as the exemplification of a Popular Front culture that comes out of the everyday: 'the feeling of the Lambeth Walk is unsectarian but not unsocial' (175).

If the section on the Munich crisis offers an example of the gap between representations of political events (the collective 'sigh of relief' that is represented as the popular response to the Munich accord) and responses to those representations in everyday life, then the discussion of the Lambeth Walk demonstrates another reading of the politics of everyday life. Here is an affective cultural practice emerging from everyday life distinct from the cultural practices associated with Fascism. It is not a 'scientific' critique of Fascist culture; it too is bound up in ritual and superstition, and for this reason offers an alternative imaginary identification that can be seen as (effectively) resistant to Fascism. The culture of the Lambeth Walk is also seen as resistant to the false promises of a mainly US commercial culture (as well as to the aggressive allure of Fascist culture) due to its ability to express the polyphonic voices of the Lambeth Walkers:

> It [commercial dance music] is no more about reality than Hitler's speeches are. Ballroom dancers sleep-walk to its strains with the same surrender of personal decision as that of uniformed Nazis. These Lambeth Walkers are happy because they find they are free to express themselves without the hypnosis of a jazz-moon or a Führer.
>
> (Mass-Observation 1939: 183)

The Lambeth Walk is seen as a cultural form that is ritualistic without being hypnotic. It is a form that prides itself in a joyful disdain of 'respected' protocols, a form that delights in an endless variation of ironic commentary, and a practice that unites without unifying.

The politics of Mass-Observation needs to be seen as a politics of everyday life. Tom Picton suggests that 'Mass-Observation did not want to change the world, they were reformist. They did not examine unemployment in Bolton, infant mortality, malnutrition, housing, health, or any of the parameters of poverty. Their approach was as fatalistic as a photograph' (Picton 1978: 2). Here politics is understood as being practised 'from above' and as being deployed *on* everyday life. Mass-Observation's politics can be seen to emerge from everyday life. So, for instance, if Mass-Observation can be seen as a social movement (which is partly how it saw itself) then its idea of changing the world would have to include the transformation of everyday life in the act of attending to it, within everyday life.

This act of transforming the everyday by being attentive to it is seen most vividly in women's experience of Mass-Observation. In this respect Mass-Observation provided a space for women's experience that has been absent from other attempts to articulate the everyday that we have looked at so far. Mass-Observation supplied a structure and an invitation to write about the everyday, but crucially one that didn't prescribe what counted as 'everyday life' or what should be privileged. This evidences a huge difference between Mass-Observation and those who insist implicitly on an equation between the everyday and metropolitan street-life. A vast number of recruits to the national panel were women and their experience in Mass-Observation evidences that for the first time the domestic everyday realm (at the time the dominant arena for the majority of women) could be taken seriously and could be transformed through conscious attention to it. This suggests a politics of the everyday that could articulate the interests of those most marginalized by official politics:

> I read in the *News Chronicle* articles about the work, and especially the account by an ordinary housewife of her day. Mass-Observation, it was something new, something to talk about; the things I do in the house are monotonous, but on the 12th, they are different somehow, letting the dog out, getting up, making the dinner, it makes them important when they have to be remembered and recorded.
>
> (Mass-Observation 1938: 70)

Being attentive to areas of life that were systematically down-graded by culture at large allowed for both an analysis and a revaluation of experiences. If the work of Simmel and Benjamin can be seen as a struggle to find a form of representation that can register the particularity of daily experiences, Mass-Observation offers an invitation to alter practically the experience of everydayness.

This politics of everyday life must be seen as similarly 'several-pronged'; if it includes a conscious attention to the everyday (and alteration of the everyday), it also includes a celebration of the non-rational, the affective and the oppositionally ritualistic within the everyday. Writing from a barrack room during the war, Tom Harrisson introduces the publication of *The Pub and the People* by stating:

> Plans are being made about the future of Britain, and these are often being made as if the prejudices and habits of ordinary people can be ignored; publication [of *The Pub and the People*] might serve some constructive purpose in reminding the planners, in their valuable work, of one of the habits they most often ignore. I say this with some feeling myself, as since the war my family have lived at Letchworth Garden City, one of the key towns of the planning movement, and one of the few places in England where no pub is allowed: this book could not have been written at all if Worktown had been Letchworth.
>
> (Mass-Observation 1943: 9)

Rather than seeing this as a nostalgic image of quaint old England, something worth fighting for, it should be seen as an image of affective and ritualistic attachments that can generate a culture that (potentially) can counter Fascism, as well as resisting the culture of the official institutions of Britain.

In Mass-Observation's several-pronged approach to everyday life, a science of everyday life is fashioned that has as its potential the purposeful destruction of the hard and fast distinction between specialist and amateur, between objectivity and subjectivity, between science and art. In its Surrealistic practice of ethnography, its attention to the mythic is both critical and celebratory, suggesting that any affective opposition to the 'forces of hatred' will have to generate imaginary and affective images as counter-attacks, as well as rational critiques. This is a science of everyday life that is being made up as it goes along, and that is making do with whatever comes to hand. It is a science significantly different from that practised by government agencies at the time. In Malinowski's supportive yet damning critique of Mass-Observation, he suggests the only question worth asking is the question of science (the answer to which, according to Malinowski, sees Mass-Observation as sorely lacking). In his articulation of science Malinowski is unswerving: 'For let us be quite clear about it: the sociologist cannot be interested in the indefinitely and infinitely varied minor diversities of feeling, idea or behaviour during the Two Minutes silence, or a Coronation or an abdication crisis' (Malinowski 1938: 118). Malinowski's science is not the science of everyday life that Mass-Observation practises. For a Surrealist ethnography, negotiating a complex historical moment, 'the infinitely varied minor diversities of feeling', might be, precisely, the very stuff of everyday life.

Mass-Observation should be seen as both modest and ambitious. At its most radical and ambitious it proposes a 'mass movement' of direct democracy that, rather than commenting on everyday life, provides the conditions for participation in the alteration of everyday life. Here dreams can become a critical response to general social conditions; likes and dislikes can become subtle indicators of dreams. Benjamin's rhetorical desire to put cultural material to work ('I need say nothing. Only exhibit') is given a practical demonstration in the modest proposal that participants 'speak for themselves' (Mass-Observation 1937d: 37–42). But this modesty can also be seen as a radical challenge to the disciplinarity of anthropology and its desire to write culture 'from above'. By establishing the conditions for a participatory practice, and by working to orchestrate the material through montage, Mass-Observation should be seen as the production of a popular poetry of everyday life.

Unlike either Benjamin or Simmel, Mass-Observation's understanding of everyday life isn't characterized by 'modernity' or the metropolis, and as such everyday life becomes a diverse ensemble of different practices and experiences. Urban modernity isn't written out of this account, but in allowing a much larger range of cultural practices to emerge (domestic cultures, residual and local customs, and so on) everyday life becomes radically heterogeneous. Mass-Observation set in motion an archival practice of the present that tried to attend to the conscious and unconscious aspects of everyday life. Within months of its launch the material archive was already unmanageable. If Mass-Observation is an example of an avant-garde 'going public', then perhaps the tendency towards bureaucracy was an inevitable condition of its continuation (Mass-Observation as an arm of government or commercial research).

Mass-Observation has a number of similarities to, and differences from, the work that this book has so far discussed. One of the biggest differences has been the way that the idea of the 'everyday' has taken centre-stage and has become the explicit 'object' of inquiry. As the front cover of *Britain* boasts: 'Mass-Observation, a movement started early in 1937 by two young men and now embracing some two thousand voluntary observers all over the country, exists to study everyday behaviour in Britain – THE SCIENCE OF OURSELVES' (Mass-Observation 1939: cover).

Notes

1   During most of the war Tom Harrisson directed Mass-Observation. In 1944 he was sent to Borneo where he remained after the war ended. In the post-war period Mass-Observation transformed itself into Mass-Observation Ltd. and became involved in market research, mainly for commercial products.

2   This archive of photographs has been singled out for comment, and for evaluating the project of Mass-Observation even though the photographs were never included in any Mass-Observation publication and can be seen to be a minor and unsuccessful (in Mass-Observation's eyes) part of the project.

3   The original quote is from Harrisson (1947). See Jeffery (1978: 20).

4   Liz Stanley (1990: 2–7) gives a range of examples of this criticism. See also the numerous criticisms that Mass-Observation analyses in Mass Observation (1938), as well as the essay by Malinowski included in that volume.

5   This point is made by Ruth Benedict in her 1934 book *Patterns of Culture*: 'To the anthropologist, our customs and those of a New Guinea tribe are two possible schemes for dealing with a common problem, and in so far as he remains an anthropologist he is bound to avoid any weighting of one in favour of the other' (Benedict 1989: 1).

6   See Taylor (1994: 152–81) and Edwards (1984). The BBC TV series about the 1920s and 1930s in Britain, *The Long Summer*, forcefully made this connection in its representation of Mass-Observation. Exceptions to this account would include the work of David Chaney, Michael Pickering and Alan Read.

7   It should be noted that Orwell doesn't 'blindly' inhabit such a class position. The examination of how sensory 'norms' affect class perception is one of the topics of his writing.

Chapter 7

HENRI LEFEBVRE'S DIALECTICS OF EVERYDAY LIFE

THE EVERYDAY THAT GRIPS Henri Lefebvre's voluminous writings on the subject is one orchestrated by the logic of the commodity, where life is lived according to the rhythm of capital. In an often repeated anecdote Lefebvre remembers his wife holding up a newly bought box of detergent and exclaiming, '*This* is an excellent product' (see Ross 1997a: 22). For Lefebvre it's as if the commodity, in an act of ventriloquy, echoes in the words of his wife. Of course the gendering of this should alert us to the way that women are seen, not simply to bear the burden of the everyday, but to be the most susceptible and the least resistant to its demand. I will return to this shortly. Yet for Lefebvre, what he sees as the postwar extension of capitalism, 'thoroughly penetrating the details of daily life' (Lefebvre 1988: 75), is an inescapable fact for everyone. Its most insistent voice is advertising; its most unrestrained form is the New Town. In postwar France the transformation and commodification of daily life took on an unprecedented force. As France 'reconstructed' in the wake of the war, modernization became synonymous with consumer culture. Blue jeans, electric cookers, fridges (figure 8), washing machines, Coca-Cola, television and so on became so many instances of the 'American temptation' (Kuisel 1993: 103–30), a temptation that was often specifically directed at women. Yet, as we shall see, however bleak Lefebvre's view of modern everyday life became, the everyday always held out the possibility of its own transformation. Secreted within the everyday were the elemental demands for everyday life to become something other (something more) than bureaucratic and commodified culture allowed.

As a philosopher, the everyday signalled for Lefebvre a speculative attempt to register the social as a totality, and in this his work can be seen

Figure 8 'This is an excellent product.' Brandt refrigerator advertisement, *Marie-Claire*, May 1955

as a continuation of Simmel's. But the everyday also signalled a frustration with philosophy and a desire to connect with the lived actuality of the present (a present seen as going through a 'consumer' revolution). As a Marxist, he saw contemporary everyday life as exploitative, oppressive and relentlessly controlled (he wrote about the terrorism of advertising [Lefebvre 1984: 106] and 'the bureaucratic society of controlled consumption' [Lefebvre 1984: 68–109]). As a romantic he sought energies within the everyday that could be used to transform it. For Lefebvre everyday life was quite simply *lived experience*, and in contemporary society this meant that together 'modernity and everyday life constitute a deep structure' (Lefebvre 1987: 11). But if it was a deep structure, everyday life was also an opaque one that was to be 'defined by "what is left over" after all distinct, superior, specialized, structured activities have been singled out by analysis' (Lefebvre [1958] 1991a: 97).[1] For traditional 'specialized' analysis, the everyday was at once too small and too big, too trivial and impossibly ambitious. For Lefebvre it was a life's work struggling to maintain a critique that he recognized as continually lagging behind the perpetually changing actuality of the everyday.

Born at the start of the century and dying at the age of 90, Henri Lefebvre's work spans nearly the entire twentieth century. This life work consists of over sixty books (see the bibliography in Shields 1999) and is marked by a heterogeneity of voices, of registers, of objectives. And yet it also pursues particular interests with a relentless fervour that didn't diminish in old age. As is appropriate for a thinker whose thought is dialectical, the heterogeneity and the obsessions can be found in the same places, accounted for via similar explanations. Born in the small town of Hagetmau in the southwest of France, he continually alternates between the rural and the urban, spending much of his life in Paris, but constantly returning to the French Pyrenees at key moments. Such movement is not just the result of the vagaries of modern living; rather it hints at a life lived across boundaries, both physical and mental. Rather than denoting 'home', the Pyrenees is a space of continual inquiry. After returning there during the war as a resistance fighter, he begins what will be his doctoral thesis on a sociological study of peasant communities in the Campan valley (Lefebvre 1962). It is amongst these villages and towns that Lefebvre thinks out his project for a critique of everyday life. It is the multiple perspective offered by a traditional and yet changing countryside mixed with a profound engagement with the transformation of urban life that can account for the huge scale of the project – a cause of both its richness and confusion. It is the unevenly modernizing towns of the French Pyrenees that will provide visual and theoretical 'moments' that will fire his critical account of everyday life and modernity.

For Lefebvre, 'moments' are those instances of intense experience in everyday life that provide an immanent critique of the everyday: they are moments of vivid sensations of disgust, of shock, of delight and so on, which although fleeting, provide a promise of the possibility of a different daily life, while at the same time puncturing the continuum of the present (see David Harvey's 'Afterword' in Lefebvre 1991b). Such moments can be glimpsed in the pages of his books, chapters that take on an almost visionary feel, made up of passages that depart from the world of academic argument to locate their author in the lived experience of actual social spaces. A Sunday morning watching people attend a village church becomes a scene that reveals the extent to which religion penetrates the everyday, while it also reminds Lefebvre of his adolescent struggles to escape Christianity (Lefebvre [1947] 1991a: 201–28). Sitting on top of a hill, looking down as the New Town of Mourenx is being constructed, becomes a moment when the production of the everyday as a readable urban script becomes undecidable as it awaits the consequences of use (Lefebvre [1962] 1995: 116–27). Other moments are supplied by Parisian experiences: looking through his window on to a view of a major intersection of roads conjures up a reverie of the rhythms that make up city life (Lefebvre 1996: 219–27); a view from another window at another time shows the shifting class relations that find expression in the suburban landscape (Lefebvre [1958] 1991a: 42–3).

This intense scrutiny of the everyday and the processes of modernization is the result of experience and observation, but it is the observation and experience of a philosophical mind. The dialectic between the practical and the theoretical, between the concrete and the abstract, requires a mutual and continual testing. There is no empirical reality that can simply be encountered so that it will reveal the forces that produced it. Nor is there a world of thought that can tell us essential truths. As Lefebvre writes, 'The limitations of philosophy – truth without reality – always and ever counterbalance the limitations of everyday life – reality without truth' (1984: 14). Philosophy for Lefebvre acts as a critical tool that can be used in the attempt to shatter the 'natural' appearance of objects and relations. Critical philosophy holds out the promise of its own dissolution as it connects with the everyday in order to transform itself (and everyday life), and in so doing mark the end of 'philosophy' as a specialized activity. Seeing philosophy as so many critical, or potentially critical, tools allowed Lefebvre a very eclectic range of philosophical references. But the combining of, for instance, the work of Marx and Nietzsche is done not in an effort to synthesize the two, but so as to allow for the fracturing of both in a critical movement to dislodge the lure of the total system.

Lefebvre's practice is philosophical and throughout his work there is a running critical dialogue with a number of thinkers, few of whom escape unscathed. The attacks that Lefebvre makes on thinkers such as Althusser, Sartre, Foucault and Barthes are polemical and extreme, but in the act of negation they allow Lefebvre to rescue something of use for his project. These critical dialogues are never abstract theoretical differences, but differences of consequence in the life-world. So, for instance, in his dispute with the work of structuralists such as the Foucault of *Les mots et les choses* ([1966] 1970) (published in English as *The Order of Things*) and the Barthes of *Le système de la mode* ([1967] 1983) (published in English as *The Fashion System*), he acknowledges their contributions to academic disciplines, but also points up the proximity between their theoretical systems and the fetishizing of systems by the new technocrats who are controlling and transforming France. As a way of differentiating his own project Lefebvre treats the project of Barthes as symptomatic of a general social trend – technocracy – while also seeing it as offering insights as to the nature of such a trend. Thus Barthes' book *Le système de la mode* is seen as constructing a rhetorical system of fashion by studying fashion magazines while ignoring the actuality of bodies wearing clothes; yet it also becomes the inverted basis for Lefebvre to analyse fashion as part of the terrorism of everyday life (Lefebvre 1984: 163–75). It is in this critical dialogue with cultural theory, coupled with a continual attention to lived experience (the uses of fashion, not just its abstract meaning), that Lefebvre articulates his dialectics of everyday life. It is necessary, in approaching Lefebvre's work on everyday life, to understand both the philosophical and cultural milieu, as well as the rapidly changing social environment. Lefebvre's work is a socially grounded (historically and geographically) critical approach to everyday life, and it, in turn, demands such an approach in attending to it.

In an essay marking the centenary of Marx's death and written towards the end of Lefebvre's life, he reasserts the centrality of everyday life for a critical Marxism: 'the commodity, the market, money, with their implacable logic, seize everyday life. The extension of capitalism goes all the way to the slightest details of everyday life' (Lefebvre 1988: 79). And as if to insist on the point: 'A revolution cannot just change the political personnel or institutions; it must change *la vie quotidienne*, which has already been literally colonized by capitalism' (80). Kristin Ross argues that in Lefebvre's work the continual references to the colonization of everyday life by capitalism should be taken literally as the continuation and transformation of the processes and forces of imperialism, and that colonialism must be seen as central to the development of capitalism (Ross 1995: 1–13). Rather than seeing colonialism as having been eradicated by the success of the struggles for independence by many African and Asian countries, modernity witnesses a continuation of colonialism in a re-ordering of the world whereby the processes of imperialism have taken on new configurations at a local and global level. What this meant in postwar France was a multiplication of colonial relations that emerge at the same time as the 'end of empire'. On the one hand the process of decolonization had profound effects not just in the liberation war in Algeria but in the way that the urban geography of French cities 'internalized' relations of colonization. Urban space articulates relations of global domination in its ethnicization of inner cities into impoverished and 'racialized' zones. On the other hand, France, like many other countries, entered into colonial relations with the United States that had inescapable consequences. Americanization becomes an umbrella term that signals all those cultural changes that are seen to stand in for the end of a particular ('traditional') way of life, and mark the move towards a cultural globalization. The continual references by the film-makers of the French New Wave (Godard, Chabrol, Varda and others) to Hollywood movies, to streamlined commodities, to American style in advertising, to American automobiles, become so many synecdoches that point to this colonized relationship. For Lefebvre such massive historical and geographical shifts don't demand simple condemnation or celebration; they demand analysis – both for the new problems that they generate and for the possibilities they signal.

These massive social changes are the material from which Lefebvre's critique of everyday life emerges. As this critique develops in response to these events, Lefebvre focuses more and more insistently on the urban as the site for apprehending the everyday. But to understand Lefebvre's orientation to such events I need to start by discussing the philosophical and cultural beginnings of his project, beginnings that would shape all his writing about everyday life.

Foundations

Martin Jay in his book on Marxism and the concept of totality puts the work of Lefebvre together with Surrealism and the emergence of a French Hegelian Marxism. Jay usefully sets up a constellation for investigating the foundations of Lefebvre's thought and even gives us a scenario that sets them all in motion. Quoting from one of Lefebvre's autobiographical works, *Le temps des méprises* (1975), he points to a decisive meeting between Lefebvre and André Breton: 'He showed me a book on his table, Vera's translation of Hegel's Logic, a very bad translation, and said something disdainfully of the sort: "You haven't even read this?" A few days later, I began to read Hegel, who led me to Marx' (Lefebvre, quoted in Jay 1984: 293). It is this constellation of the avant-garde movements of Dada and Surrealism (he remained life-long friends with Tzara) linked to the philosophical work of Hegel and its materialist reshaping in the early works of Marx that gives Lefebvre's work its thematic insistence on the everyday as a site for the investigation of alienation. Alienation and the possibility of dis-alienation receive a number of articulations in Lefebvre's work as he negotiates the various forces of this constellation. His use of the concept of 'total man' or 'total person' (humankind no longer alienated) which would result in the 'end of history' (the telos of history having been reached) follows the axis of Hegelianized

Marxism, whereas the insistence on *la fête* (the festival, particularly during the Middle Ages) as a moment 'other' to the capitalist everyday and enacting a critique of the separation of the aesthetic from the social (or of art from life) emerges from his involvement with the Surrealist avant-garde and his intense and continual study of rural France. At first glance the bacchanalian indulgence of *la fête*, with its celebration of the 'low material body' and satirical inversions of dominant social relations, seems a world away from Hegelian Marxist ideas about the end of history and the emergence of the total person. This mix of ideas, while evidencing contradictory and conflicting tendencies, is what gives Lefebvre's position its critical purchase; indeed it is the articulation of these ideas *together* that allows Lefebvre to navigate a path that avoids a simple nostalgic and romantic celebration of *la fête* on the one hand, and a dogmatic assertion of social homogeneity (the universality of the total person) on the other.

I want to argue that the combination of these positions allows Lefebvre to make two related moves: to privilege creativity for the transformation of daily life ('let everyday life become a work of art' [Lefebvre 1984: 204]) and to argue for the decline of centrally organized society. For Lefebvre, capitalist modernity can be characterized by contradictory tendencies that increase homogeneity in everyday life (a standardization in work and objects through a general commodification) at the same time as social differences are extended and deepened (the intensification of hierarchical differences of class, 'race', gender, age, etc.). These forces are combined in an experience of fragmentation as time, space and knowledge are parcelled up into a multitude of discrete units. By placing *la fête* at the 'end of history', Lefebvre suggests (and desires) a historical telos of non-hierarchical play (creativity) and the radical democratic 'right to difference'. While this suggests that Lefebvre had more in common with anarchism than with the communism of the Third International, it can be seen as a 'play' oriented reading of Marx's early writings, combining a critique of both institutional social difference and the relentless routine of modern life. Related to this is a dialogue with philosophies of history (from both the left and the right) that enables him to argue for an anti-statist and anti-bureaucratic idea of society, without promoting individualistic ideologies. The 'total person', as festive and carnivalized, is the unknown potentiality of humankind (unknown, because the effects of the materialist negation of the present can't be known in advance) for a sociability based in a radical understanding of community. Not only will this transform everyday life, it will do so from the 'bottom up' – from within the everyday.

Crucial to every aspect of Lefebvre's emerging critique of everyday life is the complex political situation of the French Left as its various factions navigate across the changing circumstances of revolutionary possibility. From the utopian moment of the prewar Popular Front and the postwar promise of the Liberation, to the growing difficulty of maintaining the Communist Party line in the face of the dogmatism, brutality and the imperialist aggression of Stalinism – the Left is characterized by a growing disenchantment with the revolution as exemplified by the Soviet Union. Lefebvre's position in the Left is an unenviable one as he remained within the Communist Party from 1928 until he was expelled in 1958 and, although he did his fair share of intellectual hatchet jobs for the party, he maintained a critical stance within the party (see Kelly 1982; Poster 1976). Part of what allowed left-wing intellectuals (outside the Soviet bloc) a certain amount of critical distance from Stalinized Marxism was an involvement with abstract philosophical and aesthetic problems. Lefebvre followed both these paths and became one of the main proponents of Hegelian Marxism in France. The form that this took was varied and changed over time, but essential to it was the restoration of some of Marx's early texts, particularly the *Economic and Philosophic Manuscripts of 1844* (Marx 1977) where Marx establishes a form of materialist humanism using Hegel's notion that human society is in a state of self-alienation. Marx's conceptualization of alienation is rooted in the production process of capitalism and is understood as being generated from the division of labour. But in more general terms he suggests that human beings are alienated from themselves (and each other) because their social conditions have postponed the expression of their human potential – the historic possibilities humans have for creative and productive work (Marx 1977: 61–74). It is this aspect of alienation from the possibilities of human development, as well as alienation between human beings and in human processes, that Lefebvre takes as central to Marx and Hegel.

In both sections of Volume I of the *Critique of Everyday Life* Lefebvre proposes, not only that the study of everyday life is a study of alienation under conditions of modernity, but that the transformation of everyday life will be brought about by the de-alienation of human beings and the creation of the total person, and that this can be seen as an 'end of history'. The logic of this is fairly straightforward: to talk about the alienation of human beings necessarily suggests that there is a state of un-alienated human life where life can finally be lived as the ideal. In more fully Hegelianized terms the dialectical conflict between the master and the slave, which can be seen as the motor of history, is finally overcome as their differences disappear. Such an overcoming would result in the realization of the idea – pure spirit – and would mean the end of history. Although such a synoptic account offers little in the way of a nuanced investigation of the dialectic, it does allow us to point to the major area of contention for a politics rooted in the transformation of everyday life (which is the central orientation of Lefebvre's project): what kind of society will result from such an overcoming? What kind of people will live in it? What are the conditions that will realize this transformation? What is the idea or spirit that will emerge?

The project of imagining a world outside the terms and conditions of the present, or as the culmination of those aspects in the present that are able to promote the ideal, is one fraught with problems. For Hegel it meant a symbolically strong state. The history of Marxism (in many ways the inheritor of these debates) can be seen as caught between, on the one hand, the radical reworking of this 'overcoming', whereby it is the state that necessarily withers away as the end of class struggle arrives, and on the other hand the seemingly inevitable growth of a state-led communism. Given the circumstances in which Lefebvre and other left-wing intellectuals found themselves, debates about these themes couldn't fail to resonate with the image of Stalin as the figurehead of an all-powerful communist state. But this Hegelian architecture was open to being employed for a number of different ends. In the Paris of the interwar years and after, it became an area of contestation, a space that allowed for a number of alternatives to the Stalinist state to be theoretically rehearsed, without necessarily having explicitly to denounce Stalin and the French Communist Party.

Although Lefebvre and his friend and colleague Norbert Gutterman had been publishing work on Hegel for several years, it was in 1933 that Hegel got his most influential introduction into Parisian intellectual society through the lectures of Alexandre Kojève. These lectures ran from 1933 to 1939 and have taken on a particular significance in intellectual history because luminaries such as Lacan, Bataille, Queneau, Breton and Merleau-Ponty attended them. Kojève's reading of Hegel's *Phenomenology of Mind* was based on the understanding that when Hegel writes of the end of history he is referring to the real historical success of the Emperor Napoleon, with whom Hegel was enamoured. So, for Kojève, the end of history in a Hegelian schema is synonymous with the emergence of a powerful head of state. But Kojève's exegesis continues this form of reasoning until the idea of the end of history becomes the legitimation for the Stalinist state. Roger Caillois recalls:

> He gave a lecture at the College [of Sociology: see chapter 4] on Hegel. This lecture left us all flabbergasted, both because of Kojève's intellectual power and because of his conclusion. You will remember that Hegel speaks of the man on horseback, who marks the closure of History and of philosophy. For Hegel this man was Napoleon. Well! That was the day Kojève informed us that Hegel had seen right but that he was off by a century: The man of the end of history was not Napoleon but Stalin.
>
> (Caillois quoted in Hollier 1988: 86)

This was in December 1937. Eleven years later, at the start of the Marshall Plan, Kojève had rethought the end of history and had concluded that Hegel had been right all along, in that history had ended at the battle of Jena, but he concluded that 'the American way of life was the one fitted to the posthistorical period' (Niethammer 1992: 67). In terms of the emerging New Left, Kojève had simply swapped one form of state capitalism for another. I think it is in the light of the New Left's refusal of both Soviet state capitalism and the United States' entrepreneurial capitalism (signalled in synecdochal form by the slogan 'neither Moscow nor Washington') that Lefebvre's accentuation of the 'end of history' and the 'total man' must be seen. If French Hegelianism was open to a number of different articulations (as the example of Kojève demonstrates), then Lefebvre's articulation must be seen in a dialogic context, explicitly as accentuating it against the conclusions of people like Kojève, against those promoting a form of statist transformation. This is achieved through the coupling of the 'total person' with the idea of la fête (the festival or carnival). Crucially, the promotion of festival as a model for the ultimate overcoming of history means that the 'end of history' is synonymous with the dissolution of the state. In subsequent years, this argument would take practical shape in the call for *autogestion* (workers' councils and forms of self-management).

La fête is a continual reference point for Lefebvre as he outlines his critique of everyday life. Festival holds an equivocal position in the everyday: it is part of popular everyday life but it is also a radical reconfiguring of daily life that is anything but 'everyday'. In Maurice Blanchot's review of Lefebvre's Critique, he suggests that the everyday becomes visible at moments of 'effervescence', 'when existence is public through and through' (Blanchot 1987: 12). For Blanchot, as for Lefebvre, such moments of effervescence are evidenced in revolutionary situations, but they can also be found in festival. In the chapter of Critique of Everyday Life entitled 'Notes Written One Sunday in the French Countryside' festival is given a vivid and ambiguous account. Here Lefebvre draws on the research he had been doing during the war, on the history of peasant society in the Pyrenees, in particular the history of medieval society, and combines it with histories of Greek and Roman culture. What interests Lefebvre is the idea of a community celebrating by excessive expenditure, by turning the world upside down:

> During the feasts there was much merry-making: dancing, masquerades in which boys and girls changed clothes or dressed up in animal skins or masks – simultaneous marriages for an entire new generation – races and other sports, beauty contests, mock tournaments . . . It is the day of excess. Anything goes. This exuberance, this enormous orgy of eating and drinking – with no limits, no rules . . .
>
> (Lefebvre [1947] 1991a: 202)

While this connects with some of the (admittedly milder) cultural practices that are privileged by Mass-Observation (particularly the Lambeth Walk),

Lefebvre's interest is in festival's ability to overturn cultural values for (potentially) revolutionary ends. Festival or carnival, then, is the overturning of established differences: differences of gender and class that have fixed hierarchical determinations. Such an overturning is not the erasure of difference; rather it is a negation that generates the possibility of re-ordering difference. The utopian possibilities of carnival are summed up in a more recent celebration of carnival culture:

> Carnival, in our sense, is more than a party or a festival; it is the oppositional culture of the oppressed, a countermodel of cultural production and desire. It offers a view of the official world as seen from below – not the mere disruption of etiquette but a symbolic, anticipatory overthrow of oppressive social structures. On the positive side, it is ecstatic collectivity, the joyful affirmation of change, a dress rehearsal for utopia. On the negative, critical side, it is a demystificatory instrument for everything in the social formation which renders collectivity impossible: class hierarchy, sexual repression, patriarchy, dogmatism, and paranoia.
>
> (Stam 1989: 95)

For Lefebvre, carnival is a moment when everyday life is reconfigured, but this different order of things is present in everyday life itself: 'Festival differs from everyday life only in the explosion of forces which had been slowly accumulated in and via everyday life itself' (Lefebvre [1947] 1991a: 202). This positive evaluation of medieval carnival can be seen as part of a more general intellectual current that will include the likes of Bakhtin, Bataille and the Situationists. Again, it can be argued that this attention to carnival is a desire to find alternative cultural formations to the two major bureaucratic state capitalist formations – the USSR and the USA. For Bataille, carnival and other festivals were seen as exemplifying the basis of human society, annihilating the distance between 'primitive' and so-called 'civilized' societies and allowing him to conceive of another kind of economy, linked to expenditure rather than profit. In particular he used the cultural practice of 'Potlatch', as practised by native Americans of the Northwest, to write about the excessive giving and spoiling of gifts (Bataille 1991). This privileging of the practice of Potlatch is linked back to Lefebvre as the Letterist International, a proto-Situationist group (whose close but troubled relationship with Lefebvre will be discussed below), entitled their journal *Potlatch* (see Wollen 1991: 46–56). Bakhtin's work on carnival (Bakhtin 1984) is, of course, emerging from another cultural context, but it too can be seen as in dialogue with some of the same socio-political forces (although under considerably more duress) and employing similar cultural material. Bakhtin's work on Rabelais, which he finished in 1940 but which was not published until 1965 (Lefebvre wrote a book on Rabelais in 1955), has been instrumental in disseminating a theorization of carnival whereby ideas of the world-turned-upside-down, the extravagance of festivals and the insistence on the corporeality of pleasure are seen as critical and potentially revolutionary responses by the dominated to the dominating. A host of historians must also be included in this list of those writing about a cultural form that has received so much attention and produced so much debate (including Le Roy Ladurie [1980], Davis [1987] and Burke [1994]).

For the purpose of looking at Lefebvre's use of *la fête* in conjunction with his Hegelian conception of the 'end of history' and the 'total person', I think it is worth considering a number of questions and criticisms that have usefully been asked of some of these other writers. The first question has to do with the revolutionary potential of the idea of carnival:

> The most common objection to Bakhtin's view of carnival as an anti-authoritarian force that can be mobilized against the official culture of Church and State, is that on the contrary it is part of that culture; in the typical metaphor of this line of argument, it is best seen as a safety-valve, which in some functional way reinforces the bonds of authority by allowing for their temporary suspension.
>
> (Dentith 1995: 73)

Or in the words of Peter Osborne, carnival can be seen as a 'licensed compensation' for the medieval everyday (Osborne 1995: 242). So, although carnival can be seen to turn the world upside down and in doing so overturn social hierarchies, it can actually work to maintain the world 'the right way up' by allowing the forces that might destroy this world order a chance to let off steam. This line of critique does problematize the assertion that carnival is simply the radical voice of subversion. But within Lefebvre's argument the medieval carnival is not itself an example of either subversion or dis-alienation but must necessarily be seen as alienated, in that it is only a *moment* when the possibility of living otherwise is glimpsed (festival in the modern world can be seen as a further alienation where that glimpse has been packaged into consumable holidays and so on). The transformation of everyday life can only be accomplished when the festival is no longer a 'few dazzling moments' (Lefebvre [1947] 1991a: 251) but has penetrated life and transformed it. The effective radicality of carnival is not at issue with Lefebvre; the value of carnival is as a promissory note signalling the possibility of another way of being – a way of being and an order of life based on the desires and frustrations of those whose interests are not at present being catered for.

Critical attention needs to be directed to the functioning of carnival as a yet-to-arrive telos of history. There is a paradox in the choice of *la fête* as signalling the end of history, in that, as an example of everyday life (or everyday life transformed), it doesn't suggest so much the end of history as the beginning. Lefebvre's invocation of medieval carnival could be seen simply as a yearning for pre-industrial history, suggesting not a working through of historical processes but a nostalgia for an unrecoverable past. This mode of nostalgia can also be seen as employing one of the key tropes of cultural theory, whereby the alienated everyday of the present is set against a more authentic way of life situated prior to industrialization, or prior to any other dramatic social change that comes to be seen as responsible for social ills. While Lefebvre's historical logic is riddled with contradictions (implicit, I think, in the logic of an 'end of history'), I think that he is struggling precisely against this jargon of authenticity. More specifically, the opposition set up by Heidegger (to whom Lefebvre continually refers) and Lukács (to whom he doesn't) of an everyday life (*Alltäglichkeit* – stressing the triviality of the daily) where people have become object-like, versus an authentic life of the spirit, is something that Lefebvre struggles to refuse (see Trebitsch 1991: xvii–xix). The particularity of *la fête* (rather than a general celebration of pre-industrial past) is of crucial importance here: Lefebvre's use of carnival continually asserts dialogic moments of struggle, where the dominated respond to their domination in excessive and festive ways, and in the end suggests the exact opposite of authenticity: the critique and contestation of authenticity. This critique is precisely the content of turning the world upside down, of cross-dressing, of the symbolic reversals of master and peasant. It is the process of taking the culture of domination, a culture ordered in the name of the authentic, and overturning it, which allows for the critique of authentic culture as interested culture. This is a far cry from the motifs of forests and *Volk* that can be found in Heidegger's *Being and Time* (see Niethammer 1992: 77–81). Perhaps Lefebvre's coupling of Hegelianism with the radical potential of carnival demonstrates that Lefebvre's intentions have as much to do with critically responding to writers such as Kojève and Heidegger as to do with creating a coherent system. Given the influence that such writers were having, Lefebvre could be seen as performing a powerful and important critique of the cultural articulations with which such philosophies were cloaking themselves, while utilizing the same philosophical architecture – an architecture that had established a high degree of intellectual currency.

If the critical debate about carnival can be seen as offering little purchase on Lefebvre, a more serious challenge might be that the Hegelian architecture that Lefebvre employs is structured on the aggressive erasure of differences (ethnic, gendered, sexual and classed differences) in the name of a universality or totality that implicitly privileges the heterosexual masculine, ethnocentric, bourgeois self. Laurie Langbauer in an article titled 'Cultural Studies and the Politics of the Everyday' suggests that such a feminist critique can be made of Lefebvre's work. While Langbauer is concerned with Lefebvre's work of the late 1960s, *Everyday Life in the Modern World*, she could also have included Lefebvre's earlier work in her discussion. Although she goes on to show how Lefebvre's work problematizes its own claims, she situates Lefebvre with a general New Left whose 'abrogation of difference remains a spectre in any attempt to constitute culture as a field' (Langbauer 1992: 48). Langbauer alerts us to the vexed question of the position of women in Lefebvre's theorization of the everyday. Here we seem to be meeting Lefebvre at his most contradictory. On the one hand, as Langbauer points out (and as I mentioned at the start of this chapter), Lefebvre sees women as both carrying the heaviest burden of the everyday and least able to recognize it as a form of alienation. Thus Lefebvre can claim that 'everyday life weighs heaviest on women' (Lefebvre 1984: 73) and go on to explain that women are in an ambiguous position as 'both consumers of commodities and symbols for commodities' (73). It is women's ambiguity in relation to the everyday which leads Lefebvre to make the startling claim that women 'are incapable of understanding' the everyday (73) and to characterize women's protests as 'clumsily formulated, directionless claims' (92). Perhaps such statements (in the 1960s) were a common enough reaction to the emergence of feminism, even a predictable one. But what is more surprising is that earlier on in the same book Lefebvre sets up a contrasting diptych that sees women in a totally different light. This diptych contrasts women's 'intimate knowledge' of poverty, 'repressed desires' and 'the endlessness of want' with 'the power of woman, crushed and overwhelmed, "object" of history and society but also the inevitable "subject" and foundation' (35). Here women not only are given a critical consciousness in relation to the everyday but are also seen as agents of a historical struggle to transform it. Perhaps this contradictory 'take' on women and the everyday is a result of the rather hurried way in which Lefebvre seems to have 'written' his books (he dictated them to a secretary) (see Shields 1999). Perhaps it is an example of Lefebvre trying to satisfy two contradictory demands. On the one hand, by distancing himself from feminism as a political movement he can try and satisfy the revolutionary Marxist who might see feminism as a distraction from the true revolutionary cause. On the other hand, the very logic of Lefebvre's dialectical approach to everyday life *should* suggest that women are going to be at one and the same time the most 'alienated' of individuals and the most active 'resistors' of such alienation.

Langbauer ends up suggesting that in contrast to Lefebvre, modern feminism should 'revise the category of the everyday from a seemingly unproblematic ground supporting shared experience, theoretical consistency, and ultimate social harmony to a site of irresolvable difference, of conflict whose resolution is not simply delayed, but theoretically impossible' (1992: 48). While I agree that such an unproblematic notion of everyday life needs problematizing, I would argue that this is not characteristic of the concept of the everyday that Lefebvre mobilizes (despite his lapses into patriarchal ideology). Although Lefebvre quite clearly sees the notion of totality as crucial to his project, it doesn't seem to be a totality that erases difference: in this 'totality' needs to be differentiated from 'universalism'. In fact, in as much as Lefebvre works with the desire for totality (rather than a dogmatic assertion of it) he seems bent on trying to offer more and more complex attempts to reveal the unevenness of capitalism and its structuring of difference. If Lefebvre's theory can partly be seen as attempting to do what Mass-Observation set about doing in practical ways (charting the everyday as heterogeneity), then for Lefebvre, 'totality' will always be a totality of differences. Lefebvre is faced with the same problem that Simmel sought to negotiate: the need to attend to the everyday in general, without assimilating the particular differences of daily life within an overarching schema.

The conceptual architecture (Hegelian) that Lefebvre initially uses is problematic and does suggest the possibility of the erasure of difference; in particular the idea of the 'total person' or 'total man' can suggest a universal subjectivity, a vague invocation of the 'true' nature of humankind. While I think that such an idea is used as a heuristic tool in Lefebvre, the danger is that it can be employed as legitimation for other projects (the openness of this architecture is demonstrated by the different inflections that Kojève gives it). As Martin Jay notes, the terms of his 1940 book, *Dialectical Materialism*, in particular the concept of 'total man', were 'vague and imprecise enough to be used by fascists as well as Marxists' (Jay 1984: 296). For Lefebvre, in the 1950s the notion of the total person was necessary if the 'theoretical conception of the human' wasn't to 'fall back into an incoherent pluralism' (Lefebvre [1958] 1991a: 68). And I guess by this he is also pointing to the need for some kind of utopian focus (however unspecifiable) for galvanizing people together for collective social transformation (the historical echo of the Popular Front). Lefebvre's vagueness on the actual nature of 'total man' and the end of history is a necessary condition of his attempt to posit a pure potentiality for humankind rather than any actuality of what an unalienated humanity is or will be. Two observations need to be made here. The first is that the conceptualization of the 'total man' is gradually played down after the 1960s. So, whatever value there was in re-accentuating Hegelianism between the wars and directly after, in the 1970s and 1980s this was no longer a major concern. The second point is to insist on the discord that results in combining *la fête* with the universalism that might be implied by some versions of Hegelian Marxism; indeed the concept of carnival can be seen as providing the terms for a critique of such Hegelian beliefs. The act of coupling Hegelian Marxism with *la fête* produces a philosophy of internal contradictions that provides the basis for its own critique and dissolution. Ideas of carnival and festival (ideas that continue throughout Lefebvre's work) do not fit with ideas of totality and universalism. The kinds of sociality implied by carnival can be much more productively seen in terms of radical heterogeneity – a moment of heterotopian possibility in a dystopian reality.

That which repeats itself constantly

La vie quotidienne (everyday life) suggests the ordinary, the banal, but more importantly, for Lefebvre, it connotes continual recurrence, insistent repetition. It is repetition that is crucial to Lefebvre's meaning of the term 'everyday life': the daily chores as well as those routinized pleasures that are meant to compensate for the drudgery. Even that which is 'out of the ordinary', for example a camping trip, is part of everyday life, because it is part of the cycle of work and leisure: the yearly holiday, *le weekend*, the birthday celebration, the office party and so on. As Lefebvre writes in *Everyday Life in the Modern World*, 'Everyday life is made of recurrences: gestures of labour and leisure, mechanical movements both human and properly mechanic, hours, days, weeks, months, years, linear and cyclical repetitions, natural and rational time' (1984: 18). If Lefebvre stresses the repetition and tempo of everyday life, then the reason for this is that by emphasizing ideas of recurrences he can articulate his most fundamental and radical working of the concept of everyday life: everyday life as the interrelationship of all aspects of life. By looking at the way the daily cycles of commuters relate to their weekly visit to the cinema, and how this might relate to an irregular regularity such as visiting a member of the family, everyday life can be seen as the relationship between different spheres. In this way the everyday can't be seen as relating to only certain kinds of activities, or social spheres: 'Everyday life is profoundly related to all activities, and encompasses them with all their differences and their conflicts; it is their meeting place, their bond, their common ground' (Lefebvre [1958] 1991a: 97).

Lefebvre's most compelling working of this theme is his analysis of leisure in the 1958 'Foreword' to *The Critique of Everyday Life*. Leisure, for Lefebvre, is a sphere of activity that needs to be seen in conjunction with social spheres such as work and the family; to see it independently of this would be to misapprehend it. One of the reasons that it can't be separated is because leisure is not one thing but many: the 'hobby' (photography, painting), the holiday, sitting in a cinema and so on. Leisure constitutes a diverse range of activities that don't contain a particular common orientation, apart from their differentiation from the world of work. But this is where Lefebvre's dialectic is in play: for him the world of leisure is both a continuation of the alienation of work and also its critique. So the example of the camping holiday bears the complex interaction of work and the negation of work: 'in the camping holiday, work and leisure are barely distinguishable, and everyday life in its entirety becomes play' (Lefebvre [1958] 1991a: 33). In as much as a camping holiday is a compensation for work, a temporary amelioration of its conditions of exhaustion as well as necessary for its efficient continuation, then it bears the stigmata of alienation ('alienation in leisure just as in work' [39]). Similarly 'camping' is, like most modern leisure, intimately bound up with commercialism. Not simply the commercialism of the 'holiday' but all those commodified desires to buy the latest in tent and camping technology. But it also articulates real needs that are other than the everyday world of work and in so doing criticizes and negates this world (for instance, camping might articulate the desire to live in a different relationship with nature). For Lefebvre, leisure in the 'modern world' is a routinized instance of a capitalist everyday life, as well as evidence of the continuation of festival. Festival might be drastically alienated by the commodification of leisure, but it is still present, and still potentially critical. In writing about how a sociology of the everyday might attend to this dialectic of leisure, he notes:

> Thus is established a complex of activities and passivities, of forms of sociability and communication which the sociologist can study. Although he [sic] cannot describe or analyse them without criticizing them as being (partially) illusory, he must nevertheless start from the fact that they contain within themselves their own spontaneous critique of the everyday. They are that critique in so far as they are other than everyday life, and yet they are in everyday life, they are alienation.
>
> (Lefebvre [1958] 1991a: 40)

This dialectical reading of leisure is a crucial aspect of Lefebvre's critique of the everyday and bears similarities to other versions of Western Marxism, for instance Herbert Marcuse's critique of the aesthetic realm (Marcuse 1972). What makes the dialectical method so crucial for Lefebvre is the idea that everyday life provides its own moments of critique, which means that the project of attending to it can be aligned with the project of transforming it. Fundamental to this is a double critique: on the one hand it is a critique of the separation of *life* into specialized areas of activity and professionalism, and on the other (but closely related to it) it is the critique of *academic and intellectual life* into specialized ways of understanding and investigating society. For Lefebvre, everyday life is a challenge to general social atomization: a separation of society and experience into discrete realms of the political, the aesthetic, the sexual, the economic and so on; of life divided into labour, love, leisure, etc. It is also a challenge to a specialized disciplinarity, which can be seen as the intellectual articulation of such divisions and separations: economics, philosophy, sociology and so on. Such disciplinary isolation must be overcome in the same way that their social cognates must be overcome.

The critique of everyday life must be seen as both attending to such separations (intellectual and social) and holding out the promise of their overcoming. By stressing the interrelatedness of all these social realms from the point of view of everyday life, Lefebvre also points out the limitations of transforming any one particular sphere in isolation. Similarly, the criticality of the study of everyday life is only guaranteed by the purposeful interdisciplinarity (or anti-disciplinarity) of the investigation. Crucial to Lefebvre's position is the critique of the separation of 'politics' from realms such as the aesthetic and the everyday, necessitating a critical politicization of the everyday that is also (and dialectically) a critique of the political realm as one divorced from the everyday. 'Thus', writes Lefebvre, 'the critique of everyday life involves a critique of political life, in that everyday life already contains and constitutes such a critique: in that it is that critique' (Lefebvre [1958] 1991a: 92). The possibility of transforming society via independent economic and political solutions is, for Lefebvre, not just a mistake, but a fundamental misunderstanding of the revolutionary project. Nowhere was this more keenly felt than in the failure of the revolution of 1917 to transform everyday life by overcoming alienation. At the start of his 1958 'Foreword' he writes rhetorically: 'is alienation disappearing in socialist society? In the USSR or the countries which are constructing socialism, are there not contradictions indicative of new – or renewed – forms of economic, ideological and political alienation?' ([1958] 1991a: 5).

In relation to this heretical scepticism (for someone who was still, but only just, a member of the Communist Party) the politicizing of the everyday can be seen as related to other attempts at critically overcoming atomized society – a reminder of avant-garde Surrealism, but also a prescient future echo of the feminist insistence that the 'personal is political'. For Surrealism the link with revolutionary Marxism was always strong but problematic; Breton's insistence on Marx's 'Change Society' was always linked to Rimbaud's 'Change Life'. Lefebvre's Surrealist heritage can be seen in his politicization of the everyday for its revolutionary potential, which would mean overcoming the discreteness of such separations of art and the everyday – 'Let everyday life be a work of art! Let every technical means be employed for the transformation of everyday life!' (Lefebvre 1984: 204). Such statements relate back to Simmel's sociological aesthetics as well as to Surrealism. But whereas Surrealism remained within the aesthetic realm, Lefebvre insists that the everyday is the only site for such transformations and locates his critique in relation to new radical social movements, where the historical possibilities of transformation are due, precisely, to the experience of certain groups of people living across and against such social separations. Again the example of feminism is useful: as a politicization of the historical experience of living across and against the separation of the public and the private as gendered realms, it evidences the possibility of a critique from within everyday life. Lefebvre's insistence on everyday life (as a space for both possible transformation and the most vivid and concrete of alienations) is linked to an understanding that 'class' needs rethinking beyond economic strictures and that not only are other forms of classification just as socially operative, their potential for critical refusal is all the more evident. As such his demand that the critique of everyday life is an investigation of alienation is explicitly linked to the practical experience and possibilities of such groups:

Is the notion of alienation an operative one? Can one derive a political strategy from it? No. Is it easily detachable from the conceptual armature of Hegelianism? Hardly. Is it unambiguous, precise, analytical? No. These are the wrong questions to put. The real question is that of the role, of the practical efficacy of alienation, as an awareness of lived experience and as a concept. It brings about self-revelation for different conditions and situations (those of women, students, the colonized, the colonizers, the masters, the workers, and so on).

(Lefebvre [1975] quoted in Reader 1987: 55)

If the Soviet revolution of 1917 had failed it was because everyday life had not been transformed. Or rather the revolution failed to release the creative potential of human beings on a daily basis.[2] Lefebvre's revolution would be continual and cultural. In 1967 the transformation of everyday life that would herald a 'Permanent Cultural Revolution' would concentrate on three areas: sexual reform and revolution; urban reform and revolution; and the rediscovery of the festival (Lefebvre 1984: 204–6).

Hypermodernization

It was only after the Second World War that capitalism succeeded in thoroughly penetrating the details of everyday life. We need new concepts in Marxism if it is to retain its capacity to help us both understand and transform this radically commodified contemporary world.

(Lefebvre 1988: 70)

These 'remarks occasioned by the centenary of Marx's death' insist that the project of Marxism must continually renew its conceptual framework if it is to have relevance for modern everyday life. It is an insistence that could be seen as the main motivation of Lefebvre's career, a career that has offered Marxism a productive range of conceptual tools. The focus of the critique of everyday life is, of course, the understanding and transformation of the contemporary world, even if it uses as old a concept as alienation for its analysis. But because everyday life is crucially a dynamic concept, it is continually responding to an observable reality that will necessarily rework its theoretical co-ordinates, offering a much-expanded analysis of alienation as it is experienced under conditions of increased modernization in the postwar period. If the first part of the critique is written under conditions of a generally optimistic nature (memories of the Popular Front, the Liberation of France and all the possibilities that that suggested), then the continuation of the project was responding to a very different situation. The 1950s and 1960s can be seen as a period of hypermodernization, a process that hit France (and

Germany) more forcefully than most other Western countries (see Ardagh 1977). Kristin Ross gives a vivid account of French social and cultural transformations in the late 1950s and early 1960s ('the years after electricity but before electronics'):

> The unusual swiftness of French postwar modernization seemed to partake of the qualities of what Braudel has designated as the temporality of an event: it was headlong, dramatic, and breathless. The speed with which French society was transformed after the war from a rural, empire-oriented, Catholic country into a fully industrialized, decolonized, and urban one meant that the things modernization needed – educated middle managers, for instance, or affordable automobiles and other 'mature' consumer durables, or a set of social sciences that followed scientific, functionalist models, or a work force of ex-colonial laborers – burst onto a society that still cherished prewar outlooks with all the force, excitement, disruption, and horror of the genuinely new.
>
> (Ross 1995: 4)

This massively accelerated modernization, with its panoply of social symptoms, can be seen in a particularly dynamic way in the double articulation of colonial processes. This double articulation is the complex colonial relations between a 'traditional' France, a general but uneven Americanization (Hollywood films, the Marshall Plan, juke boxes and so on), and the decolonization of French colonies, most importantly, Algeria. As already mentioned such processes mean that local and global relations are reconfigured as the urban fabric of France is itself transformed by such diverse forces as the returning *pied noirs* (white settlers), the increasing exploitation of 'immigrant' (Algerian) workers confined to particular *banlieus*, and the wholesale onslaught of 'international' (i.e. North American) culture industries (Hollywood, *le Big Mac*, etc.). It is in attending to such social transformations that the critique of everyday life as it continued during the postwar period gradually turned away from the emphasis on some of the philosophical themes developed before the war (though never entirely abandoning them) and increasingly concerned itself with a Marxist sociology of everyday life, which takes as its subject matter modernity and the spatial forms it generates.

Lefebvre's work, partly because of the sheer longevity of his working project, evidences a capacity to transform itself continually in the light of circumstances. The shift from a philosophical approach to a more sociologically concrete one is similar to Simmel's, though Lefebvre is adapting his thought to different social circumstances. These different circumstances are most evident in the way that Simmel and Lefebvre treat the urban environment: if Simmel offers something like a social psychology of urban modernity, Lefebvre's explicit emphasis on everyday life incorporates everything from a critique of urban planning to a poetics of movement. A critical response to 'Americanization' (or the globalization of capitalism) is seen in both Lefebvre's work and the work of Mass-Observation (the Lambeth Walk as an antidote to American commercial dance music), but Lefebvre's work extends the idea of colonization to take in a much larger range of forces and circumstances.

The concept of *la fête* and its revival continues to dominate, as it did in a variety of postwar French writing that attended to popular culture (Rigby 1991: 17–38), but increasingly the focus of Lefebvre's project is an attention to the latest aspects of social life. These are the results of observation and experience, the insights of a philosophical taxi driver.[3] The significant features of modernity are, for Lefebvre, the latest developments of the urban fabric, but not the metropolitan centre so much as the variety of suburban forms: the *bidonvilles* that house Algerian workers and the *pavilions* that house an affluent middle class in a fortress-like privacy (Lefebvre [1958] 1991a: 42–3). Rather than focusing on the glamour of new forms of travel, Lefebvre insists on the new time and space relationships that result from the urban process of suburbanization and the need for commuting. Commuting is a relationship of space and time that he refers to as 'constrained time' (Lefebvre 1984: 53) and which the Situationist International wrote about in their 1959 text, 'Situationist Theses on Traffic': 'Commuting time, as Le Corbusier rightly pointed out, is a surplus labour which correspondingly reduces the amount of "free" time' (Debord [1959] 1981c: 57).

Lefebvre's focus on what Brecht called the 'bad new things' is particularly strong in a chapter of his book *Introduction to Modernity* ([1962] 1995) entitled 'Notes on a New Town'. Here Lefebvre, at his most visionary, is watching the construction of a New Town at Mourenx, designed to cater for the increase in population being caused by the discovery of the new oil wells at Lacq. As he watches the construction of this urban text, a text that fills him with dread, he contemplates the possibilities of French state capitalism and asks 'are we entering the city of joy or the world of unredeemable boredom?' (119). The city reveals itself as a series of possibilities as well as the closure of possibilities through the production of boredom and constraint: 'in a sense the place is already nothing but traffic lights: do this, don't do that . . . Everything is clear and intelligible. Everything is trivial' (119).

It is this dialectical approach of Lefebvre's (the continual and mutual testing of an observable and dynamically changing reality with critical theory) which allows Lefebvre to develop, in the 1960s, a social theory that closely resembles aspects of the theories of postmodernism as articulated by Jameson and others in the 1980s. Indeed it appears that Lefebvre was instrumental in the moment of postmodernism's North American exemplification: the moment when Fredric Jameson, Ed Soja and Lefebvre all got lost in the Bonaventure Hotel in down-town Los Angeles. Anecdotes aside, Lefebvre might be claimed as a theorist of the everyday condition of postmodernity (*avant la lettre*) but only if such a claim is heavily qualified. In a section of *Everyday Life in the Modern World* entitled 'What Happened in France Between 1950 and 1960', he points to a number of changes that will be seen as definitive of postmodernity.

One of the most significant features of postmodernism for Jameson is the idea of 'depthlessness': 'The first and most evident [aspect of postmodernism] is the emergence of a new kind of flatness or depthlessness, a new kind of superficiality in the most literal sense' (Jameson 1991: 9). Jameson's examples for the most part remain within the sphere of aesthetic objects (books, paintings, etc.) and, while his theories have been subjected to a range of critiques for the contradictory use of these examples, the shift that he examines in relation to signs has become recognized as characteristic of the postmodern. As one critic vividly puts it, 'A garden gnome is no longer a garden gnome . . . These days one cannot help suspecting a garden gnome of being an ironic quotation' (Bürger 1991: 3). It would seem that aesthetic signs have moved from the authentic to the ironic, or from having the critical ability of parody to being merely capable of pastiche. Or to put it another way, cultural forms that once offered a fullness of experience and meaning have given way to forms that have been emptied, and so appear as depthless (Jameson 1991: 16–19). While such theorizing of the postmodern has concentrated on the aesthetic sign, Lefebvre's interest in the social changes in cultural signification has a much broader purview. Lefebvre sees the distinctive shift to be from the semiotics of the symbol to the semiotics of the signal. For Lefebvre the *symbol* relates to a society where meaning is experienced in a way that relates everyday life to the general narrative themes of a culture; by *signal* he is suggesting a much more instrumentally reduced form of meaning, a kind of 'on/off' communication exemplified by the traffic light. To some extent this is consistent with the theorizing of postmodern culture: the symbol for Lefebvre designates the signification of a society more replete than the present one. And like the discourses of postmodernism this can be taken as a nostalgic position that is continually in danger of mystifying and reifying the past.

In other ways, though, the idea of the signal suggests an important difference from theories of postmodernism. If signification in postmodern culture is seen as tending towards polysemy (towards ambiguity rather than fixed meaning), Lefebvre sees the signification of the signal as a loss of both fullness and multiplicity. The movement from the symbol to the signal is a movement that closes down the possibilities of meaning (in Bakhtinian terms, this is a movement from the dialogic to the monologic): 'the signal commands, controls behaviour and consists of contrasts chosen precisely for their contradictions (such as, for instance, red and green); furthermore, signals can be grouped in codes (the highway code is a simple and familiar example), thus forming systems of compulsion' (Lefebvre 1984: 62). Although the reign of the signal doesn't mean that symbols no longer exist, the growing ubiquity of this instrumental signification does suggest to Lefebvre a society that is becoming more and more based around prohibitions and commands. Later on, in the *Production of Space*, Lefebvre implies that the way urban space signifies is by 'dos and don'ts' (Lefebvre 1991b: 142), spaces that allow and disallow. While this can seem to offer a theory of power that dominates the urban everyday leaving little room for resistance, Lefebvre reads this dialectically and continues to emphasize agency as much as structure: urban space demands particular order because those who organize it recognize the presence of disorder. In this way it isn't assumed that the 'dos and don'ts' have been successfully deployed. In fact Lefebvre's understanding of the use of instrumental signification in everyday life might suggest the very opposite. It may well be precisely because 'the lunatics are taking over the asylum' (so to speak) that social planners try and clamp down on the 'openness' of meaning and use.

Examples like this distinguish Lefebvre's work from the work that has been associated with postmodernism. Recognizing that Lefebvre has attended to the same social phenomena as theorists of the postmodern might suggest a sobering alternative to the more 'millennialist' versions of postmodernity. For Lefebvre the social changes that mark his contemporary modernity are not to be thought of as radically different from capitalist modernity in general. Rather it is capitalist modernity itself that must be seen as a dynamically changing force that continually throws up new and unpredictable situations. As such the words of Alan Pred might suggest that Lefebvre is best thought of as a theorist of the hypermodern rather than the postmodern:

> . . . everyday life and experiences of the here and now . . .
> however clearly distinctive and dramatic they may seem,
> however radically altered they may have become
> by post-Fordist,
> post-colonial or
> post-cold war circumstances,
> are best characterized as modernity magnified,
> as capitalist modernity accentuated and sped up,
> as hypermodern,
> not postmodern.
>
> (Pred 1995: 15)

Although this necessarily qualifies Lefebvre's relationship to postmodernism it is still worth looking at other themes stressed in various accounts of postmodernity which are also articulated by Lefebvre as he analyses shifts in French society in the 1950s and 1960s. Jameson's understanding of postmodern society as 'what you have when the modernization process is complete and nature is gone for good' (Jameson 1991: ix) finds itself represented by Lefebvre as the final reduction and absorption of pre-capitalist production and traditions. Similarly, the focus on the production and accumulation of information as a significant aspect of (post)modern society, as well as the changes in the nature of time and space (time–space compression), are all part of the society that Lefebvre is observing in the late 1960s. But rather than just remark on the foresight of all this, we might ask instead why it was that such themes took so long to find an audience. Some of the most influential accounts of post-modernism seem to take as their condition of possibility a *rediscovery* of Lefebvre's critical project (for example, Harvey 1989), leaving us to ask why Anglophone academics never really discovered Lefebvre in the first place.

Not only do Lefebvre's writings of the 1960s and 1970s appear resolutely political (in the activist sense of the term), but their dynamically unsystematic approach sits uncomfortably with the hegemonic success of structuralism. The export of structuralism into Anglo-American academia might have been uneven and at times heavily contested by traditionalists, but the penetration of the academy by French structuralism and poststructuralism (in all its varied forms) was so thorough, that to speak of 'theory' in the 1970s and 1980s was to invoke a role-call of intellectual stars, most of whom had been targets of Lefebvre's scorn. By the late 1970s and early 1980s a heady brew of French structuralist and poststructuralist theory had become a kind of official opposition to purveyors of traditional values. Such waywardly unsystematic and practically political work as Lefebvre's was left without a platform.

The revitalization of Lefebvre in the Anglo-American university in recent years (still on a small scale) can be seen as a reaction to the success of this 'official opposition' through a return to older problematics. The return to a more socially grounded sense of the history and geography of culture has allowed a more responsive context for Lefebvre, particularly within the expanding field of cultural geography (for instance, in the work of David Harvey and Edward Soja). Such a shift in approaches to culture has allowed more attention to be paid to the forces of colonialism and globalization. But cultural geography's account of Lefebvre has (not unexpectedly) often resulted in a privileging of his more explicitly geographical work at the expense of a general understanding of his work as a critique of everyday life. Lefebvre's contribution to a geographical understanding of the social is, I think, substantial, and his dialectical studies of urban space as a tripartite relationship between the particularities of the locality, the forces of trans-global capitalism and the forces of the nation-state offer a usefully complex form of attention for everyday life in neo-colonial society. But while Lefebvre's work becomes more explicitly focused on urban space, this needs to be seen as the continuation of his critique of everyday life. In much of the tradition that we have been mapping out the everyday and the urban seem necessarily connected. By understanding the urban as a general condition of modern life (to be found in small towns and suburbs, etc.), Lefebvre allows for a more inclusive approach to modern everyday life. One way of insisting on the relationship between Lefebvre's urban geography and the critique of everyday life is to emphasize the dialogue that took place between Lefebvre and the Situationists in the 1960s, and to see it in the context of the quasi-revolutionary events of May 1968.

May 1968, urbanism and the Situationists

When Paris 'exploded'[4] in the spring of 1968 a number of themes that had dominated Lefebvre's writing converged and sprang into the public sphere with a ferocity that shook, but never toppled the established order. As students took control of their institutions and as workers formed strike committees and workers' councils (*autogestion*) it seemed, for a while, as if a permanent cultural revolution might result from what was appearing to be the re-emergence of the festival within the urban everyday. Here a form of revolutionary urbanism was transforming everyday life, turning it into carnival. Lefebvre's writings take on an extraordinary prescience when viewed in the light of the May events. His idea that urban processes would provide the conditions for the overturning of commodity culture, his call for the restoration of *la fête* to the city and his insistent demand to transform everyday life through a critical de-alienation are crucial themes for understanding the revolutionary moment of May 1968. Just the year before, in the books *Right to the City* (see Lefebvre 1996) and *Everyday Life in the Modern World* (see Lefebvre 1984), he reiterated his understanding of the radical potential of the festival (still present in everyday life) for transforming everyday life:

> Urban reform and revolution. There should be no misunderstandings at this point; urbanism will emerge from revolution, not the revolution from urbanism; though, in fact, urban experience and in particular the struggle for the city (for its preservation and restoration, for the freedom of the city) provide the setting and objectives for a number of revolutionary actions . . .
>
> The Festival rediscovered and magnified by overcoming the conflict between everyday life and festivity and enabling these terms to harmonize in and through urban society, such is the final clause of the revolutionary plan.
>
> (Lefebvre 1984: 205–6)

These words might sound like those of a would-be soothsayer if we didn't restore the intellectual and social context that they were party to. For one thing Lefebvre had by this time been teaching in a number of different institutions and had been involved in research with a generation of radicalized students who would play significant parts in the May events. For example, the student leader Daniel Cohn-Bendit, whose involvement in the *mouvement du 22 mars* can be seen as sparking the May events, was studying sociology with Lefebvre at Nanterre (a university *cité* on the outskirts of Paris). A more substantial relationship, however, is that between Lefebvre and the Situationist International (SI), who are often seen as the spiritual instigators of the May events. The productive ground that Lefebvre and the Situationists shared was 'the revolution of everyday life'. The details of their fiery relationship and their reciprocal influence are now buried under a barrage of resentment and acrimony (for Lefebvre's account, see Ross 1997b). It seems that the most useful approach is to see their work as differently articulating a number of shared themes, and while the working relationship between Lefebvre and the SI broke down irreparably in 1962, it is still productive to follow both articulations.

The SI was established in 1957 as an avant-garde group spread across a number of European countries and coalescing round a journal and irregular conferences in a variety of host cities. The themes of the SI were both aesthetic and social; indeed it was the indivisibility of the two that demonstrates their links back to Surrealism and it is their insistence on the social sphere as the sphere of action that caused rifts with more art-centred groups. Formed out of a number of radical art collectives (the International Letterists and the International Movement for an Imaginist Bauhaus), the SI should be seen as both politically and aesthetically avant-garde. From an SI perspective the problem with a purely artistic avant-gardism is that its revolutionary intent is too easily bought off by money, fame or institutional recuperation. Yet theirs is also a critique of political orthodoxies of both the Right and the Left. The theoretical concept most associated with the SI is Guy Debord's analysis of social relations based on reified images in his *Society of the Spectacle* (Debord [1967] 1983) and results in a relentless critique of an everyday life saturated and impoverished by the spectacle. The SI demanded revolution, and while their analysis of how this would come about is in opposition to Lefebvre's, the envisaged outcome can be seen to be similar: 'Proletarian revolutions will be festivals or nothing, for festivity is the very keynote of the life they announce. Play is the ultimate principle of this festival, and the only rules it can recognize are to live without dead time and to enjoy without restraints' (Situationist International 1966: 337).

Crucial to both the SI and to Lefebvre is an understanding of the Paris Commune as a revolutionary moment whose value had not been fully recognized by the Left. For Lefebvre the interest in the Commune of 1871 is that it can be seen as a radical negation of the urban processes that became its condition of possibility. The urban development of Paris, under Baron

Haussmann, from the 1850s to the 1870s created its own gravediggers. By recruiting masses of workers from the countryside to rebuild Paris for bourgeois rule, and by moving the workers out of the centre of Paris, Haussmannization was a condition that allowed for the possibility of the Paris Commune:

> One strong aspect of the Paris Commune (1871) is the strength of the return towards the urban centre of workers pushed out towards the outskirts and peripheries, their reconquest of the city, this belonging among other belongings, this value, this oeuvre which had been torn from them.
>
> (Lefebvre 1996: 76)

This analysis leads both Lefebvre and the SI to focus on the possibilities of the urban fabric to restore *la fête* to the city and to transform everyday life. It is ironic then that the break between Lefebvre and the SI should come about over what had been an agreement between the two parties: the SI accused Lefebvre of stealing their analysis of the Commune (see Kofman and Lebas 1996: 11–18). What adds to the irony is the SI's position with regard to ownership of ideas: 'Plagiarism is necessary, progress implies it' (Debord and Wolman 1981: 10).

The founding theoretical texts of the Situationists establish a range of concepts and practices that are central to their understanding of the urban everyday as containing the conditions of possibility for its own transformation. The idea of the *dérive* brings a number of these elements together. To *dérive* is to wander, to drift around the city. It can be seen as an important part of a more general activity – *détournment*, an approach to montage that stresses the necessity of negating elements of culture as a prelude to their transformation. A *dérive* is a practical *détournment* whereby the order of the city is negated in favour of a drift that allows the disordered forces of the city to be revealed: the play of affects and attractions of an urban psychogeography. An often quoted example of this is the friend of Guy Debord who 'wandered through the Harz region of Germany while blindly following the directions of a map of London' (Debord 1981a: 7). While this offers a certain flavour of the *dérive* it misses out on the importance of analysis and observation for psychogeography (the urban affects of place and space), and of giving yourself over to the pull of attractions of the urban environment in order to understand it. While this distinguishes it from the more purely aleatory drift of the Surrealists, it remains within a Surrealist understanding of the city. It also suggests a connection with the Surrealist-derived work of Walter Benjamin as he attempts to write the prehistory of modernity by resurrecting the nineteenth-century figure of the *flâneur* and the ragpicker. The *dérive*, in its observant aimlessness, assumes that the urban everyday can best be perceived as a form of unconsciousness. Drifting around cities is a form of urban 'free association' that is designed to reveal the hidden secrets of the urban everyday. If this focus on the urban everyday as preconscious or unconscious connects with the urban perspective of Simmel, Benjamin and Surrealism, it also, perhaps, offers another 'method' for doing Surrealist ethnography (a method that Mass-Observation, for example, might have benefited from in the Bolton project).

If the Situationist *dérive* can be illuminated by reference to Benjamin, it is because both can be seen as collage activities that can embody a dialectical approach that productively negates the coherency of modern culture by introducing other times and other spaces. In his 'Surrealism: The Last Snapshot of the European Intelligentsia', Benjamin argues that the Surrealist endeavour 'to win the energies of intoxication for the revolution' (Benjamin 1985: 237) was attempted by focusing on the outmoded spaces of the city (229). Such a claim can be seen as a description of Benjamin's work as he follows a historical process that continually foregrounds the outmoded of nineteenth-century Paris with its dioramas, arcades and such like. In Hal Foster's (Benjaminian) analysis of Surrealism, *Compulsive Beauty*, he considers the Surrealist *dérive* of André Breton's *Nadja*, with its fascination with the outmoded spaces of Paris (in particular the flea market), and suggests the analytic possibilities of the outmoded:

> To invoke such outmoded forms is to advance a twofold immanent critique of high capitalist culture . . . On the one hand, the capitalist outmoded relativizes bourgeois culture, denies its pretence to the natural and the eternal, opens it up to its own historicity. In effect, it exploits the paradox that this culture, under the spell of the commodity has any history at all. On the other hand, the capitalist outmoded challenges this culture with its own forfeited dreams, tests it against its own compromised values of political emancipation, technological emancipation, technological progress, cultural access, and the like. It may even intimate a way to tap the utopian energies trapped in these historical forms – to tap them for other political purposes in the present.
>
> (Foster 1993: 162)

This critique of capitalist culture brings the Situationist *dérive* in line with Benjamin's project and Lefebvre's understanding of the urban everyday. The dialectical approach that combines critical analysis with the rescuing and resuscitating of 'utopian energies' is located in the actuality of urban life. Common to all three is an understanding of capitalist 'progress' as uneven and radically discontinuous, while at the same time presenting itself as homogeneous. For the Situationists, as for Lefebvre, the contemporary urban everyday of capitalism is characterized by the saturation of mass cultural forms (such as TV and radio), penetrating everywhere as an act to cover over and hide the discontinuities of everyday life (Lefebvre 1996: 72). These discontinuities are the fissures in the urban fabric, the rents in the weave that reveal the 'way in which everyday life lags behind what is technically possible', 'the uneven development which characterizes every aspect of our era' (Lefebvre [1958] 1991a: 8), a process that can be seen as a kind of general *banlieuization* of the city. The discontinuous city is the city of *quartiers*, spaces of different temporalities, outmoded spaces with distinct cultural characteristics that, although in danger of becoming homogenized, can interrupt the homogenizing and hypnotizing effects of capitalist standardization through their cultural and historical differences. The city that evidences dereliction and decay alongside glamour and wealth is a city that can rupture the false historicism of modernity, a revelation that can awaken us from the dream of commodification. This is what Hal Foster sees as the potential of the Surrealist project, and what Walter Benjamin took to be 'the secret cargo' of Surrealism. For the Situationists and Lefebvre it was the basis for an analysis of the urban scene, a psychogeography that would reveal the unevenness of capitalist development, a critical geography that was practical as well as theoretical. Such an investigation meant veering off the beaten track, avoiding the official city of the tourist guide.

The Situationist *dérive* was first introduced by Ivan Chtcheglov in his 'Formulary for a New Urbanism' of 1953 (Chtcheglov 1981: 1–4), and the first reported *dérives* were by Chtcheglov (under the pseudonym Gilles Ivain) and Guy Debord. These wanderings take the two International Letterists into bars that are distinguished by their ethnic identity: the first bar is Algerian and they return there several times between 25 December 1953 and 1 January 1954. The second bar is a Yiddish-speaking bar which generates an acute sense of fear in the *dérivers*. These wanderings can be seen as a modern day form of *flânerie*: 'to be away from home and yet to feel oneself everywhere at home; to see the world, to be at the centre of the world, and yet to remain hidden from the world' (Baudelaire 1964: 9). And while it allows the unevenness of the everyday to be revealed, the unproblematic privileging of an easy spatial and social mobility is symptomatic (as well as diagnostic) of the unevenness of urban experience.

The centrality of the urban *flâneur*, as the exemplary experience of modernity, has recently been scrutinized by a number of feminist cultural historians. Pointing out that such an experience fails to reveal its own situated-ness in terms of gender and class, they show the unequal access men and women had to the spaces of modernity, and examine the spaces of femininity, spaces that have been left out of the story of modernity.[5] While the *flânerie* of Baudelaire might be seen as allowing for an *implicit* critique of modern everyday life, the *dérives* of the Situationists were intended to be part of an *explicit* social critique and their practice should be opened to a similar kind of analysis. What the

Situationists fail to reflect on is their own position as white male Parisians who are able 'to go botanizing on the asphalt', or in this case, to enact what seems to be a kind of tourist relationship with the colonized spaces of Paris and the lived experiences within them. The 'maps of influence' that the SI want to make from their psychogeographical experiments end up trapped in a language of 'atmospheres' and 'feelings' (Debord 1981d: 50–4): a language which can only attend to the effects of colonialism as exotic, repeating the discourse of orientalism. In this ethnically fragmented space of Paris, global inequalities are articulated at a local level: for instance, as part of an international proletariat, Algerian French citizens were in receipt of the worst housing in Paris (Hargreaves 1995: 12–15). Debord and Chtcheglov's *dérive* spills over into the eve of New Year 1954, the year the war for Algerian Independence began, a war that had major effects in Paris, resulting in heavy restrictions being placed on Algerian movement, restrictions based on the visibility of cultural differences for establishing an ethnically specific curfew. For all of Debord's interest in images, the SI seem unaware that they may inhabit a different representational space from those with whom they sit and chat. The radical differences of lived experience (experiences made up of different historical and spatial representation) are either ignored or played down by the Situationists and result in severe limitations to their geography of everyday life.

Perhaps the relationship between the Situationists and Lefebvre was always in danger of breaking down. The kind of politics of the everyday that Lefebvre favoured always allowed for gradual and reformist revolution. It allowed Lefebvre to have a much more amenable relationship with government agencies and institutions. For the Situationists such 'recuperation' was unthinkable. Theirs was a revolutionary agenda that demanded the total and immediate overthrow of the present. Yet the Situationists provide (however problematically) everyday life theory with a practice and an activism which is often sorely lacking in the more abstract discussions of Lefebvre and the other theorists we have discussed.

An unfinishable project

A quote from Hegel resonates across four decades of Lefebvre's writing: 'Was ist bekannt ist nicht errant' (what is familiar goes unrecognized). Lefebvre spent a large part of the century struggling to recognize the over-familiar world of the everyday. His critical perspective applies a dialectical approach to the seemingly most mundane aspects of everyday life (commuting, for instance). Such an approach continues the work of Simmel in its attempt to register the general in the particular. In bringing such attention to bear on the 'trivialities' of life he dislodges their over-familiarity. Such work is intimately connected with the avant-gardist practice of making the familiar strange. As we have seen, Lefebvre worked with and against a number of avant-gardist groups and his writing evidences a literary inclination that works to defamiliarize the familiar.

If Lefebvre can be seen to evidence an avant-garde sociology of the everyday, then the means for doing this seem closer to the work of Bertolt Brecht than to the Surrealism of André Breton. It is Brecht whom Lefebvre references in 1958 in demanding that the everyday must be defamiliarized (directly invoking Brecht's 'alienation effect' or *Verfremdungseffekt*). It would seem that a critical attention to everyday life as an alienated reality requires an alienating perspective: 'It is then that consciousness of alienation – that strange awareness of the strange – liberates us, or begins to liberate us, from alienation' (Lefebvre [1958] 1991a: 20). Everyday life in modernity evidences an all-pervasive alienation: the alienation from the recognition of alienation. In other words, alienation is the condition of being alienated from our alienation. Here, in a dialectical twist, the route to dis-alienation must start out from *more* alienation: it is only by defamiliarizing the everyday that the everyday can be recognized as alienation.

Lefebvre doesn't supply any systematic methodology for such a form of attention but he does seem to offer a set of concerns, ways of operating, that I think are invaluable for thinking critically about the everyday. In the following passage he suggests a kind of analytic perspective that transforms our perception of everyday actions by insisting that they reverberate across a number of different registers:

> Thus the simplest event – a woman buying a pound of sugar, for example – must be analysed. Knowledge will grasp whatever is hidden within it. To understand this simple event, it is not enough merely to describe it; research will disclose a tangle of reasons and causes, of essences and 'spheres': the woman's life, her biography, her job, her family, her class, her budget, her eating habits, how she uses money, her opinions and her ideas, the state of the market, etc. Finally I will have grasped the sum total of capitalist society, the nation and its history. And although what I grasp becomes more and more profound, it is contained from the start in the original little event. So now I can see the humble events of everyday life as having two sides: a little, individual, chance event – and at the same time an infinitely complex social event, richer than the many 'essences' it contains within itself.
>
> (Lefebvre [1958] 1991a: 57)

The defamiliarization of the everyday requires a plurality of approaches, a range of attentions that place it radically within a framework of critical interdisciplinarity. The everyday, Lefebvre insists, is not an 'object' or a place, but a totality of relationships.

The above quote conjures up a multitude of narratives, all of which impinge on each other. Each narrative unfolds in a different spatial organization: from the mnemonic geography of the home and the locality, to the global unevenness of world trade. These narratives would each require critical forms of attention: questions associated with feminism and political economy would need to be asked, methodological problems to do with the use of autobiographical materials and the traces of experience could be raised. In the end it is the 'tangle' of relationships to which the desire for the critique of everyday life must aspire – a desire that finally is unsatisfiable for a project that is unfinishable.

Where Lefebvre's project differs from the work that we have been looking at so far is in its commitment to the revolutionary transformation of everyday life. Where Mass-Observation saw the foregrounding of the everyday as leading to a transformation of daily life within daily life, for Lefebvre the goal of transformation must be the overcoming and obliteration of the everydayness of everyday life. The privileging of creativity and play as the basis for a social life stripped of boredom and routine places Lefebvre in a much more utopian tradition than we have seen so far. But in as much as this revolutionary energy is always within the everyday (however alienated) his utopianism is tied to the possibilities present within contemporary life. In this way a dialectical foregrounding of everyday life, which recognizes the alienation in everyday life at the same time as it attempts to grasp the utopian element that alienation tries to hide, is an act of bringing to consciousness (theoretically and practically) a non-conscious and non-apparent everyday.

Notes

1   Lefebvre's *Critique of Everyday Life: Volume I* was first published in France in 1947. It was republished in 1958 with a long and important 'Foreword'. In referencing this work I will use square brackets to make it clear to which section of the book I am referring.

2   For an account of the kinds of transformations of everyday life that did occur in the wake of the Soviet revolution, see Boym (1994).

3   David Harvey notes the importance of Lefebvre's early career as a taxi driver in his 'Afterword' to Lefebvre (1991b: 426).

4   Lefebvre's written response to the May events is given in a book entitled *The Explosion: Marxism and the French Revolution* (Lefebvre 1969).

5   See Pollock (1988); Wilson (1995); Wolff (1989). Also of interest for its attention to the suburban spaces of femininity in nineteenth-century Paris is Adler (1989).

Chapter 8

MICHEL DE CERTEAU'S POETICS
OF EVERYDAY LIFE

For what I really wish to work out is a science of singularity; that is to say, a science of the relationship that links everyday pursuits to particular circumstances.

(de Certeau 1984: ix)

T O   M O V E   F R O M   L E F E B V R E ' S writing to the work of Michel de Certeau (1925–1986) is to do something more than simply jump a generation. The shift is in many ways more fundamental. For one thing, de Certeau is sympathetically engaging with a tradition of thought (structuralism and poststructuralism) that met with little but scorn in the work of Lefebvre. Yet this doesn't quite capture the differences between the two. Perhaps it is best to locate their difference at the level of sensibility. The general surefooted-ness of Lefebvre's approach and the declamatory style of his writing are sustained by an orientation that is firmly grounded in a critical architecture (supplied by treating the everyday as an alienated condition). Michel de Certeau's writing, on the other hand, is often elliptical and elusive; often his arguments seem to meander beneath an edifice made up of a startlingly eclectic array of examples and theoretical perspectives. It marks an approach that is tentative, yet evidences an unquestioned faith in the potential of a yet to be recovered everyday. And this is perhaps the central problematic facing de Certeau: the everyday is hidden and evasive; to attempt to attend to it requires something like a leap of faith. De Certeau's work is perhaps the most wholehearted attempt to fashion an approach to the everyday from the material of the everyday itself. If he approaches it in the name of faith, then this is because 'faith' and 'belief' are the characteristics of the kinds of knowledge that circulate in the everyday. If his theorizing is labyrinthine and his arguments unsystematic, then this is because the everyday might be thought of as patterned in this way. If de Certeau's writing can be described as both suggestive and evocative, then the everyday too can be seen as textured by evocations that point to a sensory realm never fully mappable by images and words. Perhaps then with de Certeau we find a *style* for writing the everyday that comes closest to being in tune with its subject.

Assembling a poetics of everyday life

A Jesuit, a member of the psychoanalyst Jacques Lacan's *Ecole Freudienne*, a scholar in early modern mystic possessions, a critical historiographer, a committed practitioner of 'plural writing', and an ethnographer of everyday life, Michel de Certeau's writing presents the image of an itinerant thinker. In a career marked by journeys that were both intellectual and spatial (he worked in France, Brazil, California, Argentina and Chile) 'travel' figures as a constant metaphor. The theme of an active movement through time in space brings together a number of operations that will make up the materiality of the everyday for de Certeau. Whether it is reading or walking, a complex of spatio-temporal activities is at stake. Travelling suggests a journey that alters not only the traveller but also the spaces travelled; it suggests an encounter with 'other' cultures, with difference. Journeying is as apt a metaphor for de Certeau as it is for the everyday: it falls on the side of unfinished business, of becoming rather than being. In de Certeau's writing there is no finished 'system', no structure that can be overlaid on the everyday to produce neat schemas and mappable territories. De Certeau's work on the everyday is nothing if not an adventure.

The path of this adventure in theorizing everyday life is mapped across a number of single- and joint-authored works. The most significant co-ordinates are provided by the two volumes of *L'invention du quotidien* (*The Practice of Everyday Life*), first published in Paris in 1980 (de Certeau 1984; de Certeau *et al.* 1998). Taken together they present a theoretical and empirical monument to the everyday. The first volume is authored by de Certeau alone and though peppered with exemplification, articulates a generalized and theoretical approach to everyday life. The second volume consists of the work of Pierre Mayol and Luce Giard (punctuated by short essays by de Certeau) and offers a more sustained involvement with empirical material. De Certeau's work needs to be seen in conjunction with the work of his colleagues, and throughout this chapter I will insist on the productivity of reading the first volume through the material of the second. The 'Michel de Certeau' in whom I am interested includes the work of both Giard and Mayol.

The two volumes were the result of a research project (1974–8) directed by de Certeau under the auspices of the prestigious Délégation Générale à

Figure 9   Still from *Jeanne Dielman, 23 Quai du Commerce, 1080 Bruxelles*, directed by Chantal Akerman (1975). Akerman's film inspired Luce Giard's contribution to Volume II of *The Practice of Everyday Life*

la Recherche Scientifique et Technique (General Office for Science and Technology Research) (de Certeau *et al.* 1998: xiii–xxxiii). While its institutional circumstances provide an ironic setting for a project that champions the clandestine 'tactical' arts of the weak over the 'strategic' and powerful projects of 'political, economic, and scientific rationality' (de Certeau 1984: xix), they also point to the possibilities of producing 'tactical' research within a 'host' culture organized by academic protocols, 'scientific' research languages, and economic and physical structures of support and dependence. But, as is evident from the two collections entitled *Culture in the Plural* (de Certeau 1997b) and *The Capture of Speech and Other Political Writings* (de Certeau 1997a), the theoretical and practical terms for de Certeau's attention to everyday life precede the inauguration of the research for *L'invention du quotidien*. It is a historical rupture that initiates the adventure.

Brian Rigby in his *Popular Culture in Modern France: A Study of Cultural Discourse* (Rigby 1991) situates de Certeau alongside a number of other intellectuals as part of a general re-assessment of culture that emerges vividly in the wake of May 1968. For de Certeau the turn towards studying everyday culture was not about finding new cultural texts to interpret, value and celebrate; instead it was an attempt to focus investigation on the way people operate, the way they 'practise' everyday life. For de Certeau the popular culture of everyday life evidences 'ways of using the products imposed by a dominant economic order' (de Certeau 1984: xiii). Everyday life is the scene of use within 'a system that, far from being their own, has been constructed and spread by others' (de Certeau 1984: 17). What characterizes the everyday for de Certeau is a creativity that responds to this situation. By 'making do' with a ready-made culture, but also, and crucially, by 'making with' this culture (through acts of appropriation and re-employment), everyday life evidences an 'inventiveness'. In circumstances limited to the material at hand, everyday life witnesses the creative arrangements and re-arrangements of *bricolage*: 'Creativity is the act of reusing and recombining heterogeneous materials' (de Certeau 1997b: 49). But these assemblages are not just the products of an individual's will or actions; they are the products of a culture seen as heterogeneous, of culture in the plural. The heterogeneity of culture asserts itself, not just through the inventive juxtapositions that people make, but through the stubborn insistence of the body, of childhood memories and cultural histories. The 'resistance' of the everyday (de Certeau's leitmotif) is a resistance born of difference, of otherness: bodies that are at variance to the machines that they operate; traditions that are unlike those being promoted; imaginings that are different from the rationale governing the present.

For de Certeau, the journey starts in 1968, in participation in and response to the events of that Paris spring:

> One *fact* is more important than the claims or even the contestation that expressed it in terms prior to the event: a *positive* fact, a *style* of experience. A creative – that is, poetic – experience. 'The poet has lit the fuse of speech,' stated a flyer at the Sorbonne. It is a fact that we can attest to for having seen and been participants: a throng became poetic. Hidden, perhaps, until then (but that means that it was not alive), speech exploded in the relations that fostered it or that it appropriated, with the joy (or the seriousness?) of shattered categories and unforeseen bonds of solidarity.
>
> (de Certeau 1997a: 13)

Written in the summer of 1968 as an act of 'political clarification', de Certeau's description of the May events marks out some of the terms that will continually inform his investigations of popular culture and everyday life: the creativity of appropriation; a poetics of experience; a style of everyday life. Of course, that moment of emergent culture (the 'capturing of speech') could be seen as, precisely, the overcoming of everyday life, but in seeing it come to visibility (or orality) in the May events, de Certeau's project will work to find such festive and inventive poetics in a more general everyday culture. As Ian Buchanan suggests, for de Certeau 'the everyday is already extraordinary; a virtual carnival' (1997: 177). But so as not to take this as some naïve misrecognition of those aspects of the everyday that are dreary and repetitive, the virtuality of this position needs stressing. Buchanan supplies a further clarification: that 'the everyday itself be treated as always already containing the *possibility* of carnival' (179, emphasis added). To figure the everyday as a potentiality that points to an overcoming marks de Certeau's work as a continuation of Lefebvre's project, but it is a continuation that needs clarifying in relation to both similarities and differences.

Writing in 1967, Lefebvre would describe the everyday life of capitalist modernity as being characterized by its lack of style, and by its prosaic mode:

> With the Incas, the Aztecs, in Greece or in Rome, every detail (gestures, words, tools, utensils, costumes, etc.) bears the imprint of a style; nothing had as yet become prosaic, not even the quotidian; the prose and the poetry of life were still identical. Our own everyday life is typical for its yearning and quest for a style that obstinately eludes it . . . the prose of the world spread, until now it invades everything – literature, art and objects – and all the poetry of existence has been evicted.
>
> (Lefebvre 1984: 29)

The total invasion of 'prose' is, for Lefebvre, the colonization of everyday life by the commodity form: modernity is characterized by an alienation that has penetrated, not just the workplace, but crucially, everyday life itself. The seeds for overcoming this condition exist in the everyday but only as an alienated possibility.

De Certeau's work articulates a question that might jeopardize the 'success' of such an analysis:

> If it is true that the grid of 'discipline' is everywhere becoming clearer and more extensive, it is all the more urgent to discover how an entire society resists being reduced to it, what popular procedures (also 'minuscule' and quotidian) manipulate the mechanisms of discipline and conform to them only in order to evade them, and finally, what 'ways of operating' form the counterpart, on the consumer's (or 'dominee's'?) side, of the mute processes that organize the establishment of socio-economic order.
>
> (de Certeau 1984: xiv)

'Popular procedures' constitute a 'style' that is evasive. Yet it is also a style that evidences a resistance to the colonization of everyday life. So by starting out from the position that the everyday presents an obstacle (and a residue) to systematic forms of government and domination, the accounts of everyday life offered by Lefebvre and the Situationists, but also by Foucault (the specific addressee in this quote) can appear overblown. Although Lefebvre, as we have seen, argues for a nuanced version of everyday life (which dialectically positions the everyday as the sphere of cultural reproduction while, at the same time, offering moments of possible transformation), the emphasis is clearly on the extension of capitalist logic into the everyday. In comparison, de Certeau's position 'serves to confirm the unsutured nature of the social, the impossibility of the full colonization of daily life by the system, the continued fact of resistance to the temporal logic of democratic capitalism, and the ubiquitous eruption of the heterogeneous' (Poster 1997: 125).

Where the difference between de Certeau and Lefebvre is most clearly visible is in the political outcomes that result from their similar yet different staging of the everyday. For Lefebvre the outcome of analysis is a revolutionary 'praxis' that will capitalize on those 'moments' of possibility, those moments that germinate the seeds of a different everyday. For de Certeau the instrumentality of politics necessarily has to be held in abeyance; nothing could be more damaging to the study of everyday life than to greet it with a prescriptive 'political' assessment. This is not to evacuate the political from the field of everyday life; rather it is to re-imagine it for the everyday: what would a politics be like that emerged from the everyday, instead of one that was simply applied to the everyday? For de Certeau the lesson of May 1968's 'failure' is of a popular poetics being met by the language of official reform and organized politics, which results in the 'recapture of speech' and the deadening of its possibilities (de Certeau 1997a: 29–31). Writing of the 'wildcat' protests that marked 1968 and subsequent years, de Certeau explains that they 'offer a type of movement whose form is "cultural" because their participants can no longer make their requests clear within traditional sociopolitical frames of reference' (de Certeau 1997b: 112). Such requests are irruptions from everyday life, irruptions that have no chance of being heard against the blunt thunder of traditional politics.

In the wake of May 1968, 'traditional politics' was precisely the formal antagonisms that had nothing to say in response to the graffiti that emerged on the walls of Paris. The Right and the Left, *Gaullisme* and *Gauchisme*, became as one, as the *enragés* occupied a ground that was not in-between, but distinctly other. The writing on the wall spoke of demands eccentric to such an order: 'I take my desires for reality because I believe in the reality of my desires' (figure 10); 'We won't ask for anything. We won't demand anything. We'll just take and occupy' (Viénet 1992: 52–4). Such slogans resonated with a range of cultural and political references that mixed Surrealism with anarchism. If such desirous language was recaptured by the language of reform, or of reconditioned Marxism, de Certeau remained preoccupied by the echo of the desire for 'something' other.

To weigh Lefebvre and de Certeau only in terms of political outcomes is to miss some of the more productive similarities they share. Both are

Figure 10   The writing is on the wall ('take your desire for reality'). Paris graffiti, May 1968

concerned with the everyday as an ensemble of practices. Both bring the language of avant-gardism to bear on the business of attending to the everyday (collage, Brecht, Surrealism). Both note the extensive ambition of rationalism, while recognizing its mythic and irrational underside and its failure to erase ritual and superstition in general. Both concern themselves with the everyday as phenomenal and sensual: an 'aesthetic' realm that requires attention to the style and poetics of living (even if style, for Lefebvre, can't be fully realized under present conditions). Such a list of commonalities begins to make vivid connections, not just between Lefebvre and de Certeau, but across the range of writings and practices that we have so far been discussing. Indeed it is the strength of de Certeau's contribution to this 'tradition' that it allows the threads we have been uncovering to be brought together into some sort of loose weave.

What de Certeau attempts is nothing less than the production of a poetics of everyday life. Such a poetics (emerging from the practices of everyday life and allowing those practices to become visible and audible) must mark its distance from 'traditional sociopolitical frames of reference'. For de Certeau this will mean negotiating his way out of the stark polarizing language of such a tradition. It will mean having to side-step the binary logic that infects the analysis of the social. It will mean generating a poetics subtle and tactical enough to allow for the differentiation of a multiple everyday.

Beginning with the problematic that the everyday gets remaindered in forms of analysis that offer an overarching perspective of social relations, de Certeau figures everyday life as a sphere of resistance (both virtually and actually). But this 'resistance' is not synonymous with opposition. Resistance in de Certeau is closer to the use of the term in electronics and psychoanalysis:

it is what hinders and dissipates the energy flow of domination, it is what resists representation. In de Certeau's writings about everyday life, 'resistance' is as much an activity born of inertia as it is a result of inventive forms of appropriation:

> On the one hand, there are slowly developing phenomena, latencies, delays that are piled up in the thick breadth of mentalities, evident things and social ritualizations, an opaque, stubborn life buried in every-day gestures that are at the same time both immediate and millenary. On the other hand, irruptions, deviations, that is, all these margins of an inventiveness from which future generations will successively draw their 'cultivated culture'.
>
> (de Certeau 1997b: 137–8)

The 'thick breadth' of 'opaque, stubborn life' walks hand-in-hand with inventive 'deviations' in this picture of everyday life. While this might seem to echo the work of Raymond Williams, and his emphasis on 'residual and emergent' cultures that are differentiated from dominant cultures (Williams 1977: 121–7), for de Certeau the 'residual' or 'opaque, stubborn life' is not to be found simply in the continuation of cultural practices and values no longer in vogue (rural traditions, for instance). Instead de Certeau and his research colleagues want to register a cultural density around objects and practices that evoke what might be thought of as a cultural unconscious or cultural imaginary. In her writing on 'Kitchen Women Nation' Luce Giard portrays the everyday art of cooking as 'a subtle intelligence full of nuances and strokes of genius, a light and lively intelligence that can be perceived without exhibiting itself, in short, a very ordinary intelligence' (de Certeau et al. 1998: 158). But this celebration of women's know-how is also haunted by reminiscence. Each gesture, each smell, each culinary trick is thick with the condensation of memories. 'Doing cooking' is never simply the more or less inventive response to the limitations of circumstance; it always smells and tastes of the past. Cooking, like psychoanalysis, 'recognizes the past in the present' (de Certeau 1986: 4).

For Giard, cooking is situated within a 'family saga', reverberating with childhood memories and histories of migration. Her account tells of her own ambivalent feelings towards cooking; from the teenager who thought of cooking as 'a bit stupid' she learns that 'surreptitiously and without suspecting it, I had been invested with the secret, tenacious pleasure of doing-cooking' (de Certeau et al.: 153). Such pleasure offers 'a way of being-in-the-world and making it one's home' (154). But it also marks the stubbornness of memory: 'these are memories stubbornly faithful to the marvelous treasure of childhood flavors. The almond cakes, for example, about which my father, an old man already suffering, used to repeat to me the tasty secret that disappeared with his beloved grandmother, who passed away at the beginning of the century, before he was seven' (188). Cooking, eating and drinking are multiple activities: 'This glass of pale, cool, dry wine marshals my entire life in the Champagne. People may think I am drinking: I am remembering . . .' (Bachelard, quoted in de Certeau et al. 1998: 188).

If such practices are 'resistant' (and they clearly are for de Certeau and Giard), then such resistance is clearly not synonymous with being 'oppositional' or 'progressive'. Any attempt simply to mine de Certeau's work for an easily identifiable assemblage of 'oppositional' culture will miss the nuances of the project. 'Resistance' here is both a preservative and a creation of something new: rather than presenting the inverse of power, it offers a different and pluralized account of powers:

> Between the symmetrical errors of archaistic nostalgia and frenetic over-modernization, room remains for microinventions, for the practice of reasoned differences, to resist with a sweet obstinance the contagion of conformism, to reinforce the network of exchanges and relations, to learn how to make one's own choice among the tools and commodities produced by the industrial era. Each of us has the power to seize power over one part of oneself. This is why the gestures, objects, and words that live in the ordinary nature of a simple kitchen have so much importance.
>
> (213)

For Giard the resistant nature of everyday life is revealed as (partly) a 'conservative' response, precisely because industrial modernity is figured as revolutionary ('frenetic overmodernization').

The project of attending to the 'invention of everyday life' requires qualification. It is not a catalogue of data: if everyday life is inventive it also requires an invention by the writer of a language that will make possible the registering of the everyday. If *The Practice of Everyday Life* is an investigation of 'the ways in which users operate', its object 'is not so much to discuss this elusive, yet fundamental subject as to make such a discussion possible':

> This goal will be achieved if everyday practices, 'ways of operating' or doing things, no longer appear as merely the obscure background of social activity, and if a body of theoretical questions, methods, categories, and perspectives, by penetrating this obscurity, make it possible to articulate them.
>
> (de Certeau 1984: xi)

The condition of possibility for such a project is the invention of a poetics, a *poiesis* – an inventive language that will register the inventiveness, the

153

poiesis of the everyday. 'Poetics' needs to be understood both as an inquiry into the *forms* that the everyday takes and as an inventive activity within language and life: de Certeau reminds us that the etymology of 'poetics' is 'from the Greek *poiein* "to create, invent, generate"' (1984: 205). It is this inventive language of 'insinuation', of 'ruses' and 'poaching', and 'multi-form', 'tricky', 'stubborn' ways of operating that should determine the success or failure of de Certeau's project. But this aspect of de Certeau's work has remained hidden (tricky? stubborn?) for most Anglophone commentators on de Certeau. Tony Bennett writes for a number of people when he states that,

> What de Certeau's account of everyday practices most lacks . . . is anything approaching an adequate sociological or historical description of those practices that would be capable of locating them within, and accounting for them in terms of, specific social milieux. Instead, what is offered is a poetics of the oppressed, an essentially aestheticising strategy in which the prospect of understanding the specific logics informing specific forms of resistance is traded in, far too easily, for a generalised account of transgression.
>
> (Bennett 1998: 174)

Somewhere along the line, de Certeau's struggle to register that which isn't reducible to structures of domination has been interpreted simply as 'a generalized account of transgression'. The desire to extricate analysis from 'traditional sociopolitical frames of reference' has been met by their return. The language of 'law and transgression', of 'power and resistance', has stymied investigation of the heuristic possibilities opened up by de Certeau. Crucially, the productivity of de Certeau's poetics is seen as the project's biggest flaw.

De Certeau plays a tricky game. In trying to escape from the reductive language of 'bipolar' thought his writing insists on employing a series of binary terms. The first volume of *The Practice of Everyday Life* reads as a sustained orchestration of binary terms: consumption versus production; reading versus writing; tactics versus strategies; space versus place; the spoken versus the written. What makes de Certeau's manoeuvre so awkward (and seemingly so easy to mistake) is this use of binary terms to challenge the structures of binary thought. Semantically overlapping, terms such as 'strategies and tactics' refuse to be straightforward antagonists in a debate about power and resistance. Instead they allow, I will argue, the opportunity for differentiation. What de Certeau's work employs are non-oppositional binary terms. Not only do the terms 'production' and 'consumption', for example, fold back on each other, but each provides the other with the very essence that would define them:

In reality, a rationalized, expansionist, centralized, spectacular and clamorous production is confronted by an entirely different kind of production, called 'consumption' and characterized by its ruses, its fragmentation (the result of circumstances), its poaching, its clandestine nature, its tireless but quiet activity, in short by its quasi-invisibility, since it shows itself not in its own products (where would it place them?) but in an art of using those imposed on it.

(de Certeau 1984: 31)

Consumption in this account is essentially a form of production, while a 'centralized' production can only be thought of as a form of expansionist consumption. In establishing such terms, de Certeau destroys the very ground that would separate them, but not in an act of de-differentiation. In privileging consumption, de Certeau works towards a differentiation of production: productions become multiple; *whole networks of different productive assemblages emerge.*

Such productive assemblages have crucial repercussions for employing other binary terms. For instance, in mobilizing the terms 'reading and writing', de Certeau dissolves the differences between them:

We have to quit thinking that a qualitative gap exists between the acts of reading and writing. The first is a silent creativity invested in what the reader does with the text; the second is this very creativity, but made explicit in the production of a new text. Already present in reading, cultural activity merely finds a variant and a prolongation in writing. From the one to the other, no line of difference separates passivity from activity, except the line that distinguishes different ways or styles of socially *marking* the gap opened up by a practice in a given form.

(de Certeau 1997b: 145)

The only difference that can be maintained between reading and writing is the socially peculiar act of valuing the more visible activity (writing). When this has been made evident both reading and writing become practices that have to be differentiated, not according to their visibility, but by their ways of operating. But now such a differentiation would no longer be able to operate within the conventions designated by the terms 'reading' and 'writing'. This tactical use of binary terms is not without its problems and de Certeau's success with them can seem uneven. Their successful use seems to depend upon a relational logic that must relate practices to circumstances; it is a use that requires that the terms take on a metaphorical density above and beyond being verifiable and circumscribable activities (orality versus the scriptural, reading versus writing).

If commentary on de Certeau has been transfixed by a desire to uncouple these slippages and re-establish binary oppositions, it is partly because the work can be read as re-activating a split between absolute power and its lack. It can be read as straightforwardly celebrating and privileging the 'oppositional' character of the everyday and championing its general condition of resistance. De Certeau's texts have the same porous density that he finds in the everyday: they are relatively 'open' to different readings, they are capable of supplying the material for very different kinds of arguments. My account of de Certeau's 'everyday' isn't simply aimed at countering the arguments put forward by Bennett and others. My aim is to recognize de Certeau's work as a *poetics* that might allow for the everyday to emerge. I want to set about excavating this *poetics*, which I see as being at the heart of de Certeau's project, because this is the project's productivity, its potential and its invention.

Age-old ruses

> Analysis shows that a relation (always social) determines its terms, and not the reverse, and that each individual is a locus in which an incoherent (and often contradictory) plurality of such relational determinations interact. Moreover, the question at hand concerns modes of operation or schemata of action, and not directly the subjects (or persons) who are the authors or vehicles. It concerns an operational logic whose models may go as far back as the age-old ruses of fishes and insects that disguise or transform themselves in order to survive, and which has in any case been concealed by the form of rationality currently dominant in Western culture.
>
> (de Certeau 1984: xi)

What does it mean when a book on the practices of everyday life starts out by refusing to link actions to their authors? What kind of everyday is describable when 'modes of operation' and 'schemata of action' replace 'subjects and persons'? What kind of historicity is imaginable for the everyday when such activities are seen not simply as 'age-old' but as the business of 'fishes and insects'? If *The Practice of Everyday Life* is seen as attempting to register the *poiesis* of everyday life through a poetics, then it is a poetics that articulates activities rather than expresses identities – a poetics of *uses* rather than *users*. De Certeau attempts to disentangle 'people' and 'practices' by generalizing the 'operational logic' of the everyday so that it includes all living beings. While this might be seen as evidence of de Certeau's poststructuralist orientation (a 'post-humanist' 'death of the subject'), or as a form of global biological essentialism, it is equally understandable as part of his attempt to disengage from 'traditional sociopolitical frames of reference'. Such frames of reference might take comfort in ascribing resistance *to* identities (the working class, sub-cultures and so on) rather than activities. If de Certeau is going to find something new and different in the everyday (something more than the dress rehearsal of an endlessly deferred revolution or the saturation of everyday life by networks of 'micro-power') then the dropping of identity categories (already dense with the terms and conditions of limited analysis) might offer an initial tactical manoeuvre.

This is not to say that individuals and groups are missing from the swarm of examples that make up *The Practice of Everyday Life*, but in the attempt to generate 'A Practical Science of the Singular' the category of the subject is already too prolific. By relating the everyday to circumstantial practices, de Certeau liberates analysis from the burden of having to identify progressive social identities. The 'science of singularity' will be concerned with relations of difference, with instances of culture, which are already overtaken by a plurality. *The Practice of Everyday Life* is peopled with moments and practices, rather than 'subjects'; it is a book teeming with actual individuals (and groups) and individual actualities, where the familiar signposts of identity are tactically missing. The usual categories for conducting a discussion of the subject (agency, domination, resistance, consciousness, unconsciousness and so on) are not lacking, however, but are extended and altered. It will be an urban unconsciousness as much as an individual's which will guide trajectories through the city. It will be techniques, gestures, machines, buildings, beliefs, as much as the bosses and the bossed, that will be invested with the power to dominate and resist.

The slippery intricacies of the terms 'strategies' and 'tactics' can act as a guide to how the practice of everyday life can 'escape without leaving' 'the dominant social order' (de Certeau 1984: xiii). Clearly employing the metaphorics of war, de Certeau writes:

> I call a *strategy* the calculation (or manipulation) of power relationships that becomes possible as soon as a subject with will and power (a business, an army, a city, a scientific institution) can be isolated. It postulates a *place* that can be delimited as its *own* and serve as the base from which relations with an *exteriority* composed of targets or threats (customers or competitors, enemies, the country surrounding the city, objectives and objects of research, etc.) can be managed.
>
> (1984: 35–6)

A strategy 'assumes a place that can be circumscribed as *proper (propre)*' (xix). Occupying specific places, de Certeau suggestively sees strategies as *proprietorial*. The term is linked to a whole host of other terms that de Certeau will make use of: place, property, propriety, own, owning, ownership, and

157

crucially, proper (*propre* – 'clean', 'correct', 'one's own'). The terms speak of a place of appropriate manners and proper conventions, somewhere saturated by a regimen of seemly actions. The connotations of war that are associated with the term 'strategy' prepare the reader for the use that de Certeau will make of it to describe the abysmal practices of colonization, or the bleak protocols of 'scientific management', but what is more unexpected and in need of clarification is the actual and possible generalization of the term.

In Volume II of *The Practice of Everyday Life*, Pierre Mayol presents an account of everyday life in the Croix-Rousse neighbourhood of Lyons. His intention is to study the way that 'the organization of everyday life is articulated on at least two registers' (de Certeau *et al.* 1998: 8). Mayol divides these registers into 'behaviors' (walking, greeting, visiting and so on) and 'expected symbolic benefits' (linked to the consumers' 'art of coexisting' and the social unconscious or imaginary of the neighbourhood). Without explicitly mobilizing the term 'strategy' (although he does make some use of it), Mayol recognizes that a regulatory activity is in place: 'One regulation articulates both of these systems, which I have described and analyzed using the concept of *propriety*' (8). In his wonderful reading of the cultural density of bread and wine, Mayol suggests that wine drinking is subject to 'neighborhood checks' (90). While it supplies the 'festive face of the meal' and is the vehicle for an exuberant celebration of life, it is also regulated by propriety: 'Propriety thus requires the drinker to situate himself [*sic*] on the threshold immediately below the foreboding signs of reprobation, in the plausible "not too much" category that does not cast a slur on an individual's or a family's reputation' (89). For Mayol the 'strategic' form of this propriety is nuanced to the practices under consideration: rather than equate it with the disciplinary regime of a prison, Mayol describes it as 'the communal "kitty"' (8). What is crucial here are the *relations* that are established between particular actions (getting drunk, for instance) and the regulatory operations of a place. It is the *formal* character of these operations (their logic, so to speak) that is being designated by the term strategy.

Clearly, any workable political assessment of cultural practices would need to differentiate between the probity that relates to alcohol consumption and the relentlessness of colonialism (for instance). To generalize the *contents* of the term 'strategy' would constitute a dangerous aestheticism that would result in homogenized relations of power. The 'ranking' of strategies, however, is not something that *The Practice of Everyday Life* volunteers. To open up the productivity of the project requires recognizing it as a poetics, as a differentiation (always circumstantial) of the *form* of actions. The urgency and instrumentality of politics (what must we do?) is exchanged for an analysis (what's going on?). A general poetics of everyday life is being sketched out; to designate a practice as strategic is akin to claiming it as metaphorical rather than metonymical.

To further differentiate forms of action, de Certeau distinguishes between strategies and tactics:

> A *tactic* is a calculated action determined by the absence of a proper locus . . . Thus it must play on and with a terrain imposed on it and organized by the law of a foreign power . . . It takes advantage of 'opportunities' and depends on them, being without any base where it could stockpile its winnings, build up its own position, and plan raids. What it wins it cannot keep. This nowhere gives a tactic mobility, to be sure, but a mobility that must accept the chance offerings of the moment, and seize on the wing the possibilities that offer themselves at any given moment. It must vigilantly make use of the cracks that particular conjunctions open in the surveillance of the proprietary powers. It poaches in them. It creates surprises in them. It can be where it is least expected. It is a guileful ruse.
>
> (de Certeau 1984: 37)

This description of tactics extends the war analogy, but this time it is directed towards guerrilla combat. Tactics is the inventive employment of possibilities within strategic circumstances: disguise, surprise, discretion, secrecy, wit, play, bluff and so on. Crucially, tactics don't operate outside a strategy that they can confront; to do this would require a counter-strategy, they are in the ambiguous position of being inside but 'other': 'they escaped it without leaving it' (xiii).

The correlation of everyday life and war, which the terms 'strategy' and 'tactics' generate, is useful for making vivid the formal differences of actions, but the 'price' of this is that it can lead to unhelpful confusions. For instance, the descriptions of tactical practices as *guerrilla* activity hardly prepare the ground for de Certeau's claim that 'many everyday practices (talking, reading, moving about, shopping, cooking, etc.) are tactical in character' (xix). While it is precisely the *character* of activities that de Certeau is concerned with, the extension of metaphors of war does suggest a much greater degree of purposeful opposition than is evident from the examples. At this point it is worth remembering that the urgency of de Certeau's inquiry is aimed at finding out not how power is deposed (an investigation of successful 'revolutions' would surely be needed for that), but 'how an entire society resists being reduced' to 'the grid of "discipline" [which] is everywhere becoming clearer and more extensive' (xiv). These two perceptions (the extension of power and the everyday as non-reducible to it) produce the asymmetry of tactics and strategies where inventive and sluggish practices exist alongside 'proprietary powers'. Different forms and logics are at work, but their non-symmetrical combination results in the friction of 'rubbing along', rather than in direct conflict.

The most vivid example of tactical activity that de Certeau gives is *la perruque*: '*la perruque* is the worker's own work disguised as work for his [or her] employer' (25). De Certeau illustrates this: '*La perruque* may be as simple a matter as a secretary's writing a love letter on "company time" or as complex as a cabinetmaker's "borrowing" a lathe to make a piece of furniture for his living room' (25). Putting aside the gendering implicit in these examples,[1] de Certeau offers examples of tactics that, rather than confronting and opposing a 'strategic' form, take place in its blindspots. Such operations leave the 'proprietary power' relatively unscathed, while at the same time not complying to the spirit of their rationale: 'Accused of stealing or turning material to his [*sic*] own ends and using machines for his own profit, the worker who indulges in *la perruque* actually diverts time (not goods, since he uses only scraps) from the factory for work that is free, creative, and precisely not directed towards profit' (25).

Yet the example of *la perruque* also misguides the reader; it sets up the unhelpful expectation that 'resistance' is best thought of in terms of such minor victories against the system. A more 'de Certeauian' evocation of tactical practices in the factory is supplied by Robert Linhart describing his experience of working on an assembly line in a Citroën factory in Paris. Describing the relentless pace and repetition of the assembly line, Linhart contemplates the possibility of giving into its temporal logic: 'and suppose you said to yourself that nothing matters, that you need only get used to making the same movements in the same way in the same period of time, aspiring to no more than the placid perfection of a machine?' (Linhart 1981: 17). Linhart's response suggests an 'invisible' and bodily resistance:

> But life kicks against it and resists. The organism resists. The muscles resist. The nerves resist. Something, in the body and the head, braces itself against repetition and nothingness. Life shows itself in more rapid movements, an arm lowered at the wrong time, a slower step, a second's irregularity, an awkward gesture, getting ahead, slipping back, tactics at the station; everything, in the wretched square of resistance against the empty eternity of the work station, indicates there are still human inci-dents, even if they're minute; there's still time, even if it's dragged out to abnormal lengths. This clumsiness, this unnecessary movement away from routine, this sudden acceleration, this soldering gone wrong, that hand that has to do it all over again, the man who makes a face, the man who's out of step, this shows that life is hanging on. It is seen in every-thing that yells silently within every man on the line, 'I'm not a machine!'
>
> (17)

This long quote makes vivid, I think, some of the everyday practices that de Certeau recognizes as 'tactical' in form but which don't correspond to the subversive creativity that he also recognizes. This is tactics in its 'inert' and stubborn guise. This 'wretched square of resistance' insists that we see the resistance of the everyday as extending from subversive 'poaching' to a brute facticity of a body that is not a machine. Tiredness here would be 'resistant' to efficiency drives. For de Certeau, the everyday is 'far from being a local, and thus classifiable, revolt, it is a common and silent, almost sheeplike subversion – our own' (de Certeau 1984: 200). If such examples are coupled with the dreamy and stubborn reminiscences that accompany de Certeau's, Giard's and Mayol's accounts of walking, cooking, reading, drinking, etc. (remembering the town where you used to live while drinking a glass of wine, for instance), then the differences between strategies and tactics might be accounted for in relation to the temporal logics that they connect with.

Murmurs in the archive

For research in general the problem of the archive (constructed from materials from the present or the past) is both practical and theoretical: on the one hand a question of resources (what have I got?), on the other a question of method (what will I do?). To research the everyday intensifies these questions *ad infinitum*. In some ways everyday life is an archive 'yet to be catalogued', an archive that might also resist cataloguing. Inexhaustible and boundless, everyday life offers unmanageable resources that provide little guidance to the appropriateness of approach. Attempts to manage the everyday through systematic procedures and scientific attention have, perhaps, added to the 'secret' of everyday life by a studied avoidance of its mysteries. So far we have sought to track a tradition less encumbered by the desire to exhaust and manage its object. The evidence of this tradition consists of a range of imaginative responses to the archive that have resulted in a variety of projects: Georg Simmel's archive, made up of cell-like instances and micro-materials that find the general in the particular (small objects with big stories); Walter Benjamin's 'dialectical-images', constellations of new and old materials (emergent, outmoded, too early, too late), emerge from an archival practice of extraordinary diversity; for Surrealism, an archive based on collaged arrangements of the ordinary and the bizarre attempts to bring out the fantastic in the everyday; Mass-Observation's surreal empiricism gener-ates, potentially at least, an archive that could be as extensive as the everyday; and for Lefebvre the search for a differentiating totality leads him to treat the urban environment as an archive of 'moments' and forces.

Such a tradition does little to establish rules and protocols for an archival practice. Ambitious and unsystematic, this tradition, however, offers us one guiding principle: the everyday doesn't have a form of attention that is proper to it. Michel de Certeau's work is particularly useful for making this point vivid and for offering a perspective on the theoretical practices that make up this book. The theme of the proper, of propriety, falls, as we have seen, on the side of the strategic. Michel Foucault, more than anyone else, has insisted on a strategic characterization of archives and the dominating and disciplinary forms they have taken. He suggests that the 'operating model' of 'fact' collecting has been the Inquisition. He goes on to claim that, 'although it is true that, in becoming a technique for the empirical sciences, the investigation has detached itself from the inquisitorial procedure, in which it was historically rooted, the examination has remained extremely close to the disciplinary power that shaped it' (Foucault 1982: 226). Clearly indebted to Foucault, de Certeau's perspective, however, casts a more hopeful light on the archive; on the one hand it sees archival procedures as maintaining a disciplinary form, but on the other it sees the tactical aspects of the everyday as *irrepressible*. It is the tenacity of the everyday that allows archives to be a space for something more than just the systematic erasure of the everyday. I want to suggest that, following a tactical model of everyday life, de Certeau's work offers two positive ambitions for archival work. On the one hand it creates the possibility of putting together archives that don't work to erase the 'tactical' in the everyday (Mass-Observation might be understood in this way), archives that might allow the everyday a more productive forum for 'speaking for itself'. On the other it suggests the possibility that existing archives might be attended to by focusing on the everyday as a tenacious irruption and interruption within them, or as a potentiality to be extracted by a range of speculative approaches. On the one hand an archive of the everyday; on the other the everyday-ing of archives. To understand the archival ambitions of de Certeau's project two elements will need emphasizing: the psychoanalytic-like topography of the everyday; and the distinction between orality and writing.

In a historical study written in collaboration with Dominique Julia and Jacques Revel, de Certeau argues that the study of the popular culture or everyday life 'presupposes an unavowed operation': 'to conceal what it claims to show' (de Certeau *et al.* 1974: 121). De Certeau and his colleagues outline the practices of alteration and erasure that accompany a strategic and archival attention to popular culture. In their historical research into early accounts of popular culture, they find that it is at the 'very same time that street literature is pursued [by the police] with the utmost vigor that the scholars turn their attention with glee to popular books and contents' (123). Knowledge, de Certeau claims, 'remains linked to the power that authorizes it' (121). But the combination of academic cataloguing and political censorship is only one aspect of the strategic operations that greet popular culture. The other is a kind of 'rusticophilia', an approach 'which assumes the oppression of the very reality it objectifies and idealizes' (121).

This is an exoticism that erases as it celebrates – it turns the dialogic practices of the popular into a monologue. De Certeau, Julia and Revel's essay looks at historical moments in the eighteenth and nineteenth centuries when popular culture was simultaneously studied and suppressed, and suggests that more recent historical practices continue this suppression. What they find is a 'geography of the eliminated':

> Beyond the question of method and contents, beyond what it says, the measure of a work is what it keeps silent. And we must say that the scientific studies – and undoubtedly the works they highlight – include vast and strange expanses of silence. These blank spots outline a geography of the forgotten.
>
> (131)

Such practices of suppression do not mean the extinction of the everyday. As the quotation suggests, a signifying residue remains – even if it is only to be measured as an absence within the activity of suppressing it. Tactics, we must remember, are not to be found in some putative 'outside' to strategic operations. A different form of attention is needed that can listen to the silences and see the gaps within the archive as positive signs.

In a memorable passage from *The Practice of Everyday Life*, de Certeau evokes an everyday that is at one and the same time both absent and present in the archive:

> Was it fate? I remember the marvelous Shelburne Museum in Vermont where, in thirty-five houses of a reconstructed village, all the signs, tools and products of nineteenth-century everyday life teem; everything, from cooking utensils and pharmaceutical goods to weaving instruments, toilet articles, and children's toys can be found in profusion. The display includes innumerable familiar objects, polished, deformed, or made more beautiful by long use; everywhere there are as well the marks of the active hands and laboring or patient bodies for which these things composed the daily circuits, the fascinating presence of absences whose traces were everywhere. At least this village full of abandoned and salvaged objects drew one's attention, through them, to the ordered murmurs of a hundred past or possible villages, and by means of these imbricated traces one began to dream of countless combinations of existences.
>
> (1984: 21)

While the activities of use are missing, the marks they have left are not. These signs ('the presence of absences') are *just* audible to those who are prepared to 'dream of countless combinations of existences'.

De Certeau's 'everyday life' project is not simply mourning the impossibility of ever registering the everyday. Part of its power is that it continually evokes the everyday as a theoretical and practical possibility. The everyday that it does evoke is, however, never simply 'open' to easy registration: the subterranean, blind and opaque practices of everyday life are other to a field of pure visibility or strategic cataloguing. By looking at the way the everyday is evoked through the construction of new archives (the folk museum, for instance) and by looking at de Certeau's general poetics, we can see a practice that insists on the *speculative* possibilities of registering the everyday even in the least opportune environments. To see this more clearly I need to make more explicit something I have been implicitly arguing: that the relationships between the tactical and strategic forms of everyday life are being imagined as *something like* the relationship between the unconscious and the conscious 'modes' in Freudian psychoanalysis. I have already insisted that tactics draw on different temporalities from those that dominate the present and that this is analogous to the assertion in psychoanalysis of the continuation of the past (or pasts) in the present. Two other but related propositions central to psychoanalysis are crucial for an analogous understanding of the topography of everyday life and the formal aspects of strategies and tactics. The first is that consciousness cannot completely eradicate the unconscious. Freud's examples of parapraxes (slips of the tongue, bungled actions and so on) are evidence of the unconscious exerting itself on everyday consciousness. Indeed, the whole of psychoanalysis can be seen as explaining and treating the symptomatic irruptions of unconscious material as they press upon ordinary consciousness: obsessions, repetitions, remembered dreams, sublimations – not to mention the vast symptomology of the ordinary and extraordinary instances of neurosis and psychosis (for example, Freud 1977).

The second, and again related, proposition is that there is never the possibility of *direct* access to the unconscious in consciousness: *it* never declares itself but always inscribes itself in obscure and roundabout ways (dreams and neurotic symptoms, for example). Jean Laplanche and Jean-Bertrand Pontalis tell us that unconscious energies 'seek to re-enter consciousness and resume activity (the return of the repressed) but they can only gain access to the system Pcs.-Cs [Preconscious-Conscious] in compromise-formations after having undergone the distortions of censorship' (Laplanche and Pontalis 1983: 474). On the one hand then, we have unconscious energies insinuating themselves in numerous guises and disguises, operating various ruses, articulating themselves through condensations and displacements, mounting a range of attacks, and so on. On the other hand we have censorship, repression, revision and defence.

The usefulness of this 'model' for understanding the practices of strategies and tactics should be clear at a metaphorical level: de Certeau is imagining something similar happening in the everyday. The tactical side of everyday life continually irrupts in the strategic (as ruses, rebuses and creative assemblages); it can't be simply written off, or written out. Similarly, the tactical can't be attended to in a direct or unproblematic way: tactical forms are resistant to the ways of cataloguing and collecting that are the familiar staples of archival work. Strategic archival work, de Certeau would argue, is an activity of censorship, of interpretative defence, of compromise. The challenge then of de Certeau's work is to provide an archival practice that allows such 'tactical' material to proliferate, a practice that can 'listen' to the everyday and hear there the tales of repressed activity.

Psychoanalysis, though, is not easily translated into other situations and de Certeau, though he frequently refers to Freud, does not offer anything that would count as a systematic application of psychoanalysis to the everyday. For one thing psychoanalysis wouldn't fit easily with the 'subject-less' account that de Certeau wants to give. For another the everyday doesn't make for favourable circumstances to translate the diagnostic mechanisms so central to psychoanalysis (the everyday as neurotic or psychotic). Perhaps we can simply say that de Certeau hijacks the *form* of psychoanalysis without insisting on its content. Psychoanalytic form, I would argue, is crucial to understanding de Certeau's work even if it does nothing more than allow us to think our way out of a purely physical understanding of the topography of strategies and tactics. A psychoanalytic topography is one that can't be understood in purely visual or physical terms: strategies and tactics, like consciousness and unconsciousness, take place simultaneously, 'under the same roof' so to speak. While Freud battled with the problem of how to attend to the topography of the psychoanalytic subject, making use of various models (neurological, economic, etc.) and inventive analogies (children's writing toys, for example), we can limit ourselves to one intuition from Freud's 'second topography' where 'the systems are pictured as relatively autonomous persons-within-the-person' (Laplanche and Pontalis 1983: 452). Such a topography describes two radically different registers (split and relatively autonomous) that, in most situations, are hardly able to recognize one another, yet most of the time 'rub along' together (so to speak). It is the radical formal differences between the two worlds that de Certeau insists on when he describes the relationships between tactics and strategies in terms of 'otherness'. Strategy, he writes, 'is an effort to delimit one's place in a world bewitched by the invisible powers of the Other' (1984: 36). A tactic 'insinuates itself in the other's place' (xix); its space 'is the space of the other' (37).

The Practice of Everyday Life operates across another 'non-oppositional binary' that metaphorically continues to figure strategic and tactical operations. The metaphorics of 'speaking' and 'writing' are crucial to an understanding of the archive (its limits and possibilities). Voices (the 'voices' of the 'people') are, for de Certeau, strategically reconfigured within a scriptural economy (writing). By 'scriptural economy' de Certeau doesn't mean writing in general, but particular kinds of scriptural registering (statistical analysis of consumption practices, for instance [1984: 34]). Writing, in this metaphorical sense, is strategic. Jeremy Ahearne gives a useful account of the kinds of 'writing' techniques that would count as part of a 'scriptural economy': 'these techniques comprise for example operations of recording, transcription, registering, stocking and standardization, as well as the propagation and dissemination of information' (Ahearne 1995: 53). While at times de Certeau writes as if all writing is the inscription of the 'law', this needs to be understood in relation to a metaphorical understanding of language practices as social techniques related to strategic and tactical forms. Too literal a take on this division would assume that the parents' command to 'sit up straight' falls on the side of orality, while the child's scrawling writing falls on the side of the 'scriptural economy'.

Orality in de Certeau's work is given a historical depth through his work on religious history and early forms of ethnography. De Certeau's historical work centres on orality in a number of forms: the heretical speech of the possessed and religious mystics (de Certeau 1992, 2000); the policing of popular speech forms (patois) (de Certeau *et al.* 1975); and the way that oral forms 'possess' the writings of early ethnographers (de Certeau 1988: 209–43). In the two volumes of *The Practice of Everyday Life*, de Certeau uses 'speech' to relate implicitly to this work, but also to invoke the 'capture of speech' that he witnessed emerging and being recaptured in May 1968. Within the milieu of 1960s and 1970s French intellectual culture, 'speech' also held particular resonance. For instance, Julia Kristeva's *Revolution in Poetic Language* gives an account of a pre-figural or pre-symbolic language that is seen as 'analogous only to vocal or kinetic rhythm' (Kristeva 1984: 26). For Kristeva such rhythms could be found in the writing of avant-gardist poets such as Stéphane Mallarmé. Another example, and one close to de Certeau, would be the psychoanalyst Jacques Lacan who was known for an idiosyncratic speaking style, which de Certeau describes as a 'speaking body': 'Coughing, slightly grumbling, clearing the throat – like tatoos [*sic*] on the process of phonation – punctuate the chain of words and indicate all their secret of being "for the other"' (de Certeau 1986: 50). Such language practices were seen as offering a privileged access to more somatic and repressed aspects of signification: 'speech' in this sense tends to fall on the side of the unconscious. For de Certeau, as for Kristeva, the 'speaking voice' is to be found not only in actual speech: 'the literary text is modified by becoming the ambiguous depth in which sounds that cannot be reduced to a meaning move about' (de Certeau 1984: 162).

This catalogue of 'speech acts' is not intended to do much more than indicate the density that the terms 'speech', 'voice' and 'orality' have for de Certeau and the way that orality potentially extends the archive beyond any notion of straightforward empirical examples of speech. The non-oppositional division between writing and speech is not, however, without its problems. At first it is easily understood within the formal logic offered by strategies and tactics. For instance in describing the way that media forms can be seen as part of a 'scriptural economy' (even though they take oral forms), de

Certeau writes about the way that the 'voice of the people' 'is "recorded" in every imaginable way, normalized, audible everywhere, but only when it has been "cut" (as one "cuts a record"), and thus mediated by radio, television, or the phonograph record, and "cleaned up" by the techniques of diffusion' (1984: 132). If media forms can be seen as tending towards the strategic, then the tactical forms within speech can be seen as the first casualty of such mediation. What de Certeau seems to be referring to is a whole host of different practices that could be seen as cleaning up speech: from the censoring of 'dirty talk', or the control of who speaks and when, to the electronic smoothing-out (balancing) of speech through sound production (erasing click-ings, wheezings, slurpings and the like).

What is more confusing is the topographical relationship between speech and writing. De Certeau's negotiation of the binaries 'voice' and 'writing' appears contradictory. On the one hand 'voice' does not represent an outside to scriptural systems: 'These voices can no longer be heard except within the interior of the scriptural systems where they recur. They move about, like dancers, passing lightly through the field of the other' (1984: 131). This, for de Certeau, is due to the historical circumstances of mass mediation, in which the 'mass media' (TV, radio, etc.) provide one set of powerful examples. Other examples would include the regularization of language (Standard English, for example) through mass education, a regularization that is seen as de-corporealizing language. Such a historical saturation of language practices by strategic forms results in a situation where there is no ' "pure" voice, because it is always determined by a system (whether social, familial, or other) and codified by a way of receiving it' (132). Seen in this way the 'voice' (or at least a tacticalaspect of it) is equivalent to the 'speech of the body': a 'wild orchestration' that can never be 'pure' but can only 'insinuate itself into the text as a mark or trace, an effect or metonymy of the body' (155). But de Certeau also conceives of the 'voice' as precisely characterized by being outside scriptural systems: 'The place from which one speaks is outside the scriptural enterprise. The uttering occurs outside the places in which systems of statements are composed' (158). Whether or not de Certeau has moved into another mode of metaphorics (from historical to phenomenological, for instance) the inconsistencies are confusing. In understanding 'wild' sounds as the speech that can't be managed by the scriptural, de Certeau's argument might also suggest that they cannot reside there either:

> The name 'wild' both creates and defines what the scriptural economy situates outside of itself. It is moreover immediately given its essential predicate: the wild is transitory; it marks itself (by smudges, lapses, etc.) but it does not write itself. It alters a place (it disturbs), but it does not establish a place.
>
> (1984: 155)

These are difficult waters to navigate and the abstract prose of de Certeau's arguments doesn't make rigorous consistencies the norm. Seen in literal terms this contradiction does pose some serious problems when considering the archive. On the one hand we have the possibility of archives at least bearing the traces of the tactical side of life; on the other, orality is hard to imagine at all within writing. De Certeau, in the end, privileges the possibility of registering 'voices' within 'texts', and partly this is because the project of constructing a general poetics of the practices of everyday life is itself dedicated to a practice of listening, inscribing and describing. De Certeau's psychoanalytic topography allows for orality to be both inside and outside at the same time, to be repressed and censored and also to appear as a symptom (a mark, a trace). The ethnographer of the everyday, like the psychoanalyst, conducts a practice of listening.

This positive practice of listening and inscribing is vividly demonstrated in the second volume of *The Practice of Everyday Life*. In Luce Giard's account of cooking, 'speech archives' are given priority, precisely because they can register what can't be registered within Giard's 'own' writing practice. Both Giard's 'Doing-Cooking' and Mayol's 'Living' consist of ethnographic accounts that weave together description and the quotation of voices elicited from informal interviews, and both include a separate section that consists of a 'complete' transcript of one of these conversations. Luce Giard writes about the nature of these 'interviews' that were conducted for the cooking project by Marie Ferrier:

> They had as a goal neither to record opinion frequencies nor to consti-
> tute a representative statistical sample, but rather to allow us to hear
> women's voices; they talk about their way of doing-cooking, of orga-
> nizing this work, of living and experiencing it – this will give us a way
> of knowing their own language, their words, and even the inflections
> in their voices, even the rhythm of their speech. These interviews aimed
> neither to sort out underlying images nor to reveal unconscious roots,
> nor to define and classify attitude types. Their sole intention was to
> *hear women speak*: to talk about the very activity that is generally accorded
> no attention.
>
> (de Certeau *et al.* 1998: 159–60)

It is in this attempt to 'hear women speak' that the decision was made to include an 'uncut' transcript. This doesn't mean that the voices that are woven more thoroughly into the text are compromised to the point that their orality is lost or that the 'uncut' transcripts are 'free' from strategic forms: the 'quotation of voices mark themselves on an everyday prose that can only produce some of their effects – in the form of statements and practices' (de Certeau 1984: 164). In Giard's text the voices of the 'interviewees' aren't subjected to a rigorous and measuring scrutiny. What is insisted upon is the intractability of the voice:

> These voices, whose faces will remain unknown to us, make up a melodious polyphony. They are diverse, living voices that approve of, are moved, and remember themselves; voices that regret, answer, and contradict themselves. They are voices that talk simply about ordinary practices with everyday words, women's voices that talk about the life of people and things. Voices.
>
> (de Certeau *et al.* 1998: 161)

The rhythm, melodies and wild orchestrations of speech and gesture are foregrounded in a tactical reversal of usual ethnographic practices. The materials that make up Mayol's and Giard's project are not wholly different from the materials that are included in other sociological and ethnographic texts, but what is becoming different is the relationship of the authors to these materials: Giard's voice starts to take on a singularity (rather than a generality) and begins to sound like 'one of many' voices in the text, rather than a strategic 'master-voice'. The voices of the 'Kitchen Women Nation' are imagined sounding alongside her own voice which, instead of framing these other voices, provides a kind of 'harmonic descant' for them.

The attempt to make 'polyphonic' (multi-voiced) texts suggests a writing and research practice that would embrace 'artistic' forms both in content and style. The polyphony of *The Practice of Everyday Life* (the first volume) can be seen in the absolute abundance of 'quotations' from all kinds of sources – games and stories as much as historical and sociological accounts. It might also 'read' more easily as novelistic than as a consistent and deductive argument about everyday life. De Certeau's practice offers an archival practice based in heterological sources that doesn't reduce these sources to illustrations of theoretical arguments, but uses the sources to provide and provoke theory. Faced with an archive of unmanageable proportions (novels, ethnographies, sociologies, police reports, interviews, conversations, diaries, newspapers and so on), the researcher of everyday life is faced with the demand to find ways of 'listening' that are capable of hearing the tactical where it can. The two ambitions (to produce an archive of the everyday and to 'everyday' existing archives) become one: a practice of listening to the murmurs of everyday life. Michel de Certeau's general poetics of everyday life is intended to provide ways of doing this (of operating in the archive), or at least to make a start at listening to the practices of everyday life. Its success or failure should be judged in these terms.

Foregrounding the everyday

De Certeau's general poetics of everyday life evidences a tension implicit in the desire to produce 'a science of singularity' (1984: ix): on the one hand the generality of a science, and on the other the particularity of the actual. This tension isn't new and links de Certeau with the likes of Simmel, Benjamin and Freud. The problem of finding generalizable meaning in cultural practices that are only understandable and analysable within the most particular of circumstances is the problem of attending to culture. The example of psycho-analysis is again useful. Freud's understanding of the dream departed from tradition because it refused to 'treat dreams as a kind of cryptography in which each sign can be translated into another sign having a known meaning, in accordance with a fixed key' (Freud 1976: 171). Freud maintained that 'all the material making up the content of a dream is in some way derived from experience, that is to say, has been reproduced or remembered in the dream' (69) and insisted that meaning is only recoverable by attending to the particular histories of dreamers. In this way Freud refuses to produce a *general interpretation* of dreams (despite the title of his book). Freud's theory of dreams is a theory of interpretation determined by the *particularity* of the circumstances of the dreamer. It too is a 'science of the singular'. What Freud offers instead of a general interpretation of dreams is the investigation of the conditions that make the interpretation of dreams possible. Faced with the particularity of the dream's meaning Freud produces a *general poetics of dreaming*. It is this general poetics, whereby the dream can be understood in relation to a series of operations and functions (condensation, displacement, revision, wish-fulfilment and so on) that makes it 'a science of the singular'. It provides the conditions of possibility for making singularity understand-able; it provides the tools for recognizing the dream as singular and a way of attending to its *formal* generalities. In other words Freud is interested in finding the *peculiar logic* of dreaming, just as de Certeau is interested in finding the *peculiar logic* of everyday practices.

A general poetics of everyday life is a science of the singular in that it allows for the differentiation of 'the relationships that link everyday pursuits to particular circumstances' (de Certeau 1984: ix). De Certeau's project of theorizing everyday life attempts to lay the groundwork for understanding these relationships. But we shouldn't assume that this project was completed in de Certeau's lifetime, or that it is a project that *could* be easily completed. After both volumes of *The Practice of Everyday Life* had been published, de Certeau and Giard could still write,

> We know poorly the types of operations at stake in ordinary practices, their registers and their combinations, because our instruments of analysis, modeling and formalization were constructed for other objects

and with other aims. The essential analytic work, which remains to be done, will have to revolve around the subtle combinatory set of types of operations and registers, that stages and activates a making-do, right here and now, which is a singular action linked to one situation, certain circumstances, particular actors.

(de Certeau and Giard 1998: 256)

De Certeau's work should serve as a precaution when it comes to evaluating or interpreting the everyday: as in Freud, a fixed key that could unlock the puzzle of the everyday needs to be refused. The desire to produce a catalogue of minor subversions (ripped jeans, skateboarding and so on) needs to be replaced by a form of attention that necessitates the invention of a 'tool-kit' that might allow the everyday to be heard, not as background noise, but as foregrounded voice. Or rather, what is needed are 'tool-kits' that can perceive different registers of a polyphonic everyday. The singularity, the here-and-now-ness of everyday culture, requires invention in a variety of ways. It requires invention both on the everyday and in the everyday: a poetics of everyday life. De Certeau's work serves to sketch out an ambitious language for making the everyday vivid, of rescuing it from an undifferentiating scrutiny. The language that de Certeau supplies can be seen as a series of fluid and purposefully unstable categories (space and place, tactics and strategies, speaking and writing, and so on). But these language tools are also signs of passionate intensities – 'opaqueness', 'stubbornness', 'poachings', 'ruses', 'insinuations' and so on – that point to practices that swarm and proliferate as soon as the everyday becomes foregrounded.

To see *The Practice of Everyday Life* and its related texts as setting out a position in regard to the field of political action is to miss both the modesty and the ambitiousness of the project. The tactical activities that de Certeau sees as so essential to everyday life are a mixture of creative moments of getting by (making the best of things) and a host of stubborn insistencies (the past, the body, the unconscious). To imagine a transformatory politics based on the attempts to describe this everyday life is restrictive. In an effort to avoid misrecognizing de Certeau's poetics as a politics of cultural practices I have emphasized those aspects of 'tactical' life that can't easily be recuperated for an 'up-beat' politics of culture. In doing so I have underplayed aspects of the work that do celebrate the oppositional character in everyday life, and might provide some of the forms for intervention and transformation. De Certeau's project of foregrounding the everyday can be understood as a phenomenology of everyday life that takes as its precondition the possibility of discovering the peculiar logic at work in everyday practices. In this it is a massively ambitious project that demands a subtle and imaginative sensibility from those who would follow in his wake. Yet there is also a fundamental modesty at work here when it comes to suggesting actual social and cultural changes. De Certeau's practice was never simply limited to supplying theoretical attention to the everyday. As a public intellectual he continually worked with government agencies in the area of cultural policy. But if this is where we might expect to find a more resolutely 'political' orientation towards everyday life, de Certeau once again frustrates expectation. At the heart of the project is an absolute refusal to speak in the name of a vanguard that would lead the 'people' to their liberation or even betterment. Theoretically de Certeau staked his faith on the tenacious otherness of everyday life. The ambitiousness of his project was in finding ways of foregrounding this otherness. The modesty of his approach to cultural policy was determined by a similar desire. As far as this goes, a 'politics' of everyday life would simply be premature. As such his cultural policy was simply oriented to foregrounding the everyday. Only *after* the everyday is allowed to emerge would something like a politics of the everyday become possible.

For de Certeau 'the management of a society leaves in its midst an enormous "remainder"' (1997b: 134). This remainder, 'an ebb and flow of muffled voices on the architects' blueprints' (134), is the culture that de Certeau wants to see take centre stage. Such culture is evident in a variety of forms. The residual practices that 'pertain to collapsed or abandoned systems' ('certain gestures, certain objects, expressions, birthdays, and perfumes') act like punctuation 'in the text of daily activities' (1997a: 172). But alongside these epochal residues is an inventive emergent culture that, in France in the 1970s, de Certeau saw as lacking a form of representation:

> Becoming increasingly opaque, a marginalized life has no escape in our system of representations. Rural areas and cities – and not just labor unions or universities – are populated with silent subjects. And it is not because they lack ideas or criteria! But their convictions are no longer affiliations.
>
> (1997a: 9)

What is being described is a culture that can't be expressed within the cultural forms of 'democratic' capitalism (including, and perhaps especially, their oppositional forms). In a report prepared for the French Ministry of Culture and published as *L'ordinaire de la communication* in 1983, Luce Giard and Michel de Certeau combine description with specific recommendations for a *politics of possibility*. The report doesn't offer a 'revolutionary' or 'oppositional' form of politics; rather it offers a series of modest and 'everyday' proposals. In an article published at the same time as this report (and clearly 'part' of the report) they mention an example that seems as vivid as it is 'ordinary':

> In a declining industrial region, the Lorraine Coeur d'Acier station [a local radio station] established the bias of live broadcasting, each person

being able to have access to the airwaves by coming in to the studio or by calling in . . . The experiment acted as a revelation or a spur: someone astonishingly discovered that his or her coworker secretly wrote poems, and someone else confessed to being an amateur painter . . . A steelworker, overwhelmed by the experience summed it up beautifully: 'There, on the radio, it was possible to say, you'd say things to yourself, and you wanted to say it. It was possible to send words down into homes and after a while the listener would become the actor and inevitably he or she sent the words back up . . . It was a reflection of life – life is a kind of disorder, freedom is a kind of disorder.' And he concluded marvelously: 'Now I have a certain rage inside me. I want to write with an "I," and on all subjects, that way no one will stop me anymore. I want to do it.'

(de Certeau and Giard 1998: 255)

If the promotion of such speech events is a politics of everyday life, it isn't about having certain ends in mind, but about generating beginnings. Such modest and ambitious everyday politics makes connections with the project of Mass-Observation and the possibilities of 'speaking for yourself' (the radio programme mentioned above was called 'Listen to Yourself'). The cultural politics of everyday life that emerges is one that both taps into the energies present in the everyday and uses them to transform it. Such a 'politics' (if it is one) doesn't offer solutions, nor does it offer to overthrow oppression. This is a heuristic, experimental politics that puts its faith in the everyday as a means for its own transformation.

Note

1   An 'indifference' to gender is evident in much of de Certeau's work. Luce Giard's contribution to the project ('Doing Cooking') can therefore be seen as both an intervention in the project and as a partial corrective to this indifference.

Chapter 9

POSTSCRIPT
Everyday life and the future of cultural studies

IN THE WORK OF MASS-OBSERVATION, Benjamin, Simmel, Surrealism, Lefebvre and de Certeau, the everyday evidences a range of temporalities that makes it impossible to think of 'modernity' as a straightforward narrative. Everyday modernity begins to look like a patchwork of different times and spaces. I began this book by sketching an account of modernity as a contradictory picture of the everyday as both boring and mysterious, as both disconcerting and routine. The theories of everyday life we have looked at extend and deepen this sense of ambiguity. The everyday as poverty and oppression vies with the everyday as culturally rich and animated by festive forces. There is no comfort here for anyone wanting an 'object' simply to celebrate or condemn.

As we have moved from the beginning of the twentieth century to its end, the everyday, for cultural theory, has moved in and out of focus. The reasons for this are no doubt complexly related to cultural life: we have seen, for instance, the everyday come into sharp relief at moments of social and cultural crisis such as May 1968. But the vividness of the everyday is not simply related to the events of the social; it is animated by a will, a struggle to rescue the everyday from conformity. The question that the everyday makes vivid for cultural theory is the question of how to attend to the social. From Simmel onwards, this question has foregrounded (in my account at least) a notion of form, of arrangement, of aesthetic procedures, either explicitly or implicitly. The everyday makes the particularity of lived culture inescapable. But unless this is to result in an endless cataloguing, an infinite inventory, then forms must be found to make such particularity legible, meaningful or just simply productive. The tradition that this book has narrated offers a range of aesthetics for 'registering the unregistered':[1]

dialectical approaches that reveal the general in the particular; explosive juxta-positions of disparate material; productive assemblages of related phenomena; a general poetics of the singularity of living. Perhaps then, the everyday is the name that cultural theory might give to a form of attention that attempts to animate the heterogeneity of social life, the name for an activity of finding meaning in an impossible diversity.

Everyday life theory in an international frame

The everyday life theory that I have considered here needs to be recognized as operating within an international frame. This, as should be clear, does not give it a global truth; far from it. The work I've been considering is tied to specific geographies as much as specific histories. Yet these geographies are not simply gripped in the hold of what might be considered eccentric *national* cultural traditions. Lefebvre for instance is clearly relating the everyday life of postwar France to the moments of decolonization and what he came to think of as the reconfiguring of colonialism as a form of neo-colonialism. In Kristin Ross's 'Lefebvrian' book *Fast Cars, Clean Bodies: Decolonization and the Reordering of French Culture*, the everyday life of French national culture rever-berates in relation to these more global considerations. In a fascinating discussion of 1950s' French 'hygiene' adverts (for washing machines, fridges, polish and the like), Ross draws out a set of housekeeping tropes that would also be used to refer to the Algerian war (Ross 1995: 71–122). Housekeeping, as a familiar, domestic and everyday realm, echoes with the same language as France's attempt to 'keep house' (to keep its colonies in 'order'). To make the leap from 'torture' to 'shampoo' (108), and to insist on the histor-ical actuality of this relationship, suggests a historiographic practice akin to Martha Rosler's photomontages, which insert the Vietnam war into well-heeled, Western, 'colour-supplement' homes (figure 11). Rosler's photo-montage series, titled 'Bringing the War Home', demands that we read the outrages of neo-colonial wars in the domestic environments of Western everyday life. Such an orientation to the everyday has stressed a reading of commodity culture within the terms of global structures, for instance, Anne McClintock's reading of 'everyday' Victorian commodities (soap, toothpaste, biscuits, etc.) as registering the complex desires and fears of colonial attitudes (McClintock 1995).

In a recent book entitled *History's Disquiet: Modernity, Cultural Practice, and the Question of Everyday Life*, Harry Harootunian makes a number of crucial points that suggest the fruitfulness of insisting on cross-cultural figuring of everyday life. For one thing the everyday allows for a nuanced and complex account of the way 'modernity' articulates itself in different geographical settings (his continued point of reference is Japan between the two world

Figure 11   Red Strip Kitchen, from 'Bringing the War Home: House Beautiful' –
photomontage series by Martha Rosler (1967–72). With kind permission from
the artist

wars). In this regard modernity is the *global* condition of capitalism's fero-
cious success. Everyday life, however, becomes the cultural *experience* of
modernity that is never simply equivalent to what might seem to be the
homogenizing ambitions of capitalism. For one thing everyday life becomes
an arena for cultural survivals and revivals, the reconfiguring of specific traditions under the domain of the modern. In Harootunian's words:

> If modernity was driven by the desiring machine of capitalism, promising
> to install its regime of production and consumption everywhere, the
> everyday, serving as a minimal unification of the present and signaling

the level of lived experience and reproduction would, in fact, negotiate the compelling demands of homogeneity through the mediations of a past that constantly stood in a tense, often antagonistic, relationship to the present of the new.

(Harootunian 2000: 63)

It is precisely by bringing together the global generality of modernization with the specificity of *regional* and *historical* cultural continuities and discontinuities, that the everyday is seen as a particularly appropriate perspective for cross-cultural studies of modernity. For Harootunian it allows the measure of the 'not quite the same' to be taken across different cultures. In other words a focus on everyday life would insist on the uneven experiences of modernity on an international and intranational scale (for instance, the different everydays of rural and urban communities).

Harootunian's *History's Disquiet* is mainly a theoretical book. He considers some of the same theorists as I've considered here (specifically Lefebvre, Benjamin and Simmel). But Harootunian also points to a range of Japanese intellectuals working in the 1930s who insisted that philosophy should become 'everyday'. The writing of philosophers such as Tosaka Jun, Harootunian tells us, anticipates the thought of Lefebvre in crucial ways. Yet within Anglophone cultural studies it is the name of Lefebvre that is known, not that of Tosaka Jun. This example, of course, needs multiplying and extending globally. 'Non-Western' cultural theory remains invisible. If the project of everyday life studies is to go in search of the hidden and the ignored, then, this should apply to its theoretical resources as much as to the cultural practices it pursues. In this sense one *direction* that everyday life theory would want to take would be geographical: to cast the everyday within an international frame of theories and practices.

The everyday is not, as we have seen, simply reducible to the significations of material culture or the characteristics of national cultures. The everyday, in important and challenging ways (especially in the work of de Certeau), is about the density of cultural life and its refusal to be contained by the parameters of what would pass for 'national life'. This doesn't mean that ideas of national culture aren't going to be important, merely that they wouldn't be the end point of everyday life studies. In many ways the idea of the national is going to be the ground that a study of the everyday seeks to recode and pluralize. As far as this goes a cross-cultural approach to everyday life might start, not from the perspective of known and identifiable cultural differences, but (perhaps more polemically these days) from a sense of a common global 'invisibility' to everyday life. Thus an attempt to foreground the murmuring voices of the everyday could (as in de Certeau's work) make connections between (for instance) peasant cultures in Brazil and North African factory workers in France (de Certeau 1984: 15–17). This is not to suggest a global sameness to the everyday, but to map out formal contiguities across specific socio-cultural situations.

Finally then I'd like to think that if a cross-cultural attention to the everyday keeps alive something of the problematic spirit that is the subject of this book it may well provide an opportunity to *re-imagine* cultural studies. In other words it might help to re-animate cultural studies in imaginative ways. To adopt something of the inventiveness of these approaches, as well as to extend 'everyday life theory' in more international ways, seems to me to be a worthwhile ambition.

Note

1   Thanks to Stephen Clucas for this formulation.

Bibliography

Adam, Barbara (1995) *Timewatch: The Social Analysis of Time*, Cambridge: Polity Press.

Ades, Dawn (1986a) 'Photography and the Surrealist Text', in Rosalind Krauss and Jane Livingston, *L'Amour Fou: Photography and Surrealism*, London: Arts Council of Great Britain, pp. 153–89.

—— (1986b) *Photomontage*, London: Thames & Hudson.

Adler, Kathleen (1989) 'The Suburban, the Modern and "Une Dame de Passy"', *The Oxford Art Journal*, 12.1: 3–13.

Adorno, Theodor (1980) 'Letters to Walter Benjamin' [1935–8], translated by Harry Zohn, in Theodor Adorno, Walter Benjamin, Ernst Bloch, Bertolt Brecht and Georg Lukács, *Aesthetics and Politics*, London: Verso, pp. 110–33.

—— (1992) *Notes to Literature: Volume II*, New York: Columbia University Press.

Adorno, Theodor, Benjamin, Walter, Bloch, Ernst, Brecht, Bertolt and Lukács, Georg (1980) *Aesthetics and Politics*, London: Verso.

Ahearne, Jeremy (1995) *Michel de Certeau: Interpretation and its Other*, Cambridge: Polity Press.

Anderson, Perry (1979) *Considerations of Western Marxism*, London: Verso.

—— (1992a) *A Zone of Engagement*, London: Verso.

—— (1992b) 'Components of a National Culture' [1968], in Perry Anderson, *English Questions*, London: Verso, pp. 48–104.

Aragon, Louis (1987) *Paris Peasant* [1926], translated by Simon Watson Taylor, London: Picador.

Ardagh, John (1977) *The New France: A Society in Transition 1945–1977*, Harmondsworth: Penguin.

Axelrod, Charles D. (1994) 'Towards an Appreciation of Simmel's Fragmentary Style' [1977], in David Frisby, ed. *Georg Simmel: Critical Assessments*, 3 vols., London and New York: Routledge, section 5, number 41: 32–45.

Bakhtin, Mikhail (1984) *Rabelais and his World*, translated by Hélène Iswolsky, Bloomington: Indiana University Press.

Barthes, Roland (1973) *Mythologies* [1957], translated by Annette Lavers, London: Granada.

—— (1983) *The Fashion System* [first published in 1967 as *Le système de la mode*], translated by Matthew Ward and Richard Howard, Berkeley, Los Angeles and London: University of California Press.

Bataille, Georges (1985) *Visions of Excess: Selected Writing 1927–1939*, translated by Allan Stoekl, Manchester: Manchester University Press.

—— (1991) *The Accursed Share: Volume I*, translated by Robert Hurley, New York: Zone Books.

Bataille, Georges, Leiris, Michel, Grialue, Marcel *et al.* (1995) *Encyclopaedia Acephalica*, translated by Iain White, Dominic Faccini, Annette Michelson *et al.*, London: Atlas.

Battersby, Christine (1991) 'Situating the Aesthetic: A Feminist Defence', in Andrew Benjamin and Peter Osborne, eds., *Thinking Art: Beyond Traditional Aesthetics*, London: ICA, pp. 31–43.

Baudelaire, Charles (1964) *The Painter of Modern Life and Other Essays*, translated by Jonathan Mayne, New York: Da Capo.

Bauman, Zygmunt (1989) *Modernity and the Holocaust*, Cambridge: Polity Press.

Benedict, Ruth (1989) *Patterns of Culture* [1934], Boston: Houghton Mifflin.

Benjamin, Andrew (1989) 'Traditions and Experience: Walter Benjamin's "On Some Motifs in Baudelaire"', in Andrew Benjamin, ed. *The Problems of Modernity: Adorno and Benjamin*, London and New York: Routledge, pp. 122–40.

Benjamin, Andrew and Osborne, Peter, eds. (1991) *Thinking Art: Beyond Traditional Aesthetics*, London: ICA.

—— (1994) *Walter Benjamin's Philosophy: Destruction and Experience*, London and New York: Routledge.

Benjamin, Walter (1982) *Illuminations*, translated by Harry Zohn, London: Fontana.

—— (1983a) *Charles Baudelaire: A Lyric Poet in the Era of High Capitalism*, translated by Harry Zohn, London: Verso.

—— (1983b) *Understanding Brecht*, translated by Anna Bostock, London: Verso.

—— (1985) *One Way Street and Other Writings*, translated by Edmund Jephcott and Kingsley Shorter, London: Verso.

—— (1989) 'Konvolut N: Re the Theory of Knowledge, Theory of Progress', in Gary Smith, ed. *Benjamin: Philosophy, Aesthetics, History*, Chicago: The University of Chicago Press, pp. 43–83.

—— (1998) 'An outsider attracts attention' in Siegfried Kracauer, *The Salaried Masses: Duty and Distraction in Weimar Germany*, translated by Quintin Hoare, London: pp 109–114.

—— (1999) *The Arcades Project*, translated by Howard Eiland and Kevin McLaughlin, Cambridge, Mass.: Harvard University Press.

Bennett, Tony (1998) *Culture: A Reformer's Science*, London: Sage.

Bentley, Nancy (1995) *The Ethnography of Manners: Hawthorne, James and Wharton*, Cambridge: Cambridge University Press.

Berman, Marshall (1983) *All That is Solid Melts into Air: The Experience of Modernity*, London: Verso.

Biernacki, Richard (1994) 'Time Cents: The Monetization of the Workday in Comparative Perspective', in Roger Friedaland and Deirdre Boden, eds. *NowHere: Space, Time and Modernity*, Berkeley: University of California Press, pp. 61–94.

Blanchot, Maurice (1981) *The Gaze of Orpheus and other Literary Essays*, translated by Lydia Davis, New York: Station Hill.

—— (1987) 'Everyday Speech' [1959], translated by Susan Hanson, *Yale French Studies*, 73: 12–20.

Bloch, Ernst (1989) *The Utopian Function of Art and Literature: Selected Essays*, translated by Jack Zipes and Frank Mecklenburg, Cambridge, Mass.: The MIT Press.

Boym, Svetlana (1994) *Common Places: Mythologies of Everyday Life in Russia*, Cambridge, Mass.: Harvard University Press.

Brecht, Bertolt (1980) 'Against Georg Lukács', translated by Stuart Hood, in Theodor Adorno, Walter Benjamin, Ernst Bloch, Bertolt Brecht and Georg Lukács, *Aesthetics and Politics*, London: Verso, pp. 68–85.

Breton, André (1924) 'Manifesto of Surrealism', reprinted in Breton (1972a).

—— (1935) 'Speech to the Congress of Writers', reprinted in Breton (1972a).

—— (1960) *Nadja* [1928], translated by Richard Howard, New York: Grove Press.

—— (1972a) *Manifestoes of Surrealism*, translated by Richard Seaver and Helen R. Lane, Ann Arbor: University of Michigan Press.

—— (1972b) *Surrealism and Painting*, translated by Simon Watson Taylor, New York: Harper & Row.

Brodersen, Momme (1996) *Walter Benjamin: A Biography*, London: Verso.

Buchanan, Ian (1997) 'De Certeau and Cultural Studies', *New Formations*, 31: 175–88.

—— (2000) *Michel de Certeau: Cultural Theorist*, London, Thousand Oaks, New Delhi: Sage.

Buck-Morss, Susan (1986) 'The Flaneur, the Sandwichman and the Whore: The Politics of Loitering', *New German Critique*, 39: 99–140.

—— (1989) *The Dialectics of Seeing: Walter Benjamin and the Arcades Project*, Cambridge, Mass.: The MIT Press.

Bürger, Peter (1984) *Theory of the Avant-Garde*, translated by Michael Shaw, Manchester: Manchester University Press.

—— (1991) 'Aporias of Modern Aesthetics', in Andrew Benjamin and Peter Osborne, eds. *Thinking Art: Beyond Traditional Aesthetics*, London: ICA, pp. 3–15.

Burke, Peter (1994) *Popular Culture in Early Modern Europe*, Aldershot: Scholar Press.

Caillois, Roger (1959) *Man and the Sacred*, translated by Meyer Barash, Glencoe, Ill.: Free Press.

Calder, Angus and Sheridan, Dorothy, eds. (1985) *Speak for Yourself: A Mass-Observation Anthology 1937–1949*, Oxford: Oxford University Press.

Chafe, William H. (1986) *The Unfinished Journey: America Since World War II*, Oxford: Oxford University Press.

Chaney, David and Pickering, Michael (1986) 'Authorship in Documentary: Sociology as an Art Form in Mass-Observation', in John Corner, ed. *Documentary and the Mass Media*, London: Edward Arnold.

Chtcheglov, Ivan (1981) 'Formulary for a New Urbanism' [1953], in Knabb (1981), pp. 1–4.

Clark, T. J. (1985) *The Painting of Modern Life: Paris in the Art of Manet and his Followers*, London: Thames & Hudson.

Clarke, John, Critcher, Chas and Johnson, Richard, eds. (1979) *Working Class Culture: Studies in History and Theory*, London: Hutchinson.

Clifford, James (1986) 'Introduction: Partial Truths' in James Clifford and George E. Marcus, eds. *Writing Culture: The Poetics and Politics of Ethnography*, Berkeley: University of California Press, pp. 1–26.

—— (1988) *The Predicament of Culture: Twentieth-Century Ethnography, Literature, and Art*, Cambridge, Mass.: Harvard University Press.

Clifford, James and Marcus, George E. eds. (1986) *Writing Culture: The Poetics and Politics of Ethnography*, Berkeley: University of California Press.

Cohen, Margaret (1993) *Profane Illumination: Walter Benjamin and the Paris of Surrealist Revolution*, Berkeley: University of California Press.

Coombes, Annie E. (1994) *Reinventing Africa: Museums, Material Culture and Popular Imagination*, New Haven: Yale University Press.

Cowan, Ruth Schwartz (1989) *More Work For Mother: The Ironies of Household Technology from the Open Hearth to the Microwave*, London: Free Association Books.

Crow, Thomas (1985) 'Modernism and Mass Culture in the Visual Arts', in Francis Frascina, ed. *Pollock and After: The Critical Debate*, London: Harper & Row, pp. 233–66.

Davis, Murray S. (1994) 'Georg Simmel and the Aesthetics of Social Reality' [1968], in David Frisby ed. *Georg Simmel: Critical Assessments*, 3 vols., London: Routledge, section 5, number 42, pp. 46–60.

Davis, Natalie Z. (1987) *Society and Culture in Early Modern France*, Cambridge: Polity Press.

de Certeau, Michel (1984) *The Practice of Everyday Life* [1980], translated by Steven Rendall, Berkeley: University of California Press.

—— (1986) *Heterologies: Discourse on the Other*, translated by Brian Massumi, Manchester: Manchester University Press.

—— (1988) *The Writing of History* [1975], translated by Tom Conley, New York: Columbia University Press.

—— (1992) *The Mystic Fable: Volume I – the Sixteenth and Seventeenth Centuries*, translated by Michael B. Smith, Chicago: University of Chicago Press.

—— (1997a) *The Capture of Speech and Other Political Writings*, translated by Tom Conley, Minneapolis: University of Minnesota Press.

—— (1997b) *Culture in the Plural* [1974], translated by Tom Conley, Minneapolis: University of Minnesota Press.

—— (2000) *The Possession at Loudun* [1970], translated by Michael B. Smith, Chicago: University of Chicago Press.

de Certeau, Michel and Giard, Luce (1998) 'A Practical Science of the Singular' [1983], in Michel de Certeau *et al.* (1998), pp. 251–6.

de Certeau, Michel, Giard, Luce and Mayol, Pierre (1998) *The Practice of Everyday Life, Volume II: Living Cooking* [1980], translated by Timothy J. Tomasik, Minneapolis: University of Minnesota Press.

de Certeau, Michel, Julia, Dominique and Revel, Jacques (1975) *Une politique de la langue: la Révolution française et les patois: l'enquête de Grégoire*, Paris: Gallimard.

—— (1986) 'The Beauty of the Dead: Nisard' [1974], in Michel de Certeau, *Heterologies: Discourse on the Other*, translated by Brian Massumi, Manchester: Manchester University Press, pp. 119–36.

de Man, Paul (1986) *The Resistance to Theory*, Manchester: Manchester University Press.

Debord, Guy (1981a) 'Introduction to a Critique of Urban Geography' [1955], in Knabb (1981), pp. 5–8.

—— (1981b) 'Perspectives for Conscious Alterations in Everyday Life' [1961], in Knabb (1981), pp. 68–75.

—— (1981c) 'Situationist Theses on Traffic' [1959], in Knabb (1981), pp. 56–8.

—— (1981d) 'Theory of the Dérive' [1958], in Knabb (1981), pp. 50–4.

—— (1983) *Society of the Spectacle* [1967], Detroit: Black & Red.

Debord, Guy and Wolman, Gil J. (1981) 'Methods of Detournement' [1956], in Knabb (1981), pp. 8–14.

Dentith, Simon (1995) *Bakhtinian Thought: An Introductory Reader*, London and New York: Routledge.

Devereaux, Leslie and Hillman, Roger, eds. (1995) *Fields of Vision: Essays in Film Studies, Visual Anthropology and Photography*, Berkeley: University of California Press.

Donzelot, Jacques (1980) *The Policing of Families: Welfare versus the State*, translated by Robert Hurley, London: Hutchinson.

Doyle, Arthur Conan (1993) *The Adventures of Sherlock Holmes*, London: The Folio Society.

—— (1995) *Sherlock Holmes: Four Great Novels*, Bristol: Parragon Book Services.

Durkheim, Emile (1995) *The Elementary Forms of Religious Life* [1912], translated by Karen E. Fields, New York: Free Press.

Eagleton, Terry (1986) *Against the Grain: Selected Essays*, London: Verso.

—— (1990) *The Ideology of the Aesthetic*, Oxford: Blackwell.

Edwards, Stephen (1984) 'Disastrous Documents', *Ten-8* 15: 12–23.

Evans, Jessica (1997) 'Introduction to "Nation, Mandate, Memory"', in Jessica Evans, ed. *The Camerawork Essays: Context and Meaning in Photography*, London: Rivers Oram Press, pp. 145–7.

Featherstone, Mike (1992) 'Postmodernism and the Aestheticization of Everyday Life', in Scott Lash and Jonathan Friedman, eds. *Modernity and Identity*, Oxford: Blackwell, pp. 265–90.

—— (1995) *Undoing Culture: Globalization, Postmodernism and Identity*, London: Sage.

Felski, Rita (1995) *The Gender of Modernity*, Cambridge, Mass.: Harvard University Press.

Ferguson, Harvie (1996) *The Lure of Dreams: Sigmund Freud and the Construction of Modernity*, London and New York: Routledge.

Fisera, Vladimir, ed. (1978) *Writing on the Wall – France, May 1968: A Documentary Anthology*, London: Alison & Busby.

Fiske, John (1986) *Understanding Popular Culture*, London: Routledge.

—— (1992) 'Cultural Studies and the Culture of Everyday Life', in Lawrence Grossberg, Cary Nelson and Paula Treichler, eds. *Cultural Studies*, London and New York: Routledge, pp. 154–73.

Foster, Hal (1993) *Compulsive Beauty*, Cambridge, Mass: The MIT Press.

Foucault, Michel (1970) *The Order of Things: An Archaeology of the Human Sciences* [first published in 1966 as *Les mots et les choses*], London: Tavistock.

—— (1982) *Discipline and Punish: The Birth of the Prison*, translated by Alan Sheridan, Harmondsworth: Penguin.

—— (1984) *The History of Sexuality. Volume I: An Introduction*, translated by Robert Hurley, Harmondsworth: Penguin.

Freud, Sigmund (1973) *Introductory Lectures on Psychoanalysis* [1916–17], translated by James Strachey, Harmondsworth: Penguin.

—— (1975) *The Psychopathology of Everyday Life* [1901], translated by Alan Tyson, Harmondsworth: Penguin.

—— (1976) *The Interpretation of Dreams* [1900], translated by James Strachey, Harmondsworth: Penguin.

—— (1977) *Case Histories 1: 'Dora' and 'Little Hans' – Pelican Freud Library, Volume VIII* [1905], translated by Alix and James Strachey, Harmondsworth: Penguin.

Friedan, Betty (1965) *The Feminine Mystique*, Harmondsworth: Penguin.

Frisby, David (1984) *Georg Simmel*, London: Methuen.

—— (1985) *Fragments of Modernity: Theories of Modernity in the Work of Simmel, Kracauer and Benjamin*, Cambridge: Polity Press.

—— (1992a) *Simmel and Since: Essays on Georg Simmel's Social Theory*, London and New York: Routledge.

—— (1992b) *Sociological Impressionism: A Reassessment of Georg Simmel's Social Theory*, London and New York: Routledge. First published 1981.

Gardiner, Michael E. (2000) *Critiques of Everyday Life*. London and New York: Routledge.

Geist, Johann (1983) *Arcades: The History of a Building Type*, translated by Jane O. Newman and John H. Smith, Cambridge, Mass.: The MIT Press.

Gersham, Herbert S. (1974) *The Surrealist Revolution in France*, Ann Arbor: University of Michigan Press.

Giedion, Siegfried (1969) *Mechanization takes Command: A Contribution to Anonymous History*, New York: Norton.

Greenhalgh, Paul (1988) *Ephemeral Vistas: The Expositions Universelles, Great Exhibitions and World's Fairs, 1851–1939*, Manchester: Manchester University Press.

Hamper, Ben (1992) *Rivethead: Tales from the Assembly Line*, London: Fourth Estate.

Hargreaves, Alec G. (1995) *Immigration, 'Race' and Ethnicity in Contemporary France*, London and New York: Routledge.

Harootunian, Harry (2000) *History's Disquiet: Modernity, Cultural Practice, and the Question of Everyday Life*, New York: Columbia University Press.

Harrison, Charles and Orton, Fred, eds. (1984) *Modernism, Criticism, Realism*, London: Harper & Row.

Harrisson, Tom (1937) *Savage Civilisation*, London: Victor Gollancz.

—— (1938) 'Public Busybody No. 1', *Daily Mirror*, 6 December: 14.

—— (1940a) 'M.O.I. Defended', *Picture Post*, 10 August: 31.

—— (1940b) 'What is Public Opinion?' *Political Quarterly*, 11: 368–83.

—— (1942) 'Notes on Class Consciousness and Class Unconsciousness', *Sociological Review*, 34.3–4: 147–64.

—— (1947) 'Introduction', in Bob Willcock, 'Polls Apart', unpublished survey of Mass-Observation.

—— (1970) 'Introduction', in Mass-Observation, *The Pub and the People* (first published 1943), Welwyn Garden City: Seven Dials Press.

—— (1976) *Living through the Blitz*, London: Collins.

Harrisson, Tom, Jennings, Humphrey and Madge, Charles (1937) 'Anthropology at Home', *The New Statesman and Nation*, 30 January: 155.

Harvey, David (1989) *The Condition of Postmodernity*, Oxford: Blackwell.

Haxthausen, Charles W. and Suhr, Heirdrun, eds. (1990) *Berlin: Culture and Metropolis*, Minneapolis: University of Minnesota Press.

Hodgkinson, Anthony W. and Sheratsky, Rodney E. (1982) *Humphrey Jennings: More than a Maker of Films*, London: University Press of New England.

Hollier, Denis, ed. (1988) *The College of Sociology 1937–39*, translated by Betsy Wing, Minneapolis: University of Minnesota Press.

—— (1989) *Against Architecture: The Writings of George Bataille*, translated by Betsy Wing, Cambridge, Mass.: The MIT Press.

—— (1992) 'The Use-Value of the Impossible', translated by Liesl Ollman, *October*, 60: 3–24.

—— (1997) *Absent Without Leave: French Literature Under the Threat of War*, translated by Catherine Porter, Cambridge, Mass.: Harvard University Press.

Huyssen, Andreas (1986) *After the Great Divide: Modernism, Mass Culture and Post-modernism*, Basingstoke: Macmillan.

Jacknis, Ira (1985) 'Frank Boas and Exhibits: On the Limitations of the Museum Method of Anthropology', in George W. Stocking, Jr., ed. *Objects and Others: Essays on Museums and Material Culture*, Madison: The University of Wisconsin Press.

Jackson, Kevin, ed. (1993) *The Humphrey Jennings Film Reader*, Manchester: Carcanet Press.

Jackson, Peter (1992) *Maps of Meaning: An Introduction to Cultural Geography*, London and New York: Routledge.

Jameson, Fredric (1991) *Postmodernism, or the Cultural Logic of Late Capitalism*, London: Verso.

Jay, Martin (1984) *Marxism and Totality: The Adventures of a Concept from Lukács to Habermas*, Cambridge: Polity Press.

Jeffrey, Tom (1978) *Mass-Observation: A Short History*, Occasional Paper, Centre for Contemporary Cultural Studies, The University of Birmingham.

Jennings, Humphrey (1993) 'Surrealism' [1936], in Kevin Jackson, ed. *The Humphrey Jennings Film Reader*, Manchester: Carcanet Press, pp. 219–21.

—— (1995) *Pandaemonium: The Coming of the Machine as seen by Contemporary Observers*, edited by Mary-Lou Jennings and Charles Madge, Basingstoke: Macmillan.

Jennings, Mary-Lou, ed. (1982) *Humphrey Jennings: Film-Maker, Painter, Poet*, London: BFI.

Jones, Karen and Williamson, Kevin (1979) 'The Birth of the Schoolroom', *Ideology and Consciousness*, 6: 59–110.

Kafka, Franz (1994) *The Trial* [1925], Harmondsworth: Penguin.

—— (1997) *The Castle* [1926], Harmondsworth: Penguin.

Kaplan, Alice and Ross, Kristin, eds. (1983) *Everyday Life*, special issue of *Yale French Studies*, 73.

Kelly, Michael (1982) *Modern French Marxism*, Oxford: Blackwell.

Kern, Steven (1983) *The Culture of Time and Space 1880–1918*, Cambridge, Mass.: Harvard University Press.

Knabb, Ken, ed. (1981) *Situationist International Anthology*, Berkeley: Bureau of Public Secrets.

Kofman, Eleonore and Lebas, Elizabeth (1996) 'Last in Transposition – Time, Space and the City', in Henri Lefebvre, *Writings on Cities*, translated and edited by Eleonore Kofman and Elizabeth Lebas, Oxford: Blackwell, pp. 3–60.

Kojève, Alexandre (1969) *Introduction to the Reading of Hegel*, translated by James H. Nicols, Jr., New York: Basic Books.

Kracauer, Siegfried (1995) *The Mass Ornament: Weimar Essays*, translated by Thomas Y. Levin, Cambridge, Mass.: Harvard University Press.

—— (1998) *The Salaried Masses: Duty and Distraction in Weimar Germany*, translated by Quintin Hoare, London: Verso.

Kramarae, Cheris, ed. (1988) *Technology and Women's Voices: Keeping in Touch*, London: Routledge & Kegan Paul.

Krauss, Rosalind (1987) *The Originality of the Avant-Garde and Other Modernist Myths*, Cambridge, Mass.: The MIT Press.

Krauss, Rosalind and Livingston, Jane (1986) *L'Amour Fou: Photography and Surrealism*, London: Arts Council of Great Britain.

Kristeva, Julia (1984) *The Revolution in Poetic Language*, translated by Margaret Waller, New York: Columbia University Press.

Kuisel, Richard (1993) *Seducing the French: The Dilemma of Americanization*, Berkeley, Los Angeles and London: University of California Press.

Langbauer, Laurie (1992) 'Cultural Studies and the Politics of the Everyday', *Diacritics*, 22.1: 47–65.

—— (1993) 'The City, the Everyday, and Boredom: The Case of Sherlock Holmes', *differences*, 5.3: 80–120.

—— (1999) *Novels of Everyday Life: The Series in English Fiction 1850–1930*, Ithaca and London: Cornell University Press.

Laplanche, Jean and Pontalis, Jean-Bertrand (1983) *The Language of Psycho-analysis*, translated by Donald Nicholson-Smith, London: Hogarth Press.

Lash, Scott and Friedman, Jonathan, eds. (1992) *Modernity and Identity*, Oxford: Blackwell.

Lefebvre, Henri (1955) *Rabelais*, Paris: Les Editeurs Français Réunis.

—— (1962) *La Vallée de Campan – étude de sociologie rurale*, Paris: Presses Universitaires de France.

—— (1968a) *Dialectical Materialism* [1940], translated by John Sturrock, London: Jonathan Cape.

—— (1968b) *The Sociology of Marx*, translated by Norbert Gutterman, Harmondsworth: Penguin.

—— (1969) *The Explosion: Marxism and the French Revolution*, translated by Alfred Ehrenfeld, London: Monthly Review Press.

—— (1975) *Les temps des méprises*, Paris: Stock.

—— (1984) *Everyday Life in the Modern World* [1968], translated by Sacha Rabinovitch, New Brunswick: Transaction Publishers.

—— (1987) 'The Everyday and Everydayness', *Yale French Studies* 73: 7–11.

—— (1988) 'Towards a Leftist Cultural Politics', in Cary Nelson and Lawrence Grossberg, eds. *Marxism and the Interpretation of Culture*, Chicago: University of Illinois Press, pp. 75–88.

—— (1991a) *Critique of Everyday Life: Volume I* [1947/1958], translated by John Moore, London: Verso.

—— (1991b) *The Production of Space* [1974], translated by Donald Nicholson-Smith, Oxford: Blackwell.

—— (1995) *Introduction to Modernity* [1962], translated by John Moore, London: Verso.

—— (1996) *Writings on Cities*, translated and edited by Eleonore Kofman and Elizabeth Lebas, Oxford: Blackwell.

Leiris, Michel (1934) *L'Afrique fantôme*, Paris: Gallimard.

—— (1989) *Brisées: Broken Branches*, translated by Lydia Davis, San Francisco: North Point Press.

—— (1991) *Scratches: Rules of the Game – Volume I* [1948], translated by Lydia Davis, Baltimore: The Johns Hopkins University Press.

—— (1992) *Manhood: A Journey from Childhood into the Fierce Order of Virility* [1939], translated by Richard Howard, Chicago: University of Chicago Press.

—— (1997) *Scraps: Rules of the Game – Volume II* [1955], translated by Lydia Davis, Baltimore: The Johns Hopkins University Press.

Le Roy Ladurie, Emmanuel (1980) *Carnival: A People's Uprising at Romans 1579–1580*, translated by Mary Feeney, London: Scolar Press.

Levine, Donald N. (1989) 'Simmel as a Resource for Sociological Metatheory', *Social Theory*, 7: 161–74.

Lewis, Helena (1988) *Dada Turns Red: The Politics of Surrealism*, Edinburgh: Edinburgh University Press.

Linhart, Robert (1981) *The Assembly Line*, translated by Margaret Crosland, London: John Calder.

Lukács, Georg (1991) 'Memories of Georg Simmel', translated by Margaret Cerullo, *Theory, Culture and Society*, 8.3: 145–50.

Lynd, Robert S. and Lynd, Helen Merrel (1929) *Middletown: A Study in Modern American Culture*, New York: Harvest.

McClintock, Anne (1995) *Imperial Leather: Race, Gender and Sexuality in the Colonial Contest*, London and New York: Routledge.

MacIntyre, Alasdair (1984) 'The Idea of a Social Science' [1967], in Charles Harrison and Fred Orton, eds. *Modernism, Criticism, Realism*, London: Harper & Row, pp. 214–27.

Madge, Charles (1933) 'Surrealism for the English', *New Verse*, 6: 14–18.

—— (1934) 'The Meaning of Surrealism', *New Verse*, 10: 13–15.

—— (1937a) 'Anthropology at Home', *The New Statesman and Nation*, 2 January: 12.

—— (1937b) 'Press, Radio, and Social Consciousness', in C. Day Lewis, ed. *The Mind in Chains: Socialism and the Cultural Revolution*, London: Frederick Muller, pp. 147–63.

—— (1976) 'The Birth of Mass-Observation', *Times Literary Supplement*, 5 November: 1395.

Malinowski, Bronislaw (1922) *Argonauts of the Western Pacific*, London: Routledge.

—— (1938) 'A Nation-Wide Intelligence Service', in Mass-Observation, *First Year's Work 1937–38*, edited by Charles Madge and Tom Harrisson, London: Lindsay Drummond, pp. 83–121.

Marcus, Laura and Nead, Lynda, eds. (1993) *The Actuality of Walter Benjamin*, special issue of *New Formations*, 20.

Marcuse, Herbert (1972) *Negations: Essays in Critical Theory*, translated by Jeremy J. Shapiro, Harmondsworth: Penguin.

Marx, Karl (1968) *The Eighteenth Brumaire of Louis Bonaparte* [1852], in Karl Marx and Friedrich Engels, *Selected Works – In One Volume*, London: Lawrence & Wishart, pp. 96–179.

—— (1976) *Capital: A Critique of Political Economy – Volume I* [1867], translated by Ben Fowkes, Harmondsworth: Penguin.

—— (1977) *Economic and Philosophical Manuscripts of 1844*, London: Lawrence & Wishart.

Marx, Karl and Engels, Friedrich (1968) *Selected Works – In One Volume*, London: Lawrence & Wishart.

—— (1973) *Manifesto of the Communist Party* [1848], Beijing: Foreign Language Press.

Mass-Observation (1937a) *Mass-Observation*, introduction by Julian Huxley, London: Fredrick Muller.

—— (1937b) *May 12th Mass-Observation Day Surveys*, edited by Humphrey Jennings and Charles Madge, London: Faber & Faber.

—— (1937c) 'Poetic Description and Mass-Observation', *New Verse*, 24: 1–6.

—— (1937d) 'They Speak For Themselves: Mass-Observation and Social Narrative', *Life and Letters*, 17: 37–42.

—— (1938) *First Year's Work 1937–38*, edited by Charles Madge and Tom Harrisson, London: Lindsay Drummond.

—— (1939) *Britain*, Harmondsworth: Penguin.

—— (1943) *The Pub and the People: A Worktown Study*, London: Gollancz.

—— (1982) 'A Note on Images', in Mary-Lou Jennings, ed. *Humphrey Jennings: Film-Maker, Painter, Poet*, London: BFI.

—— (1983) *The Tom Harrisson, Mass-Observation Archive: File Reports, Series: 1937–1949*, Brighton: Harvester Press Microform Publications.

Mayhew, Henry (1967) *London Labor and the London Poor*, 4 vols. [1861–2], London: Frank Cass.

Mercer, Neil (1989) 'Mass-Observation 1937–40: The Range of Research Methods', *Working Papers in Applied Social Research*, 16, Manchester: University of Manchester.

Morris, Meaghan (1990) 'Banality in Cultural Studies', in Patricia Mellencamp, ed. *Logics of Television: Essays in Cultural Criticism*, Bloomington and Indianapolis: Indiana University Press, pp. 14–43.

—— (1998) *Too Soon, Too Late: History in Popular Culture*, Bloomington and Indianapolis: Indiana University Press.

Mulford, Jeremy, ed. (1982) *Worktown People: Photographs from Northern England 1937–38*, Bristol: Falling Wall Press.

Müller, Lothar (1990) 'The Beauty of the Metropolis: Toward an Aesthetic Urbanism in Turn-of-the-Century Berlin', in Charles W. Haxthausen and Heirdrun Suhr, eds. *Berlin: Culture and Metropolis*, Minneapolis: University of Minnesota Press, pp. 37–57.

Nadeau, Maurice (1987) *The History of Surrealism*, translated by Richard Howard, London: Plantin Publishers.

Nelson, Cary and Grossberg, Lawrence, eds. (1988) *Marxism and the Interpretation of Culture*, Chicago: University of Illinois Press.

Niethammer, Lutz (1992) *Posthistoire: Has History come to an End?* translated by Patrick Camiller, London: Verso.

Orwell, George (1962) *The Road to Wigan Pier*, Harmondsworth: Penguin.

Osborne, Peter (1995) *The Politics of Time: Modernity and Avant-Garde*, London: Verso.

Petro, Patrice (1993) 'After Shock/Between Boredom and History', *Discourse: Journal of Theoretical Studies in Media and Culture*, 16.2: 77–99.

Pickering, Michael and Chaney, David (1986) 'Democracy and Communication: Mass-Observation 1937–1943', *Journal of Communication*, 36.1: 41–56.

Picton, Tom (1978) 'A Very Public Espionage', *Camerawork*, 11: 2.

Plant, Sadie (1992) *The Most Radical Gesture: The Situationist International in a Postmodern Age*, London and New York: Routledge.

Pollock, Griselda (1988) 'Modernity and the Spaces of Femininity', in Griselda Pollock, *Vision and Difference: Femininity, Feminism and the Histories of Art*, London and New York: Routledge, pp. 50–90.

Poster, Mark (1976) *Existential Marxism in Postwar France: Sartre to Althusser*, Princeton: Princeton University Press.

—— (1997) *Cultural History and Postmodernity: Disciplinary Readings and Challenges*, New York: Columbia University Press.

Pred, Allan (1995) *Recognizing European Modernities: A Montage of the Present*, London and New York: Routledge.

Raine, Kathleen (1967) *Defending Ancient Springs*, London: Oxford University Press.

Rammstedt, Otthein (1991) 'On Simmel's Aesthetics: Argumentation in the Journal *Jugend*, 1897–1906', *Theory, Culture and Society*, 8.3: 125–44.

Ray, Paul C. (1971) *The Surrealist Movement in England*, Ithaca: Cornell University Press.

Reader, Keith A. (1987) *Intellectuals and the Left in France Since 1968*, Basingstoke: Macmillan.

—— (with Khursheed Wadia) (1993) *The May 1968 Events in France: Reproductions and Interpretations*, Basingstoke: Macmillan.

Rigby, Brian (1991) *Popular Culture in Modern France: A Study of Cultural Discourse*, London and New York: Routledge.

Ross, Kristin (1988) *The Emergence of Social Space: Rimbaud and the Paris Commune*, Minneapolis: University of Minnesota Press.

—— (1995) *Fast Cars, Clean Bodies: Decolonization and the Reordering of French Culture*, Cambridge, Mass.: The MIT Press.

—— (1997a) 'French Quotidian' in Lynn Gumpert, ed. *The Art of the Everyday: The Quotidian in Postwar French Culture*, New York: New York University Press, pp. 19–29.

—— (1997b) 'Lefebvre on the Situationists: An Interview', *October*, 79: 69–83.

Sadler, Simon (1998) *The Situationist City*, Cambridge, Mass.: The MIT Press.

Sandberg, Mark B. (1995) 'Effigy and Narrative: Looking into the Nineteenth-Century Folk Museum', in Leo Charney and Vanessa R. Schwartz, eds. *Cinema and the Invention of Modern Life*, Berkeley: University of California Press.

Scannell, Paddy and Cardiff, David (1991) *A Social History of Broadcasting – Volume I: 1922–1939, Serving the Nation*, Oxford: Blackwell.

Schivelbusch, Wolfgang (1977) *The Railway Journey: The Industrialization of Time and Space in the 19th Century*, New York: Berg.

Schor, Naomi (1992) 'Cartes Postales: Representing Paris 1900', *Critical Inquiry*, 18: 188–241.

Shields, Rob (1999) *Lefebvre, Love and Struggle: Spatial Dialectics*, London and New York: Routledge.

Sieburth, Richard (1989) 'Benjamin the Scrivener', in Gary Smith, ed. *Benjamin: Philosophy, Aesthetics, History*, Chicago: University of Chicago Press, pp. 13–37.

Simmel, Georg (1968) *The Conflict in Modern Culture and Other Essays*, translated by K. Peter Etzkorn, New York: Teachers College Press.

—— (1971) *On Individuality and Social Forms*, edited by Donald N. Levine, Chicago: University of Chicago Press.

—— (1990) *The Philosophy of Money* [1900/1907], translated by Tom Bottomore and David Frisby, London and New York: Routledge.

—— (1991) 'The Berlin Trade Exhibition' [1896], *Theory, Culture and Society*, 8.3: 119–23.

—— (1997) *Simmel on Culture*, edited by David Frisby and Mike Featherstone, London: Sage.

Situationist International (1966) 'On the Poverty of Student Life' (1966), in Knabb (1981), pp. 319–37.

Smith, Gary, ed. (1989) *Benjamin: Philosophy, Aesthetics, History*, Chicago: University of Chicago Press.

Smith, Woodruff D. (1991) *Politics and the Sciences of Culture in Germany 1840–1920*, Oxford: Oxford University Press.

Soja, Edward W. (1989) *Postmodern Geographies: The Reassertion of Space in Critical Social Theory*, London: Verso.

—— (1996) *ThirdSpace: Journeys to Los Angeles and Other Real-and-Imagined Places*, Oxford: Blackwell.

Spacks, Patricia Meyer (1995) *Boredom: The Literary History of a State of Mind*, Chicago: University of Chicago Press.

Spender, Humphrey (1982) 'Interview', in Jeremy Mulford, ed. *Worktown People: Photographs from Northern England 1937–38*, Bristol: Falling Wall Press, pp. 11–24.

Stam, Robert (1989) *Subversive Pleasure: Bakhtin, Cultural Criticism, and Film*, Baltimore: The Johns Hopkins University Press.

Stanley, Liz (1990) 'The Archeology of a 1930s Mass-Observation Project', *Sociology: Occasional Paper 27*, Manchester: University of Manchester.

Stanton, Gareth (1997) 'In Defence of Savage Civilisation: Tom Harrisson, Cultural Studies and Anthropology', in Stephen Nugent and Cris Shore, eds. *Anthropology and Cultural Studies*, London: Pluto Press, pp. 11–33.

Stewart, Susan (1993) *On Longing: Narratives of the Miniature, the Gigantic, the Souvenir, the Collection*, Durham, NC and London: Duke University Press.

Stocking, George W. Jr., ed. (1985) *Objects and Others: Essays on Museums and Material Culture*, Madison: University of Wisconsin Press.

—— (1987) *Victorian Anthropology*, New York: The Free Press.

—— (1996) *After Tylor: British Social Anthropology 1888–1951*, London: Athlone Press.

Summerfield, Penny (1985) 'Mass-Observation: Social Research or Social Movement?', *Journal of Contemporary History*, 20: 439–52.

Sussman, Elisabeth, ed. (1991) *On the Passage of a Few People through a Rather Brief Moment in Time: The Situationist International 1957–1972*, Boston: ICA.

Tagg, John (1992) *Grounds of Dispute: Art History, Cultural Politics and the Discursive Field*, Basingstoke: Macmillan.

Taylor, John (1994) *A Dream of England: Landscape, Photography and the Tourist's Imagination*, Manchester: Manchester University Press.

Thompson, E. P. (1985) 'Imagination Power – Review of Pandaemonium by Humphrey Jennings', *New Society*, 25 October: 164–5.

—— (1993) *Customs in Common*, Harmondsworth: Penguin.

Thompson, Kenneth (1982) *Emile Durkheim*, London: Tavistock.

Torgovnick, Marianna (1990) *Gone Primitive: Savage Intellects, Modern Lives*, Chicago: University of Chicago Press.

Trebitsch, Michel (1991) 'Preface', in Henri Lefebvre, *Critique of Everyday Life: Volume I*, translated by John Moore, London: Verso, pp. ix–xxviii.

Ulmer, Gregory L. (1985) 'The Object of Post-Criticism', in Hal Foster, ed. *Postmodern Culture*, London: Pluto Press, pp. 83–110.

Vidler, Anthony (1991) 'Agoraphobia: Spatial Estrangement in Georg Simmel and Siegfried Kracauer', *New German Critique*, 54: 31–45.

Viénet, René (1992) *Enragés and Situationists in the Occupation Movement, France, May '68*, New York: Automedia.

Waldberg, Patrick (1997) *Surrealism*, London: Thames & Hudson.

Watson, Sophie and Gibson, Katherine, eds. (1995) *Postmodern Cities and Spaces*, Oxford: Blackwell.

Weber, Max (1991) *The Protestant Ethic and the Spirit of Capitalism* [1904–5], translated by Talcott Parsons, London: HarperCollins.

Williams, Raymond (1977) *Marxism and Literature*, Oxford: Oxford University Press.

Williams, Rosalind H. (1982) *Dream Worlds: Mass Consumption in Late Nineteenth-Century France*, Berkeley: University of California Press.

Wilson, Elizabeth (1995) 'The Invisible Flâneur', in Sophie Watson and Katherine Gibson, eds. *Postmodern Cities and Spaces*, Oxford: Blackwell, pp. 59–79.

Wohlfarth, Irving (1986) 'Et Cetera? The Historian as Chiffonnier', in *New German Critique*, 39: 143–68.

Wolff, Janet (1989) 'The Invisible Flâneuse: Women and the Literature of Modernity', in Andrew Benjamin, ed. *The Problems of Modernity: Adorno and Benjamin*, London and New York: Routledge, pp. 141–56.

Wolin, Richard (1989) 'Experience and Materialism in Benjamin's *Passagenwerk*', in Gary Smith, ed. *Benjamin: Philosophy, Aesthetics, History*, Chicago: University of Chicago Press, pp. 210–27.

—— (1994) *Walter Benjamin: An Aesthetic of Redemption*, Berkeley: University of California Press.

Wollen, Peter (1991) 'Bitter Victory: The Art and Politics of the Situationist International', in Elisabeth Sussman, ed. *On the Passage of a Few People Through a Rather Brief Moment in Time: The Situationist International 1957–72*, Boston: ICA, pp. 20–61.

—— (1993) *Raiding the Icebox: Reflections on Twentieth-Century Culture*, London: Verso.

Zola, Emile (1992) *The Ladies' Paradise*, Berkeley: University of California Press.

Index